© 2011 Pascal Perich

RICH COHEN is a *New York Times* bestselling author, as well as a contributing editor at *Vanity Fair* and *Rolling Stone*. He has written seven books, including *Tough Jews, Israel Is Real,* and the widely acclaimed memoir *Sweet and Low.* His work has appeared in *The New Yorker, The Atlantic Monthly, Harper's Magazine,* and *The Best American Essays.* He lives in Connecticut with his wife, three sons, and dog.

The **Fish** That **Ate** the **Whale**

Sam "the Banana Man" Zemurray and the fruits of his labor

The Fish That Ate the Whale

The Life and Times of America's Banana King

Rich Cohen

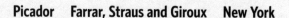

Picador   Farrar, Straus and Giroux   New York

www.picadorusa.com
www.twitter.com/picadorusa • www.facebook.com/picadorusa
picadorbookroom.tumblr.com

Picador® is a U.S. registered trademark and is used by Farrar, Straus and Giroux
under license from Pan Books Limited.

For book club information, please visit www.facebook.com/picadorbookclub
or e-mail marketing@picadorusa.com.

Designed by Abby Kagan

Map copyright © 2012 by Jeffrey L. Ward

Frontispiece: Photograph of Samuel Zemurray reprinted by permission of
Eliot Elisofon/Time & Life Pictures/Getty Images

Picador ISBN 978-1-250-03331-4

Picador books may be purchased for educational, business, or promotional use. For information
on bulk purchases, please contact Macmillan Corporate and Premium Sales Department at
1-800-221-7945 extension 5442 or write specialmarkets@macmillan.com.

First published in the United States by Farrar, Straus and Giroux

First Picador Edition: June 2013

20   19   18   17   16   15   14   13   12   11

To my sister, Sharon,
for thirty-five years of New Orleans

Power is based on perception. If you think you got it, you got it, even if you don't got it.
>
> —**Herb Cohen**, *You Can Negotiate Anything*

In my beginning is my end.   —**T. S. Eliot**, "East Coker"

There's always a guy.   —**Jerry Weintraub**, in conversation

Contents

x • Contents

Preface

Samuel Zemurray, who led the United Fruit Company for roughly twenty-five years, from the early 1930s to the mid-'50s, was an emblematic figure of the American Century—those decades that saw the United States grow from a regional power into an empire. In Sam the Banana Man, as Zemurray was known to friends and enemies alike, the story of the age is collapsed to the scale of a single life: the ascent from humble origins, the promise and ambition, the sudden, dazzling, disorienting wealth, the corruption, brutality, propaganda, wars, and overreach—and the grinding late-day melancholy.

When he arrived in America in 1891 at age fourteen, Zemurray was tall, gangly, and penniless. When he died in the grandest house in New Orleans sixty-nine years later, he was among the richest, most powerful men in the world. In between, he worked as a fruit peddler, a banana hauler, a dockside hustler, and the owner of plantations on the Central American isthmus. He battled and conquered United Fruit, which was one of the first truly global corporations. United Fruit, in its day, was as ubiquitous as Google and as feared as Halliburton. More than a business, it was the spirit of the nation abroad, akin to the Dutch East India Company, its policies backed by the threat of U.S. gunboats. As the president of United Fruit, Zemurray became the most important man in Central America—he could change the course of history with a phone call—a symbol of the best and worst of the United States: proof that America is the land of opportunity, but also a classic example of the Ugly American, the corporate pirate who treats foreign nations as the backdrop for his adventures. In South America, when people shouted "Yankee, go home!" it was men like Samuel Zemurray they had in mind.

I first learned about Zemurray as a sophomore at Tulane University. The Banana Man had been a generous donor to Tulane, and many of the buildings on campus are named for him or members of his family; the university president lives in the mansion on St. Charles Avenue where Zemurray spent some of his best years. I was transfixed by the story the moment I heard it in a seminar taught by Joseph Cohen, a relation to me in spirit alone. Unlike lectures in other classes, this was an epic, gaudy in character and incident, filled with mercenary soldiers and dirty wars, financial battles and the sort of political shenanigans familiar from the smoky back rooms of my hometown, Chicago.

Zemurray's life is a parable of the American dream—not history as recorded in textbooks, but the authentic cask-strength version, a subterranean saga of kickbacks, overthrows, and secret deals: the world as it really works. This story can shock and infuriate us, and it does. But I found it invigorating, too. It told me that the life of the nation was written not only by speech-making grandees in funny hats but also by street-corner boys, immigrant strivers, crazed and driven, some with one good idea, some with thousands, willing to go to the ends of the earth to make their vision real. It meant anyone could write a chapter in that book, be part of the story, vanish into the jungle and reemerge as a figure of lore. Of course, you would not make the mistakes Zemurray made. You would harm no one, and disturb nothing, and never pay off, and never kick back, and never compromise or lose your bearings. You would do it in a new sin-free way, win-win, which of course is also part of the American character, perhaps the most defining part: the notion that, if we were only given one more chance, we could finally get it right.

It's what people mean when they speak of American exceptionalism: unlike the Europeans, we do not yet know you can't be both powerful and righteous. So we set out again and again, convinced that this time we'll avoid the mistakes of the previous generations. It's this kind of confidence that gives a people the strength to rule abroad; the moment that confidence goes, the empire is doomed. When Zemurray was young, he seemed to believe he was different. He would make an honest fortune in a way that benefited the impoverished people of the South. His tragedy was not that he was worse than other businessmen, but that, despite all his brilliance and good intentions, he was no better.

In the end, what I took from Zemurray's story, and what made it redeeming, was not the evils and excesses of United Fruit but the optimism that characterized his life, the belief that he could indeed be both triumphant and loved. It's this infuriating faith that made him such a quintessentially American figure. If you want to understand the spirit of our nation, the good and bad, you can enroll in college, sign up for classes, take notes and pay tuition, or you can study the life of Sam the Banana Man.

The Fish That Ate the Whale

Prologue

Sam Zemurray spoke with no accent, except when he swore, which was all the time. He was a big man, six foot three, rangy, nothing but muscle and bone, with the wingspan of a condor, hooded eyes, and a crisp, no-nonsense manner. If you saw him in the French Quarter, walking fast, you got out of the way. He lived uptown. If he was down here, it meant he was working.

It was a brisk night in the winter of 1910. Zemurray stood under the clock in front of the D. H. Holmes department store taking in the cheap twinkle of Canal Street. He wore a dark overcoat. At thirty-three years old, he was already a colorful figure. People passed around Sam Zemurray stories as if they were snapshots: in this one, you saw the town he left in Russia; in that one, the ship that brought him to America; in this one, the train that carried him to Alabama; in that one, the first bananas he purchased on the wharf in Mobile; in this one, the Central American isthmus where he cleared the jungle and made his fortune. After ten years in the South, he was known by a variety of nicknames: Z, the Russian, Sam the Banana Man, El Amigo, the Gringo.

He'd arrived on the docks at the start of the last century with nothing. In the early years, he'd had to make his way in the lowest precincts of the fruit business, peddling ripes, bananas other traders dumped into the sea. He worked like a dog and defied the most powerful people in the country. By 1905, he owned steamships, side-wheelers that crossed the Gulf of Mexico, heading south empty, returning with bananas. It was said he had traveled the breadth of Honduras, from Puerto Cortés to

Tegucigalpa, on a mule. Because he wanted to know the terrain, get his hands in the black soil.

A few minutes before midnight, three men came around the corner. The obvious leader—you could tell by the happy flash in his eyes—was Lee Christmas of Livingston Parish, a onetime railroad engineer who had gone wild on the isthmus. It was Christmas, the most famous mercenary in the Americas, who turned "revolution" into a verb. As in, *Let's go revolutin'!* *The New York Times* called him a real-life Dumas hero. Wherever he went, he was followed: by hit men, by police, by foreign agents trying to fathom his next move. Why, look here! Two such men lurk in the shadows across Bourbon Street—members of the United States Secret Service, with shiny shoes and flat faces, with lumps where their pistols dig into the fabric of their government coats. When Zemurray needed an army, he went to Christmas and Christmas did the rest, gathering a crew of exiles and adventure seekers in the dives of the French Quarter.

Christmas was in the company of two friends, key players in what was a conspiracy: Guy "Machine Gun" Molony, a veteran of the Boer War and a former New Orleans cop who could assemble a Vickers repeating rifle in under three minutes, hence the nickname, and General Manuel Bonilla, a tiny man, as brown as a bean, with a hawk nose and black eyes.

Zemurray was in the process of overthrowing a foreign government—he had been warned by Philander Knox, the U.S. secretary of state, who ordered federal agents to tail him and his cohorts in New Orleans, but didn't care. If Sam failed, he faced ruin. But if he succeeded, he would become a king in banana land. General Bonilla had been president of Honduras. With the right kind of help, he would be president again.

Zemurray studied the Secret Service agents across the street. Pulling a bankroll from his pocket, snapping off tens and twenties, he told Christmas, "You've got to lose them."

Then, just like that, Zemurray crossed Canal Street and disappeared uptown.

Christmas and his men went the other way, into the rabbit warren of the French Quarter, with its wrought-iron balconies, saloons, and hotels, all the gut-bucket joints where mercenaries waited for a job. They crossed Rampart to Basin Street, the entrance of the Tenderloin. In earlier times, the houses of ill repute had been scattered throughout

New Orleans. A dozen years before, at the urging of the reformer Alfred Story, they had been relocated in a defined district, a neighborhood of once grand houses gone to seed. These blocks, running a mile in each direction—from Basin Street to Custom House, from Custom House Street to Robertson, from Robertson Street to St. Louis, from St. Louis Street back to Basin—had become the most notorious red-light district in America. Much to the fury of the reformer, it was known as Storyville. The best houses, mansions with front porches and plush couches and piano players in the parlors, were at the front of the district on Basin Street. Farther back, the houses took on a seedier aspect. Bordellos gave way to single rooms, each with a window where a girl beckoned. On the edge of the district, the women performed in hallways, even in thresholds. Each year, a company printed a blue book that mapped the houses and rated every whore in various categories, from deportment to personality to stamina.

The previous five nights, Christmas, Molony, and Bonilla had gone to the same house, the grandest of them all, a Victorian mansion on Basin Street run by Madam May Evans. The federal agents followed as far as the opposite corner, posting themselves in a circle of lamplight. The first nights, the agents stayed till dawn, when the mercenaries staggered to rooms they rented near the river. But the last few nights, when the music stopped and the house went dark, the agents returned to headquarters to write their report, which was sent to the Department of State. Secretary Knox believed Zemurray was up to no good in Honduras.

Lee Christmas knocked on the front door, then vanished into Madam May's. From somewhere in the district came the sound of a spasm band, street urchins playing homemade instruments for nickels and dimes. The men took their positions in the house: Bonilla in a dark room upstairs, where he sat and looked out the window, eyes never leaving the agents; Christmas and Molony in the parlor, in deep chairs, drinking with the girls as a man in a dinner jacket played piano.

They told stories about mercenary heroes: Narciso López, who left New Orleans with a hundred men, landed in Cuba, and nearly reached Havana before he was caught and strung up in a public square; William Walker, who captured Nicaragua with eighty-four soldiers, "the Immortals," but was later stood against a wall in Trujillo, Honduras, and shot full of holes. After each story, Christmas would raise his glass and say, "That son of a bitch was a man!"

The agents quit at three a.m. "It's nothing but a drunken brawl in the district," they told their superior.

When Bonilla saw them leave, he hurried downstairs and told the others the police had gone.

Christmas looked out the window, and then, in his rough cowboy way, said, "Let's go."

A car was waiting on a side street. As the men climbed in, Christmas said to Bonilla, "Well, compadre, this is the first time I've ever heard of anybody going from a whorehouse to a White House!"

The car headed west on Canal Street. Past the old cemetery and through the swamp—swamp the way all of this had been swamp before the Frenchmen came with compass and chain. The road deteriorated beyond town, became rutted and bumpy, more Indian trail than highway. The countryside was spooky, huge magnolias, bait shops, houses on stilts, water lapping at the supports. They drove along Bayou St. John, past inlets, tributaries, green peninsulas. The smell of the bayou— crawfish, tidal marsh, vine—was overwhelming. The car stopped near the old Spanish Fort, where the bayou spills into Lake Pontchartrain. A ship was waiting—a forty-two-foot yacht. The men went aboard, ducked into a cabin. Within minutes the ropes had been pulled and the ship was speeding across the lake.

The bayous have always been the back door into New Orleans, a smuggler's paradise where the brackish waters are dotted by islands that vanish in flood tide. Take out a map and you can trace the route followed by Lee Christmas and his men that morning. They sailed to the Middle Ground, the shipping channel in the center of the lake, then continued along the shore opposite the city, slipping in and out of bays, the captain on the lookout for navy and coast guard. They went through the Rigolets, a corkscrew of marsh that dumps into Lake Borgne, the entrance to the Mississippi Sound. They passed Grassy Island, Cat Island, Bay St. Louis, and Pass Christian in the dark. On December 24, 1910, they dropped anchor off Ship Island, a sandbar near the center of the sound. The church towers of Gulfport, Mississippi, were visible in the distance.

"What now?" asked Molony.

"We wait for El Amigo," said Christmas.

It was one of Zemurray's conditions: he wanted his involvement in the operation kept a secret. With this in mind, he was to be identified, if he had to be identified at all, only as El Amigo.

A boat appeared on the horizon, a speedy little craft that zipped across the sound, reaching the yacht in a spray of white water. A man reached out a hand, pulling Christmas aboard, then Molony, then Bonilla. It was Zemurray, in his long black coat.

He led the way to a cabin filled with weapons—grenades, rifles, a machine gun, enough ammunition to fight a war—then stood in the galley, cooking breakfast. Steak and eggs, a bottle of whiskey. He drank a shot himself—to ward off the cold—then went to the pilot house. The engines started and the boat glided into Pass Christian, a fishing village on Bay St. Louis.

Zemurray walked into town, leaving his soldiers to play poker on an overturned rifle case. Bonilla won the big hands. "Sometimes, boys, you have to lose with a winning hand so that later you can win with a losing hand," he told them.

"Shut up and deal," said Christmas.

Zemurray returned with more weapons. When everything was stowed, he signaled the captain, who raised anchor and motored across the sound, where another ship, the *Hornet*, a fearsome armor-clad cruiser that had seen action in the Spanish-American War, was waiting. Zemurray had bought the ship secretly, through a third party, for his mercenaries.

The men spent an hour carrying weapons onto the warship. When everything was loaded, Zemurray noticed Bonilla shivering.

"Jesus Christ, Manny, what's wrong with you?"

"Just a little chill, amigo."

Zemurray took off his overcoat and draped it across the shoulders of the tiny general, saying, "I've shot the roll on you, and I might as well shoot the coat, too."

Zemurray said goodbye to the men, then stood on the deck of his ship watching the *Hornet* pass the barrier islands and sail into the open sea.

Green

1

Selma

Sam Zemurray saw his first banana in 1893. In the lore, this is presented as a moment of clarity, wherein the future was revealed. In some versions, the original banana is presented as a platonic ideal, an archetype circling the young man's head. It is seen from a great distance, then very close, each freckle magnified. As it was his first banana, I imagine it situated on a velvet pillow, in a display alongside Adam's rib and Robert Johnson's guitar. There is much variation in the telling of this story, meaning each expert has written his or her own history; meaning the story has gone from reportage to mythology; meaning Sam the Banana Man is Paul Bunyan and the first banana is Babe the Blue Ox. In some versions, Sam sees the banana in the gutter in Selma, Alabama, where it's fallen from a pushcart; in some, he sees it in the window of a grocery and is smitten. He rushes inside, grabs the owner by the lapel, and makes him tell everything he knows. In some, he sees it amid a pile of bananas on the deck of a ship plying the Alabama River on a lazy summer afternoon.

The most likely version has Sam seeing that first banana in the wares of a peddler in the alley behind his uncle's store in Selma. The American banana trade had begun twenty years before, but it was still embryonic. Few people had ever seen a banana. If they were spoken of at all, it was as an oddity, the way a person might speak of an African cucumber today. In this version, Sam peppers the salesman with questions: What is it? Where did you get it? How much does it cost? How fast do they sell? What do you do with the peel? What kind of money can you make? But none of the stories mentions a crucial detail: did

Zemurray taste that first banana? I like to imagine him peeling it, eating the fruit in three bites, then tossing the skin into the street the way people did back then. Tossing it and saying, "Wonderful." In future years, Zemurray always spoke of his product the way people speak of things they truly love, as something fantastical, in part because it's not entirely necessary. When he mentioned the nutritional value of bananas in interviews, he added, "And of course it's delicious." Putting us at a further remove from Zemurray is the fact that the kind of banana he saw in Selma in 1893, the banana that made his fortune, the variety known as the Big Mike, went extinct in the 1960s.

Sam Zemurray was born in 1877, in the region of western Russia once known as Bessarabia. It's Moldavia today. He grew up on a wheat farm, in a flat country ringed by hills. His father died young, leaving the family bereft, without prospects. Sam traveled to America with his aunt in 1892. He was to establish himself and send for the others—mother, siblings. He landed in New York, then continued to Selma, Alabama, where his uncle owned a store.

He was fourteen or fifteen, but you would guess him much older. The immigrants of that era could not afford to be children. They had to struggle every minute of every day. By sixteen, he was as hardened as the men in Walker Evans's photos, a tough operator, a dead-end kid, coolly figuring angles: Where's the play? What's in it for me? His humor was black, his explanations few. He was driven by the same raw energy that has always attracted the most ambitious to America, then pushed them to the head of the crowd. Grasper, climber—nasty ways of describing this kid, who wants what you take for granted. From his first months in America, he was scheming, looking for a way to get ahead. You did not need to be a Rockefeller to know the basics of the dream: Start at the bottom, fight your way to the top.

Over time, Sam would develop a philosophy best expressed in a handful of phrases: *You're there, we're here*; *Go see for yourself*; *Don't trust the report*.

Though immensely complicated, he was, in a fundamental way, simple, earthy. He believed in staying close to the action—in the fields with the workers, in the dives with the banana cowboys. You drink with a man, you learn what he knows. ("There is no problem you can't solve if you understand your business from A to Z," he said later.) In a famous exchange, when challenged by a rival who claimed he could not understand Zemurray's accent, Zemurray said, "You're fired. Can you understand that?"

Selma, Alabama, was the perfect spot for a kid like Sam: an incubator, a starter town, picturesque yet faded, grand but still small enough to memorize. A manufacturing center in the time of the Confederacy, it had since been allowed to dilapidate. There was a main street, a fruit market, a butcher shop, a candy store, a theater with plush seats, a city hall, churches. There were brick houses with curtains in the windows and swings on the porches—the white side of town. There were shotgun shacks, blue and yellow and red, fronted by weedy yards—the Negro side of town. There were taverns and houses of worship where Christian gospel was mixed with African voodoo. There were banks, savings and loans, fraternal orders. There was a commercial district, where every store was filled with unduly optimistic businessmen.

Though the biography of Zemurray's uncle has been forgotten, we can take him as a stand-in for the generation of poor grandfathers who came first, who worked and worked and got nothing but a place of honor in the family photo in return. Sometimes described as a grocery, sometimes as a general store, his shop was precisely the sort that Jewish immigrants had been establishing across the South for fifty years. Such concerns were usually operated by men who came to America because they were the youngest of many brothers, without property or plans. These people went south because, in the early days of the American republic, it was not inhospitable to Hebrews. Many began as peddlers, crossing the country with a mountain of merchandise strapped to their backs. You see them in ancient silver prints and daguerreotypes, weathered men humping half the world on their shoulders, pushing the other half in a cart—bags of grain, dinnerware, tinware, lamps, clothes, canvas for tents, chocolate, anything an isolated farmer might want but could not find in the sticks.

When they had saved some money, many of these men opened stores, which meant moving all that merchandise under a roof in a town along their route. Even now, as you drive across the South, you will see their remnants baked into the soil like fossils: an ancient veranda, a ghost sign blistered from years of rain—LAZARUS & SONS, HOME OF THE 2 PENNY BELT. These men were careful to open no more than one store per town, partly because who needs the competition, partly because they worried about attracting the wrong kind of attention. They stocked everything. What they did not stock, they could order. The most successful grew into great department stores: S. A. Shore in Winchester, Alabama, founded by Russian-born Solomon Shore, father of Dinah; E. Lewis & Son Dry Goods in Hendersonville, North Carolina, founded by Polish-born Edward Lewis; Capitol Department Store in Fayetteville, North Carolina, founded by the Russian Stein brothers. Others, having started by extending credit to customers, evolved into America's first investment banks. Lehman Brothers, founded by Henry Lehman, a Jewish immigrant from Bavaria, began as a dry goods store in Montgomery, Alabama, in 1844. Lazard Frères, founded by three Jewish brothers from France, began as a wholesale business in New Orleans in 1848. The store owned by Zemurray's uncle was probably of this variety: having begun as a young man carrying merchandise, it grew into a neat grocery on Broad Street.

Selma closed early. By ten p.m., the bustling of the marketplace had given way to the swamp stink and cicadas, but there was always action for those who knew where to look: in the private clubs where merchants played faro and stud, in the juke joints that stayed open from can till can't. According to those who knew him, Sam did not care for crowds and parties. He had a restless mind and a persistent need to get outdoors. He liked to be alone. You might see him wandering beneath the lamps of town, a tough, lean young man in an overcoat, hands buried deep in his pockets.

He stacked shelves and checked inventory in his uncle's store. Now and then, he dealt with the salesmen who turned up with sample cases. He stood in the alley, amid the garbage cans and cats, asking about suppliers and costs. There was money to be made, but not here. He interrogated customers. He was looking for different work and would try anything, if only for experience. His early life was a series of adventures, with odd job leading to odd job. Much of the color that would later entertain magazine writers—Sam's life had the dimensions of a fairy tale—were accumulated in his first few years in Selma.

He worked as a tin merchant. Well, that's how it would be described in the press. "Young Sam Z. bartered iron for livestock, chickens and pigs." According to newspaper and magazine accounts, he was in fact employed by a struggling old-timer who was less tin merchant than peddler, the last of a vanishing breed, the country cheapjack in a tattered coat, sharing a piece of chocolate with the boy. Now and then, he might offer some wisdom. *Banks fail, women leave, but land lasts forever.* He combed trash piles on the edge of Selma, searching for discarded scraps of sheet metal, the cast-off junk of the industrial age, which he piled on his cart and pushed from farm to farm, looking for trades—wire for a chicken coop in return for one of the razorbacks in the pen. After the particulars were agreed on, Sam was told to get moving, *Catch and tie that animal, boy.* It was Zemurray's first real job: racing through the slop with a rope in his hand. "In those days," he told a reporter from *Life*, "I could outrun any pig in Dixie." Paid a dollar a week, he kept the job just long enough to know he would rather be the man who owned the hog than the man who collected the junk, and would rather be the man who discarded the sheet metal than the man who owned the hog.

A series of jobs followed, tried on and thrown off like thrift-store suits. He was a housecleaner and a delivery boy. He turned a lathe for a carpenter. By eighteen, he had saved enough to send for his brothers and sisters, half a dozen pale young Jews who turned up in Alabama in the last years of the nineteenth century.

But his real life began only when he saw that first banana. He devised a plan soon after: he would travel to Mobile, where the fruit boats arrived from Central America, purchase a supply of his own, carry them back to Selma, and go into business.

2

Ripes

Zemurray took his money and went south. Wisteria bloomed along the railroad tracks. Towns drifted by. He could smell the ocean before he could see it. He was like a kid on the frontier, who, a day after the harvest, folds his savings into a roll and goes to try his luck in town.

Mobile was a seedy industrial port filled with all the familiar types: the sharpie, the financier, the scoundrel, the chucklehead, the sport. Sam was a bit of everything. He could be shrewd, but he could also be naïve. He was greedy for information. He took a room in a seamen's hotel near the port. The waterfront was crossed by train tracks—dozens of lines converged here. Boxcars crammed with coal, fruit, cotton, and cane stood on the sidings. The railroad conductors were the aristocrats of the scene. They drank coffee in the station house, smug in their checkered caps. The docks were crowded with stevedores, most of them immigrants from Sicily. The train sheds were crowded with peddlers, most of them Jewish immigrants from Poland and Russia. They bought merchandise off the decks of ships and sold it from carts in the streets of Mobile.

One evening, Sam stood on the wharf watching a Boston Fruit banana boat sail into the harbor. The Boston Fruit Company, which would become United Fruit, dominated the trade, with a fleet that carried bananas from Jamaica to Boston, Charleston, New Orleans, and Mobile. Zemurray would have seen one of the smaller ships that made the trip to the Gulf ports, a cutter with sails and engine. The funnel sent up black smoke. The pier strained under the weight of unloaders who appeared, as if out of nowhere, whenever a ship landed. As soon as the boat was anchored, these men swarmed across the deck, ants on a sugar pile, working in organized teams.

In the South, in the days before mechanical equipment, bananas were unloaded by hand, the workers carrying the cargo a stem at a time—from the hold, where the shipment was packed in ice, onto the deck of the ship. A banana stem is the fruit of an entire tree—a hundred pounds or more. Each stem holds perhaps a hundred bunches; each bunch holds perhaps nine hands; each hand holds perhaps fifteen fingers—a finger being a single banana. It was backbreaking work, and dangerous, not just for the shoulders and arms but also for the central nervous system. As any banana cowboy would tell you, banana plants are prized nesting places for scorpions. When the stems are cut down, the killers go along for the ride, from the banana plantation to the jungle railroad, to the wharf, to the ship, across the Gulf to Mobile, or New Orleans, or Boston, where they spring out, stinging the first stevedore they happen upon.

Most workers on the banana docks were West Indians who arrived in the southern ports on the ships that carried the cargo. Early last century, newspaper reporters looking for local color often wrote about these hired hands, painting them in barbarous shades of minstrel blue. They described dark skin, big lips, grinning faces, heavy haunches, their shirts as white as their eyes, lifting and hauling, working as one man. They pictured them in sunlight and gaslight, moving like shadows along the docks, docile, content, occasionally breaking into hymns and psalms and strange tribal music that chilled their white overseers. "Most of them are Jamaican negroes," Frederick Upham Adams wrote in *Conquest of the Tropics*, "black as the ace of spades and care-free as the birds who sing in the adjacent park. Fat negro 'mammies' trudge in with handcarts loaded with food and sweetmeat delicacies dear to the negro taste. . . . Powerful clusters of electric lights flash out in the vast covered shed which protects the docks, and the myriad lights of the ship add their glow to the general effect."

Sam would have watched closely as the workers formed lines that snaked from the deck of the ship down a ramp, and across the pier to the waiting boxcars. (He wanted to learn every detail of the trade.) Each stem was passed from man to man until it reached the open door of the train, where an agent from the company examined it for bruises, freckles, color. If the stem passed muster, it was loaded into the car, which was air cooled and straw filled. When the car was full, the door was swung shut and locked. An empty car was rolled into its place. This continued for hours—a shift might run from three p.m. until midnight. When a train was packed, the switchman signaled and the cargo was carried across the South.

The bananas that did not pass muster were dumped on the side of the yard, where they were further divided. Some were designated as turnings, meaning they were on their way to being worthless. At the end of the day, they were sold at a discount to store owners and peddlers. You could see them, with their carts piled high, trundling through the streets, calling, "Bananas, bananas for sale! A nickel a bunch! Yes, we have bananas, we have bananas for sale!"

The bananas that did not make the cut as greens or turnings were designated "ripes" and heaped in a sad pile. A ripe is a banana you have left in the sun that has become as freckled as a Hardy boy. These bananas, though still good to eat, delicious even, would never make it to the market in time. In less than a week, they would begin to soften and stink. As far as the merchants were concerned, they were trash. When defining a ripe, Boston Fruit used the following standard: one freckle, turning; two freckles, ripe.

Sam noticed everything—the care with which the bananas were handled, the way each boxcar was filled and rolled to a siding, how men from the banana company, college men, moved through the crowd barking orders—but paid special attention to the growing pile of ripes. Anything can cause a banana to ripen early. If you squeeze a green banana, it will turn in days instead of weeks; ditto if it's nicked, dented, or banged. A ripe banana will cause those around it to ripen, and those will cause still others to ripen, until an entire boxcar is ruined. Before refrigeration was perfected, as much as 15 percent of an average cargo ended up in the ripe pile.

Sam grew fixated on ripes, recognizing a product where others had seen only trash. It was the worldview of the immigrant: understanding how so-called garbage might be valued under a different name, seeing nutrition where others saw only waste. He was the son of a Russian farmer, for whom food had once been scarce enough to make even a freckled banana seem precious.

After the ship had been unloaded, after the trains had carried off the green bananas, after the merchants and peddlers had taken away the turnings, Sam walked down to the pier to talk to the company agent. They spoke as the sun went down, the man with the Ivy League elocution and the kid with the Russian accent, who rolled his *r*'s and spit his vowels. Zemurray had $150. That was his stake. He figured it would go further if it was spent on ripes. He was no fool. He knew what this meant—that he would have to move fast, that he was entering a race with the clock. Three days, five at the most. After that, he would be left with a pile of glue. But he believed he could make it. As far as he was concerned, ripes were considered trash only because Boston Fruit and similar firms were too slow-footed to cover ground. It was a calculation based on arrogance. I can be fast where others have been slow. I can hustle where others have been satisfied with the easy pickings of the trade.

Zemurray's first cargo consisted of a few thousand bananas. He did not spend all his money but retained a small balance, which he used to rent part of a boxcar on the Illinois Central. The trip to Selma was scheduled to take three days, meaning he would have just enough time to get the fruit to market before the sun did its worst. In most cases, a fruit hauler would spend a few dollars extra for a bed in the caboose, but since the freight charge used the last of his money, Zemurray traveled in the boxcar with his bananas, the door open, the country drifting by. It seems appropriate: Zemurray sleeping beside his first haul, attending to his product like a baby in a nursery.

The train left on a Tuesday morning, say, the sun fiery above the smoky freight-yard dawn, the clank of wheels over switches, the ocean drifting away. Color and country: blue in the morning, green at midday, red in the evening. Zemurray sat in the boxcar doorway. The train traveled maddeningly, infuriatingly, exceedingly slow. In the country, it went the speed of a trotting mule. In the towns, it was no faster than a man walking. In the cities, it stopped altogether, sometimes for hours, waiting for cargo and crew. Zemurray paced the railroad bed, hands on his hips, muttering.

Stoplights. Temporary holds. What was supposed to be three days was turning into five, six. With each hour, the bananas became more pungent. He spoke to the conductor, who commiserated, saying, "What a terrible shame."

In a Mississippi train yard, where the redbrick buildings, feed stores, and tinsmiths crowded close to the tracks, a brakeman, hearing Sam's story, said, "You've got good product there. If you could just get word ahead to the towns along the line, I'm sure the grocery owners would meet you at the platforms and buy the bananas right off the boxcars."

During the next delay, Zemurray went into a Western Union office and spoke to a telegraph operator. Having no money, Sam offered a deal: if the man radioed every operator ahead, asking each of them to spread the word to local merchants—*dirt-cheap bananas coming through for merchants and peddlers*—Sam would share a percentage of his sales. When the Illinois Central arrived in the next town, the customers were waiting. Zemurray talked terms through the boxcar door, a tower of ripes at his back. *Ten for eight. Thirteen for ten.* He broke off a bunch, put the money in his pocket. The whistle blew, the train rolled on. He sold the last banana in Selma, then went home in the dark. When he tallied his money, it came to $190. His first real success: after accounting for expenses Sam had earned $40 in six days.

Zemurray had stumbled on a niche: ripes, overlooked at the bottom of the trade. It was logistics. Could he move the product faster than the product was ruined by time? This work was nothing but stress, the margins ridiculously small (like counterfeiting dollar bills), but it was a way in. Whereas the big fruit companies monopolized the upper precincts of the industry—you needed capital, railroads, and ships to operate in greens—the world of ripes was wide open. Within a few weeks of his return to Selma, Zemurray set out again, then again, then again. It was in these months, on train platforms and in small towns, that Zemurray first came to be known as Sam the Banana Man.

Historians later described the young Zemurray as a fruit peddler, no different from other poor Jews who pushed carts through Manhattan's Lower East Side, except instead of a wagon, Sam worked from a boxcar. (He was "Sam the Banana Man," according to *Life*, "who once used railroads as pushcarts.") It made sense, but only in a shallow way. In truth, Sam Zemurray was more interesting and unique—as a salesman of a perishable product, he was a kind of existentialist, skirting the line between wealth and oblivion, health and rot, a rider of railroads, a chaser of time, crossing the country in a boxcar filled with reeking produce. It was life: move the fruit now or you're ruined forever. He became a gambler by necessity—a risk taker, a salesman, a brawler. "The little fellow," as the big wheels in Boston called him, but the little fellow would build a kingdom from ripes.

3

The Fruit Jobber

By the end of the nineteenth century, the world of the banana men—which was a world of shipping companies, warehouses, plantations, ripening rooms, loading bays, and docks—had settled into a hierarchy. If you step back, you can see it laid out in a cross section, like an exhibit in a museum: at the top, you have the owners of the companies, men who sit in boardrooms and trade stock. One of the largest was Boston Fruit, dominated by old New England families. But there were others, as many as fifty small and midsized importers. They had names like Tropical Trading and Transport Company, Colombian Land Company, Snyder Banana. Beneath them were sea captains who rented cargo space. These were the sort of salts whose portraits hang in dockside taverns: bearded sailors in peacoats, their storm-tossed ships painted in the background. Such men were the backbone of the trade, which depended on speed. There were tales of ruthless sailors who did whatever it took. Captain Gus, for example, who, rather than losing days in quarantine, dumped a passenger sick with fever into the sea. Then came the bureaucrats: dock agents, purchasers, inspectors, and overseers who worked the wharves, filled the hotels and taverns, and spoke only of bananas. Then the stevedores, loaders and unloaders, African Americans and Sicilians who went everywhere with their baling hooks, always present, never seen.

Finally, at the bottom of the trade, in the cellar beneath the basement, came the banana peddler, also known insultingly as the fruit jobber. (For the rest of his life, no matter how high he climbed, the executives at United Fruit referred to Zemurray as "the fruit jobber.")

Almost all were foreign born: Jews from Russia, Greeks from Anatolia, Italians from Sicily. It was the only work many could get. Bananas were especially disreputable, with the taint of cholera and the stink of the docks. Most jobbers were small men, feisty, excitable, voluble, prone to anger. When they argued, it made a kind of symphony. You saw the crowd whenever a ship came in, fighting for position. Sam, big, deliberate, strong, and slow, stood out from the beginning. Nothing could make him hurry. He had the sort of calm that cannot be taught. Years later, in a letter to Franklin Roosevelt, Supreme Court justice Felix Frankfurter described Zemurray as "one of the few statesmen among businessmen that I have encountered. He has the qualities that one usually finds in a great personality: simplicity as well as size."

Sam had filled out since his first years in Selma, become a man. In his prime, he was six foot etcetera, a buck eighty-five in boots, broad across the shoulders with powerful arms. He was a kind of colossus; dismissals of him as "the little fellow" were comical. In meetings where rivals expected a stooped immigrant, his size registered with shock. It was ten points on the board before the game even began.

He moved to Mobile soon after he went into ripes. Better to live near the docks. Now and then, if business was slow, he took a job. He worked on a ship as part of a cleaning crew, scrubbing decks. He worked in a warehouse as a watchman. I'm not sure where he lived. In a cheap rental in the old part of the city, perhaps; in a boardinghouse by the harbor. He had soon made his name as a uniquely resourceful trader: the crazy Russian who bought the freckled bananas. He was pure hustle. Every morning, before first light, he was at the docks with a pocketful of bills. Foghorns blew, train wheels rattled, smoke drifted across the sky. He purchased every ripe and overripe and about-to-be-ripe he could lay his hands on. The importers were happy to get money for what, in other towns, was considered trash. He sorted these bananas, then loaded them onto the boxcars of the Illinois Central: the overripes went to markets in Mobile or towns nearby; the ripes went to stores fifty or a hundred miles up the line; the about-to-be-ripes might keep as far as Memphis or Birmingham.

Because Zemurray discovered a patch of fertile ground previously untilled, his business grew by leaps and bounds. In 1899, he sold 20,000 bananas. In 1903, he sold 574,000. Within a decade, he would be selling more than a million bananas a year. When Andrew Preston, the president of United Fruit, visited Mobile in 1903, he asked to meet Samuel Zemurray, the Russian selling the ripes. No photos of this meeting were taken, no minutes recorded, but it was significant: the titan who began the trade shaking hands with the nobody who would perfect it. Preston later spoke of Zemurray with admiration. He said the kid from Russia was closer in spirit to the banana pioneers than anyone else working. "He's a risk taker," Preston explained, "he's a thinker, and he's a doer."

Zemurray signed a contract with United Fruit that year, putting their arrangement in writing. Though I've not been able to find the original document, I have found its language summarized in a lawsuit the attorney general of the United States brought against the Illinois Central, which, according to the Justice Department, had been unfairly favoring Zemurray. The lawsuit defines the fruit jobber's relationship with United Fruit thus: "An importer of bananas had a contract with Z, under which all ripe bananas and all bananas that were turning ripe became his property."

In other words, all the bananas shipped by United Fruit, which amounted to nearly half the bananas in the world, were in the process of becoming Zemurray's. Everything turning was turning into Sam's.

A few years before, Zemurray seemed like a fool buying garbage. Now look what he'd accomplished! Selling hundreds of thousands of bananas a year, he'd become one of the biggest traffickers in the trade. And he'd done it without having to incur the traditional costs. His fruit was grown for him, harvested, and shipped for free. He was like a bike racer riding in the windbreak of a semitruck—the semitruck being United Fruit. By his twenty-first birthday, he had a hundred thousand dollars in the bank. In today's terms, he would have been a millionaire. If he had stopped there, his would have been a great success story.

4

Brown to Green

Samuel Zemurray took a partner circa 1903. This was out of character. He was the solitary sort, a late-night walker and party avoider. He liked to make decisions on his own—better to ask forgiveness than permission. But he had gone as far as he could go with ripes. He wanted to move into the more respectable precincts of the trade; that's where the real money was. For this, he would need capital and help, someone to kick in cash and tend the office while he traveled.

Ashbell Hubbard is gone now, dead and buried, forgotten. No shadow, rumor, trail. If his name survives, it's as a footnote in the story of Zemurray. Here was a poor bastard who lacked the nerve, who sold out too early, who quit the game a minute before the number came in. He was a product of the scene, having grown up in Mobile, a sort of elder statesman respected by everyone in the trade. In him, Zemurray would have recognized a member of the club, a mild-mannered man who could reassure investors concerned by Sam's risk taking. (Hubbard had his own contract with United Fruit, which also helps explain the partnership.) In Zemurray, Hubbard would have recognized the raw talent of the rising star. They joined with an ambitious goal: to traffic yellows and greens. This meant contracting Central American farmers for a percentage of each harvest, which Zemurray and Hubbard would import to Mobile, New Orleans, Galveston. For Sam, who had always kept down costs, this meant assuming a new level of risk.

The Hubbard-Zemurray Company started with $30,000 in capital. The men rented an office in Mobile. There was frosted glass with a name on the door, shipping schedules, railroad tables tacked on a wall. After hours, they stopped in one of the bars on the water, where they could catch up on gossip and market talk, the smallest bit of information meaning possible advantage. By then, a group of men had gathered around Zemurray, banana men who seemed to defer to him, though he was the youngest on the scene. This ability to attract followers would prove crucial. Though he said little, he was recognized as a leader. His team was better, stronger, tighter. In my mind, young Sam, this kid who demanded fierce loyalty, resembles, crazy as it might sound, John Wayne, the gawky youth who turned up in that early Raoul Walsh Western, slouching in imitation of his own childhood hero Tom Mix, the first cowboy star. Zemurray was big and slow like that, gruff, easy, earthy, and charming, with a booming voice that commanded respect. Walking into a portside dive where the men were drinking, he would frown and say, "All right, boys, time to work."

In 1905, Zemurray and Hubbard purchased Thatcher Brothers Steamship Company, which was in bad financial shape. This acquisition ran upward of $10,000. Sam put up some of the money, Ashbell did the same. The balance was covered by United Fruit at the direction of Andrew Preston. (According to colleagues, Preston followed Zemurray's progress as the general manager of the Yankees might follow a flamethrower making his way through the minors.) Such partnerships were the way of United Fruit, the style that earned the company the nickname El Pulpo, the Octopus. They wrapped their tentacles around every start-up in the industry. In those days, U.F. either owned a piece of you or was intent on your destruction. United Fruit took a 25 percent stake in Hubbard-Zemurray but remained a silent partner.

Around this time, Hubbard and Zemurray acquired the Cuyamel Fruit Company, founded in the 1890s by the speculator William Streich, who bought a hundred acres on the Cuyamel River in Honduras and then ran out of money. Cuyamel was subsequently purchased by a consortium of Cincinnati businessmen, who invested several hundred thousand more dollars in equipment, steam shovels, and engines that turned to rust in the fields, as they followed Streich into insolvency. The banana lands were littered with defunct concerns and failed businessmen. You would see them in taverns near the harbor, in dirty suits and panama hats, cadging drinks and boasting: *I used to own this; I was once head of that; I was mayor of this; I was boss of that.* If you're going to build in the jungle, build fast. Anything left for a season is lost. It turns first into a ruin, then into a story, then is forgotten altogether.

What had Zemurray purchased?

A strongbox filled with deeds that might or might not be honored. The acquisition of Cuyamel—it cost him $20,000—was a gamble. For the moment, the key purchase was Thatcher Brothers, picked like a plum from the bottom of the market. With Thatcher, Zemurray became the owner of steamships. This changed his status immediately.

It's worth lingering on the ships, as they would remain important for years. Once fancy ocean liners, they had since fallen into disrepair. Chipped and rusty, they retained a certain elegance. An upper deck, a hurricane deck, a side-wheel, a dining room. The ships once made a regular run from Liverpool, England, to Argentina—they were said to be the fastest across the Atlantic. They were warhorses and would remain in constant operation for fifty years, filled with dandies in the beginning, filled with bananas in the end. Standing in the pilothouse, the world would look different to Zemurray, his field of operation suddenly expanded. The entire Gulf of Mexico was now open, all the waterfront towns, markets, inlets, and deltas of the Central American isthmus.

5

Bananas Don't Grow on Trees

In the jungle, after a heavy rain, you can hear the banana trees growing. If you're a tourist lost in the lowlands, it's the ominous sound of the coming end, creepy crawlies in the depths of the lagoon. If you're a banana man walking in your fields at sundown, it's money.

A banana plant, under the best conditions, can grow twenty inches in twenty-four hours. The thought can make you sick: groves of stems and monstrous leaves expanding while we sleep, desiring, it seems, to cover completely the sunny parts of the world. Which, of course, makes it an ideal crop for a businessman. It's never out of season. A single plant can bear fruit as many as three times a year for twenty years or more. And when the stem is finally kaput, and by now you're old and rich, you dig up the rhizome, hack it to pieces, plant each piece, and watch those grow. Thus another twenty years go by.

The scientific name for the plant, *Musa paradisiaca*, the fruit of paradise, carries evidence of a medieval legend—that it was the banana, not the apple, that the snake used to tempt Eve in the Garden of Eden, a belief that, considering the shape of the fruit and the nature of man's Fall, makes sense. According to another legend, the banana was a holy fruit from the East, sustenance for the wise men of India, the peels rotting in piles beside the bodhi tree where the Buddha attains enlightenment, where men are freed from the wheel, where the banana cowboy puts down his guns.

This notion—carefree men living on wild bananas—comes, probably, from a sense of the fruit as the perfect, shrink-wrapped-by-God product of the jungle. You are hungry, reach up and take a bite. In fact, the fruit does not begin to ripen until picked and cannot be eaten from a tree without retching. Even in ancient times, those who ate bananas had to harvest them, then wait for the harvest to ripen in palm-frond huts, a system copied by United Fruit.

According to scientists, the banana has its origins in the jungles of Southeast Asia, in the wilderness of our first world. These jungles have all the conditions a banana needs to thrive—conditions replicated everywhere on the equator. Sandy soil known as loam, high humidity, high temperatures, and at least 180 inches of rain a year. A frost will wipe out an entire crop. In cataloging the home country of the banana, where the fruit grows wild, the anthropologist Herbert Spinden of the Peabody Museum included "Northeast India, Burma, Cambodia and parts of Southern China, as well as the large islands of Sumatra, Java, Borneo, the Philippines and Formosa."

There are dozens of edible species in the Far East, and dozens more that will cause you pain or put you to sleep forever. The best include the Cavendish, the kind we eat today; the plantain, which has to be cooked to be enjoyed; the dwarf banana known as the Lady Finger; and the Jamaican Red, which has a pinkish peel and tastes like the banana Curious George eats.

The Gros Michel, or Big Mike, the banana that built the trade, was a hybrid created in 1836 on a farm in Jamaica. The work of the French botanist Jean François Pouyat, this banana was prized for its taste and durability. With its thick skin and slow ripening time, the Big Mike was easy to ship—throw a few stems on deck, raise anchor, go.

Some facts about the banana:

It's not a tree. It's an herb, the world's tallest grass. Reaching, in perfect conditions, thirty feet, it's the largest plant in the world without a woody trunk. Its stem actually consists of banana leaves, big, thick elephant ears, coiled like a roll of dollar bills. As the plant grows, the stem uncoils, revealing new leaves, tender at first, rough at last. The fruit appears at the end of a cycle, growing from a stem that bends toward the ground under its own weight. Because the plant is an herb, not a tree, the banana is properly classed as a berry. The plant grows from a rhizome, which, in the way of a potato, has no roots. It's outrageously top-heavy and can be felled, as entire fields sometimes are, by a strong wind. Though the plant can be grown all over the world—

I grew one in Connecticut, for a little while—it will, with two exceptions, bear fruit only in the tropics. Iceland and Israel are the exceptions: Iceland because it grows on the slopes of a volcano; Israel for reasons that remain mysterious. Various attempts to farm bananas commercially in the continental United States—California, Louisiana, Mississippi, southern Florida—have failed. The tree bears a red flower, a delicate, bloody thing, a few days before it fruits.

The banana's great strength as a crop is also its weakness: it does not grow from a seed but from a cutting. When the rhizome is chopped into pieces and planted, each piece produces a tree. (Even though the plant is not technically a tree, I am going to keep calling it that.) In fact, the banana does not have a seed—I mean, yes, there is a stone at the bottom of the fruit, but try to plant it and watch what happens. Nothing. Time and evolution have rendered that stone as useless as your appendix. This means terrific savings in seed and in the shipping of seed and so on, but it also means each fruit—I'm going to go ahead and keep calling it a fruit, too, because I feel funny calling a banana a berry—is a clone, a replica of all the others of its species. Which means nice corporate uniformity but also poses a terrific danger—if a parasite or a disease mutates to kill one banana, it will eventually kill all members of that species. That's what happened to the Big Mike and is happening now to the Cavendish.

The banana made its way west slowly, from region to region, over eons. Rhizomes were carried by Muslim traders, who got them from traders in the Far East. The first Arabic reference appeared in the writings of the poet Mas'udi, who, in AD 956, expressed his love for a dish called kataif—almonds, honey, nut oil, banana—popular in Damascus, Constantinople, and Cairo. By 1050, bananas had arrived in West Africa. (The word "banana" is said to have originated in Africa.) In the fifteenth century, bananas were carried to the Canary Islands, soon after they had been captured and colonized by Castilian adventurers from Spain. In 1516, Friar Tomás Berlanga carried bananas to the New World—two rhizomes, which he planted in Santo Domingo because, he said, his garden needed variety. In the first years of the modern banana trade, all the fruit in the Americas was descended from these two rhizomes.

According to Gonzalo Fernández de Oviedo, who wrote the earliest history of the New World—he was fourteen when Columbus set sail— Friar Berlanga gave pieces of rhizome to whoever happened to visit Santo Domingo, encouraging them to plant bananas across the region. Within a generation, banana leaves were casting shadows on all the Caribbean islands. "And they have even been carried to the mainland," wrote Fernández, "and in every port they have flourished." When Berlanga was made bishop of Panama, he brought rhizomes with him, which is how the banana was introduced to the isthmus.

For the first 350 years of its American life, the banana was consumed locally, usually within a mile of its birthplace. The fruit was delicious, but the notion that it might become an export, harvested in the way of coffee beans, was unimaginable. There was the occasional shipment, freaks that turned up too early. A stem was carried into the harbor at Salem, Massachusetts, in 1609, for example—the first bananas to reach the British colonies. But for the most part, the banana lands were too remote for North American trade. Even later, when a few stems did materialize, the fruit was seen as a curious luxury—the opposite of the place it held in the South. According to Charles Morrow Wilson, author of *Empire in Green and Gold*, "Perhaps not one *Norteamericano* in ten thousand had ever seen or tasted a banana in 1870." As late as 1876, bananas were put on display at the World Exposition in Philadelphia in the way of a winged Pegasus. Many historians reference that expo as the moment the banana was introduced to the United States. It was priced by the slice, each wrapped in foil, at ten cents a pop.

When steam power became a reality, merchants finally recognized the banana as a commercial product.

So appeared the first banana men, pioneers who moved to sleepy Central American ports in the 1850s. Puerto Limón in Costa Rica, Puerto Cortés in Honduras. They came in the way of Spanish conquistadores, looking to establish themselves as property owners, members of a social class that would not have them back home. They resembled figures in the Western tales of Owen Wister: men who have left everything, have run away, are restless, wanted. In photos, they look like outlaws in straw hats, guns at their sides. Most arrived in the wrong clothes, disembarking in wool coats, the sweat beading on their foreheads. Some worked as traders, bartering for tropical birds, crafts, coffee beans. These men, many of whom opened stores, were the first Americans to deal in bananas: purchased from a peasant who grew a dozen stems beside a shack, sold to a sea captain who, looking them over, said, *I'll give it a try*. There were the Melhado brothers, who opened a store in Trujillo, Honduras, in 1854, and continued to sell bananas as well as cattle, mahogany, and rubber until 1926. Many of the original companies were ad hoc partnerships between merchants like the Melhados and sea captains in need of cargo. The names of the early firms read like Latin classifications of defunct species, evidence of ancient creation: *The Blue Fields Supply & Steam, The Limon Ocean Fitters*. It was an immigrant trade from the start—there was something slapdash about it. If you were the father of a girl, and that girl brought home a boy, and that boy said he worked in bananas, you and your daughter would have a talk.

The first true banana merchant was Carl Augustus Frank, a German immigrant who lived near the harbor in New York. In the 1860s, Frank was a steward on a Pacific mail ship. He prepared manifests, met dock agents, greased local police, handled mail, and made deals with merchants who rented cargo space. On a trip in 1865 or thereabouts, he spotted bananas growing in the right-of-way along some train tracks. Frank, who'd never seen a banana before, examined the fruit, then bought a bunch from a peddler in Aspinwall, Colombia. The transporting of that bunch was moonlighting. Frank snuck them aboard as you'd sneak aboard a stowaway. He reached New York in eleven days, a terrifically short run. Most of the bananas were still green and could be sold at a premium. Frank turned a profit in excess of 100 percent on his investment.

Many banana firms had a creation story that mirrors Carl Frank's: some shipping agent or sea captain happened on the strange fruit in the Caribbean, bought a stem for next to nothing, caught a strong wind, which is the breath of God, that carried him home in record time, the bananas green or turning when he arrived, the result being a huge profit, an astounding return. The banana men, the early ones, would spend the rest of their careers trying to recapture the thrill of that initial score.

In 1867, Frank set up shop as a full-time banana importer. His office was at 229 Fulton Street. Two desks, a mailbox, maps, shipping tables, a storefront that portended a flood of industry. That New York—the

New York of stevedores and sailors, penny-a-night flops and laudanum-laced knockout drops—is gone, demolished, built over, forgotten. The banana business, in other words, had its beginning in a vanished land, where the funnel of the steamship was the tallest object on the skyline of the city. Frank was joined by his brother Otto. He would stay on Fulton Street while Carl traveled the isthmus, searching for bargains. The Franks leased land in Panama, where they planted their own rhizomes, vertical integration even then being the dream of the banana man. They rented space on mail ships and contracted with store owners and merchants in New York. Within a year, the brothers were selling as many bananas as they could ship.

The Franks were followed into the trade by dozens of importers, many of whom worked out of ports in the American South. Most survived no more than a season or two. In those ancient days, every firm operated in the same basic manner. A company agent would arrive in the port of a banana country. If he had worked out a deal with a grower in advance, he was met by a farmer with stems; if not, he would wander the country, posting flyers that invited farmers to meet him with their bananas. In Honduras, most early growers were Sicilians who had come in the same wave that flooded America in the 1880s. The company agent would inspect each bunch, selecting and rejecting, then turn the cargo over to local boat owners, lighters, who carried the bananas on rafts out to a steamship that waited in the deep water beyond the reef.

By 1880, the trade was booming, with dozens of companies operating up and down the Atlantic coast of the United States. The trading houses were filled with banana men. In New York, the industry leaders met at the Hoffman House on Madison Square. These were the men who created the first market for the banana, which was still expensive but getting cheaper all the time. In the industrial age, when food sat in grimy piles in general stores, the banana men sold their product as a natural wonder, the most hygienic of foods, germproof in its skin. It was these men who decided the fruit should be marketed not as a delicacy for the rich but as a staple for the poor. Hence the effort to lower the price. Hence the effort to resist all taxes and duties demanded by the nations of the isthmus. In the last years of the nineteenth century, the sale of bananas doubled and doubled again. One day no one could identify the yellow fruit, the next day the banana was more popular than the apple. In 1898, *Scientific American* instructed readers on how to best consume a banana: "The fruit is peeled by slitting the skin longitudinally and giving it a rotary motion with the hands."

Like most booms, it could not last. Not because there was anything wrong with the product: the banana is perfect. Not because there was any scarcity in demand: people loved bananas from the start—the average American now consumes seventy a year. But because supply was uncertain. The banana, as I've said, is terribly vulnerable: to wind, cold, heat, rain, lack of rain, flood, disease. Most firms got their fruit from a single farm or valley, greatly increasing this vulnerability. The entire supply of many early traders could be wiped out by one bad storm. This became painfully clear in 1899, the Year Without Bananas. There had been a heat wave, a flood, a drought, a hurricane. The market sheds were shuttered, the pushcarts stood empty. Dozens of firms went under. It was like the natural disaster that wipes out all but a few impossible-to-kill species. The handful that did survive came away smarter, having learned basic lessons that would dictate how the business was organized in the future:

1. **Get big**   A banana company needs to be fat enough, with enough capital in reserve, to weather inevitable freak occurrences, such as an earthquake or a hurricane.
2. **Grow your own**   A banana company needs its own fields so it can control planting and harvesting, thus avoiding ruinous competition in the event of a down season.
3. **Diversify**   A banana company needs plantations scattered across a vast terrain, stems growing in far-flung countries, so that a disaster that wipes out the crop of a particular region will not destroy the firm's entire supply.

If you study these lessons, you will understand the development of the banana business, how it grew from mom-and-pop trading posts into an all-powerful behemoth.

In certain ways, Sam Zemurray was without precedent. The schnorrer, the pushcart nebbish, the fruit jobber from the docks. He came from nowhere to create not just a fortune but an archetype; he was the gringo in platonic form. He seemed to strive for the sake of striving, to hustle to prove it could be done. Swinging his machete as the sun beats down, face bathed in sweat. You see him astride his white mule, in the doorway of the cantina, his voice as gruff as the voice of William Holden in *The Wild Bunch*, saying, "If you're on a man's side, you stay on that man's side, or you're no better than a goddamn animal."

Was there a precursor?

Of course there was. (The world is a mere succession of fortunes made and lost, lessons learned and forgotten and learned again.) In truth, Zemurray was following a path blazed by three men who had gone into the jungle a generation before. Here I speak of the titans who built the greatest banana company in the world: United Fruit, El Pulpo, the Octopus, reviled even now, decades after its empire collapsed in the South.

Every story needs a villain.

6

The Octopus

United Fruit, in its early years, is the tale of three lives, three men, three dreamlike adventures:

First, Lorenzo Baker of Wellfleet, Massachusetts, son and grandson of commercial fishermen, himself something of a throwback. He might have stepped out of the pages of Robert Louis Stevenson with muttonchops gone gray before he was forty. He never smiled, never laughed; he scowled or stormed off. That's what people remembered. He was born on Bound Brook Island, a spit of land off Cape Cod "on or about July 4, 1840." By age fourteen, he was working on a schooner. By sixteen, he was earning a full percentage. By twenty-one, he was a captain. He stayed in the pilothouse after the ship landed and the men had gone to get drunk in Provincetown. He loved seaports: boats, hundreds of them, schooners and draggers, masts stripped of sails, nets caked with guts, sailors playing poker as the lights of town glowed in the distance. By thirty, Baker had saved enough to buy a majority share in an eighty-five-ton, three-mast fishing boat called the *Telegraph*. He paid $8,000 to be a principal owner, every penny he had. A week after he took possession, he was approached on the docks by a rough character wearing the sort of coat that cattlemen wore on the Plains. Having acquired the title to a gold mine, the man wanted Baker to carry him and nine other prospectors with their equipment three hundred miles up the Orinoco River to Ciudad Bolívar in Venezuela, from where they would continue on horseback.

When Christopher Columbus sighted the Orinoco in August 1498, he believed he had stumbled across one of the rivers that flowed out of the Garden of Eden. In a letter to King Ferdinand of Spain, Columbus said he had discovered the site of the terrestrial Elysium, "which none can enter save with God's leave." The basin of the river was explored by Alexander von Humboldt in 1800—he wrote of its pink dolphins—but the upper river was not navigated until 1951. Being asked to sail three hundred miles into the interior was like being asked to sail off the earth.

Why did Captain Baker say yes?

The money: $8,500 in cash. Five hundred more than Baker paid for his share in the *Telegraph*. Even if the worst happened, he would walk away rich enough to invest in a new boat without the help of creditors.

Baker landed in Ciudad Bolívar on April 20, 1870. The *Telegraph*'s log records it as the successful delivery of "10 gold prospectors and 4 tons of machinery." The equipment was gathered on a pier, picks and axes wet with rain. Baker was paid the balance of his fee in French and Spanish gold, then stood on the deck of the *Telegraph* watching the mineros fade into the jungle.

Baker had trouble sailing down the river—currents, shallows. When he reached the sea, the *Telegraph* was taking on water. She limped away from the coast like a sailor stumbling away from a fight. He landed in Port Antonio, Jamaica, where the ship was put in dry dock, its hull caulked and repaired.

Ten days later, when the *Telegraph* was returned to the water, Baker began to look for ballast. With this in mind he purchased bamboo, ginger, and allspice. As the cargo was being loaded, he sat in a bar near the water to have a taste of local rum. He was drinking planter's punch when he saw *his* first bananas.

What are those? he asked, pointing to the fruit piled on the wharf.

Baker found himself in conversation with a dock agent who explained the particulars: texture, hardiness, market life—ten days to two weeks. The agent brought Baker a ripe banana.

How do you open it? asked the captain.

It was peeled. He took a bite. The flavor of the banana, the warmth of the rum, the sun beating down, the trade wind—it was perfect, a once-in-a-lifetime experience.

He bought 160 bunches at 24 cents a bunch. They were loaded onto the deck of the *Telegraph*. Then Baker raced the clock that started ticking as soon as the stems had been cut. The trip from Port Antonio to New York usually took two weeks—you could do it faster if conditions were perfect, but if the wind died it could take much longer. This was the gamble at the core of the business, the risk taken by the first banana men. You lived at the whim of forces beyond your control. Your life was weather. The early trade was less industry than art.

Baker caught a favorable wind out of Port Antonio. As in an old-time cartographer's illustration, you see the face of God blowing a gust that billows the sails and speeds the *Telegraph* across the water. He reached Jersey City in eleven days—the bananas were still green. The dock swarmed with agents, go-getters working on commission who examined everything that came in, hunting for bargains. Baker sold his bananas for $2 a bunch: a tremendous return, a jackpot he tried to replicate for years. He would sail to Port Antonio, have a glass of planter's punch, load the *Telegraph* with bananas, then light out. He ran into a squall on his second trip. As the *Telegraph* pitched wildly, the entire cargo slid into the sea. He developed a routine: bananas in summer, mackerel in winter, oysters in spring. In July 1871, he sailed into Boston with the biggest load of bananas the city had ever seen.

Andrew Preston was on the docks the afternoon that load came in. A buyer for Seaverns & Morrison, a Boston produce dealer, Preston took a special interest in perishables. He made a career of recognizing a prize at a distance. He got his hands on everything: pineapples, persimmons, pomegranates. When Baker heaved his cargo onto Long Wharf, it was the first time Preston had ever seen bananas. Stacked in piles, they looked obscene. For years, magazines refused to run ads that pictured a banana—a photo of a woman eating a banana was verboten into our own time.

Preston bought Baker's entire haul. The bosses at Seaverns & Morrison were not pleased. I mean, here's this kid, and yes, he's a good kid, a hard worker, but he's blown the budget on a single product, which we don't know how to store or sell. Okay, fine, he let his heart run away, but then, as soon as that cargo was unloaded, he went out and bought another, then another, as many bananas as Baker could import. In this way, what started as an annoyance at Seaverns & Morrison became a problem. Andrew Preston would not stop talking about bananas. Like Baker before him and like Zemurray after, he had spotted a niche. He knew bananas were going to be huge, just knew it! I assume many people have comparable hunches—*quadraphonic stereos are going to be huge! Beanie Babies are going to be huge!*—but most are forgotten because most were wrong.

Preston was right. He quit Seaverns & Morrison and went to work with Baker. For years, the men had an informal arrangement: Baker carried the bananas to Preston, who sold them across an ever-expanding territory. Preston meant to change the model of the business. It had been low volume, high price; he would make it high volume, with cheap bananas sold up and down the economic scale. To achieve this, Baker and Preston had to increase supply and control quality. In the early days, Baker carried whatever happened to be available—the Cavendish, the Lady Finger, the Jamaican Red. In the future, he would ship only the Big Mike: a buyer has to know what he's going to get. The Big Mike had the advantage of being tough—stack it and it will not bruise. Its skin was moister when peeled than the skin of other bananas, which is why people stopped slipping on banana peels when Big Mike went extinct.

In 1877, Baker moved to Port Antonio to better control supply. The roles of the men became plain, a division that would characterize the industry: Preston stayed in Boston, where he managed the market; Baker stayed in the tropics, where he handled the product. When sales boomed, the partners decided to form a corporation. They had reached a point where the only way forward was to expand. For this, they needed capital. But when they went to the banks, their loan applications were denied as too risky: *one bad season, you're done.* They established a partnership of investors instead, each of whom would put up money in return for stock. Boston Fruit was founded in 1885. The original investors were Preston, Baker, and ten other Bostonians, most of whom invested $1,500.

By 1897, Boston Fruit had $4 million in assets and was growing fast. Yet the company kept running into the same wall: supply could not keep up with demand. Sooner or later, prices would rise, destroying the business model that made the company successful. What's more, all their bananas came from Jamaica, making Boston Fruit vulnerable. That's why Preston was turned away by the banks: too much could go wrong. Though Preston and Baker were making big money—by 1899, Boston Fruit controlled 75 percent of the U.S. banana market—they were regarded as akin to mushroom harvesters, entirely dependent on the rain.

When the worst happened in 1899, the Year Without Bananas, Preston went back to the banks. Only this time, he went with a pitch: Some think the problem is we've grown too big, but the real problem is that we're still too small. We must get bigger, much bigger. We must grow so many bananas in so many places that no single storm can ever put us in such dire straits again. In other words, United Fruit was born of disaster. As Bo Diddley might sing, it was the son of a lightning bolt, sired by a hurricane.

There were two ways for the company to grow: Preston could scout property, plant fields, and harvest bananas, or he could find someone who had done these things already.

By his fiftieth birthday, Minor Keith owned land in six republics on the isthmus, and the hundred-peso note of Costa Rica showed his face: small, dark, and filled with mischief. *Fortune* magazine described him as "an apple-headed little man with the eyes of a fanatic." He had grown monstrously fat, a tiny, corpulent tycoon squeezed into expensive shoes. Brooklyn born, he traveled everywhere before making his way to Costa Rica in 1871, where his older brother Henry, because of family connections, had been hired to build a railroad across the isthmus. Henry, who knew little about trains, met Minor in Puntarenas on the Pacific. Spreading out a map, Henry traced a route that looked easy: fifty-four miles of flat ground and modest hills from Puntarenas to Puerto Limón. Wanting to see the terrain up close, they crossed the country by foot and mule—the brothers in Western gear, boots dragging on the ground. They climbed the Cordillera, the spine of mountains that runs the length of the isthmus. After three days, they reached San José, 3,500 feet above sea level. The country grew more rugged as they went. The valleys were choked with undergrowth. Most of the jungle was uninhabited, forsaken, diseased, the home of yellow fever and cholera. The Indians never lived there. They built their villages in the high country. The Spanish did the same. It was a factor in the success of the banana companies: the cheap prices paid for land by the gringos was considered a windfall by local owners, who believed the lowlands a dangerous waste with no value at all.

From the last hill, the Keith brothers could see Puerto Limón tucked into a cove on the Caribbean. They followed a path into town, then walked into the first tavern. When Minor told the bartender how they had come—across the Cordillera by mule—he bought them drinks. "There's an old saying," said the bartender. "A man who makes the trip to the Caribbean by land once is a hero, the man who does it twice is a fool."

For now, let the Keiths be heroes—soon enough, they will be fools.

The first railroad tie was laid a few months later. In the public announcement, Henry Keith said the train would reach the Cordillera within a year. It's not clear when he realized the work was going to be a lot harder than he'd imagined. A few days into the job is my guess. Laying track on the isthmus is a nightmare. There is no bedrock in the jungle. As soon as a section of rail had been laid, it began to shift. Now and then, after a big rain, an entire stretch would slide into a valley. Weeds wrapped around the ties, roots buckled the beds. The workers were tormented by heat and disease. More than three hundred died the first year; just four miles of track were completed.

Halfway through the second summer, Henry Keith was not feeling well. Feverish, hot to the touch. And his eyes—*my God, his eyes!* Yellow fever. Minor told his brother to go home to Brooklyn, recover, then return. But less than a month later, Henry was back in Puerto Limón. Soon after that, he was dead. Minor moved into his brother's tent and carried on. He sent for his little brother Charlie, as he had been sent for. When that brother died, he sent for his youngest brother, John. When John died, he continued alone. This made him a hero in Costa Rica, a man whose commitment could not be questioned, who fed his own brothers to the jungle.

The railroad made its first run on December 7, 1885. Fifteen years, at least four thousand dead. The conductor stopped short of the Devil's Elbow, a precarious stretch in the mountains where the track crossed a rickety bridge. He was afraid it would collapse. Minor argued with the man, then grabbed an American flag and sat on the cow catcher. Looking ahead, he shouted, "Go!" The train reached Puntarenas at eleven p.m., where it was greeted by a huge crowd. Keith gave a short speech, his command of Spanish being barely serviceable: "*Señores: suplico darme su perdón: yo no ser hablador; ser puramente trabajador.*" Gentlemen, please pardon me; I no be speaker. I be purely worker.

In his spare time, Minor Keith roamed Central and South America, exploring its cities and towns. It was in this way that he saw *his* first bananas—a stem of fat fingers creaking in the warm wind. That was 1873, on the Caribbean coast of Colombia, where the Big Mike made its first appearance on the Spanish Main. Not long after, Keith heard that the Frank brothers of New York were planting bananas along the tracks of the Panama Railroad. And selling them in New York! He went to see Carl Frank, who explained the business. The early traders did not fear competition. It seemed there would never be enough bananas to meet the demand.

It was Carl Frank who sold Minor Keith the rhizomes he planted along the Costa Rican railroad. Keith thought bananas would serve as a cheap food for his own workers, but soon realized, as Frank had before him, that there was a tremendous market for bananas in the North. He formed the Tropical Trading and Transport Company to carry his fruit but sold most of his crop to other suppliers. Though he considered himself a railroad man—it was his dream to build a train from New York to Tierra del Fuego—his business was supported by bananas. He planted rhizomes across the region. By 1882, he was growing bananas in Colombia, Ecuador, Costa Rica, Nicaragua, Honduras, Guatemala, and Mexico. In 1883, he shipped 110,801 stems; in 1890, he shipped more than a million. In 1894, Keith signed a contract with Boston Fruit. He agreed to sell the company his entire banana harvest.

Despite this, Keith's economic situation was perilously uncertain. It was the nature of train building: you lived at the whim of creditors. You might appear rich, but if a lender called in a loan, you were done. Keith owed millions of dollars to banks, money he borrowed to complete his railroad. In late 1898, one of these lenders, Hoadley and Company of New Orleans, went bankrupt. The creditors who took over gave Keith ninety days to repay $1.5 million.

Preston and Baker followed these developments. Keith was their biggest supplier. If he went under, so would they. Boston Fruit had money but needed bananas. Minor Keith had bananas but needed money. In March 1899, Minor Keith, forty-nine years old, boarded a ship for Boston.

The men met in the office of Boston Fruit. Everything was settled in less than an hour. There would be neither loan nor temporary arrangement. The men would merge companies instead—a permanent solution to perpetual problems: money for Keith, fruit for Preston and Baker. The new enterprise, called the United Fruit Company, was incorporated in New Jersey on March 30, 1899. Stock in United Fruit was then traded for stock in the existing concerns: 31,755 shares of United Fruit for all 5,000 shares of Boston Fruit; 39,964 shares of United Fruit for Minor Keith's holdings. This left the company with $20 million in capital as well as 212,349 acres in the Dominican Republic, Cuba, Jamaica, Costa Rica, Honduras, and Colombia. Preston was the company's first president and director, Keith its vice president.

United Fruit issued two hundred thousand shares of stock, which offered for $100 dollars apiece. Even after initial swaps and sales, the company still held 184,000 unsold shares. With this in hand, Preston put the second part of the plan into effect—a cunning way to bring order to a chaotic industry. He traveled from port to port, stopping in every city where bananas moved in numbers. He took aside dozens of importers and jobbers, giving each the same pitch: join us; get big; survive. In return for shares in their small companies, these men would receive United Fruit stock. (It was like selling talking parrots for a thousand dollars apiece and taking payment in thousand-dollar talking parrots, Lorenzo Baker explained later.) After the Year Without Bananas, most of the traders who survived were willing to swap independence for security. In its first six months, United Fruit merged with twenty-seven banana companies. It was like that movie *The Blob*—the beast absorbs everything into its own terrible body.

The names of these firms read like names on the sides of sunken clipper ships:

Colombian Land Co.
Snyder Banana Co.
J. D. Hart Co.

J. M. Ceballos & Co.
Orr & Laubenheimer Co.
Camors, McConnell & Co.
New Orleans–Belize Royal Mail & Central American Steamship Co.
W. W. & C. R. Noyes
John E. Kerr & Co.
J. H. Seward Importing & Steamship Co.
Aspinwall Fruit Co.
West Indian Fruit Co.
Monumental Trading Co.
West India Trading Co.
Henry Bayer & Son
Camors-Weinberger Banana Company
J. B. Cefalu & Brother
S. Oteri
Bluefields Steamship Co.
W. L. Rathbun & Company

One of United Fruit's acquisitions stood out: the Vaccaro Brothers Company, a banana export business run by three Sicilians from New Orleans. Later called Standard Fruit, the concern, which eventually regained its independence, would become part of Dole, now one of the most powerful companies in the fruit business. For years, the banana trade was defined by these three names: United, Cuyamel, Standard.

This was the age of trusts, when steel and oil concerns combined to monopolize their industries. It was also the age of trustbusters, when the government went after any would-be Rockefeller who tried to get a stranglehold on a trade. (The Sherman Anti-Trust Act passed in 1890.) With this in mind, Preston was careful to control no more than 49 percent of the business in any market. He wanted to get big enough to dominate but stay small enough to avoid prosecution. The independents who survived this wave—a tidal wave that remade everything that came before—were *allowed* to survive by United Fruit. They were left to stand as proof of healthy competition. In other words, even its rivals existed so U.F. could prosper.

The company solidified its control by amassing the Great White Fleet, the ships that ruled the Caribbean. Within a decade, the fleet—each vessel painted white to reflect the tropical sun—was carrying not just bananas but also the mail and cargo of Central America. In the case of a strike or disagreement, the company could simply shut down the commerce of the region.

U.F. was in possession of just four ships at the time of incorporation, sailboats with auxiliary steam called fruiters. Preston replaced these tubs with a fleet of powerhouses: the *Farragut*, the *Dewey*, the *Schley*, the *Sampson*, "twin-screw 280-footers" with engines that drove a furious pace—Honduras to Boston in fourteen days; Honduras to New Orleans in five. What began as a summer business for Captain Baker became a twelve-month operation, with banana plants bearing every week of the year. The company introduced its first refrigerated vessel in 1903, a river freighter named *Venus* that had been refitted by a Canadian scientist with a primitive contraption of ice blocks, animal hair, air ducts, and fans. Told of this, Lee Christmas, drinking in the French Quarter, slammed his fist on the bar and said, "Ain't it just like them gah-damned Yankees to commence by refrigeratin' *Venus*? So they take the *Venus* and pad her stern with cow hairs, and put fans and ice bins in her belly! That's Boston, brother! That's Boston!"

By 1910, United Fruit owned one of the largest private navies in the world: 115 ships that sailed under a flag designed by Preston's daughter Bessie—a white diamond bounded by blue and red triangles: the isthmus, the sun, the encroaching seas. The pride the company took in its fleet was captured in an old company mural: a native weighed down by a bushel of bananas, pushing aside a palm frond to reveal a ship at anchor in the bay, aglow with the light of civilization.

United Fruit bought vast tracts of jungle in these years, which were cleared and filled with buildings, turned into settlements of clapboard and steel. "It's in Guatemala that one begins properly to appreciate the great civilizing influence of the United Fruit Company," *National Geographic* reported in 1903.

By 1905, the banana trade *was* United Fruit. The company owned the most ships, planted the most fields, had the most money, and controlled both supply and demand: supply by planting more or less rhizomes, demand by increasing the market. Beginning around this time,

U.F. stationed an agent at South Ferry terminal in New York, where the Ellis Island Ferry landed. Handing a banana to each immigrant who came off the boats, the agent said, "Welcome to America!" This was to associate the banana with the nation, a delicacy of the New World, though none of the bananas were grown in the United States, were in fact as foreign as the men and women coming off the boats. At the same time, U.F. began selling baby food made from bananas, which would hook customers when they were tiny. In 1920, the company introduced a hot banana drink meant to take the place of coffee—it failed. There was banana flour and banana bread. In 1924, U.F. published a book of recipes meant to jack up sales, for example:

CORN FLAKES WITH BANANAS

Fill a cereal bowl half full of corn flakes, and cut one half of a ripe banana on top of this, and serve with heavy cream, and sugar if desired (though it will be found that for the average taste the banana supplies the necessary sugar element in a natural form).

Each of these efforts associated the banana with the beginning—of your life, of your day, of your career as an American. In this way, the banana, which had been exotic, was turned into a staple, the most familiar, necessary, obvious thing in the world. In this way, business boomed. By 1908, United Fruit was shipping thirty-six million stems a year—60 percent of all bananas consumed in the United States. By then, the company had become a dominant player in Central America.

United Fruit dealt with its competition in one of two ways: absorb or crush. Even in the United States, where the dominance of the company was not fully understood—you really had to go down there and see for yourself—people began to ask, *Should any company be this powerful?* Questions persisted. Finally, a decade after the behemoth incorporated, Andrew Preston's fears were realized.

A lawsuit brought by the American Banana Company of Mobile was joined by the Justice Department. It charged United Fruit with violating the Sherman Anti-Trust Act, which was meant to break up "combinations" of companies that banded together to corner a market.

It's difficult to imagine a company in more clear violation. Between 1899 and 1905, United Fruit had acquired dozens of independent concerns, rolling them into a monolith that dominated trade. Gone were the mom and pop haggling on the docks; gone were the pushcart operators setting their own prices.

According to the Justice Department, the formation of United Fruit, this Ottoman Empire of a trust, robbed consumers of a crucial benefit of competitive trade: a better product at a lower price. The U.F. lawyers argued that the size of the company had done just the opposite, resulting in a dependable supply of cheap bananas. In fact, said the lawyers, there were still not enough to satisfy demand, meaning there was plenty of room for any independent trader who wanted to get into the business.

In 1909, the case reached the Supreme Court. It's interesting to consider what might have happened if the Justice Department had won its case against United Fruit as it won its case against Standard Oil two years later. If U.F. had been broken up, if the monster had been divided into a half dozen little monsters, American history in Latin America might have been very different. An isthmus without El Pulpo is an isthmus in which the United States is not demonized in the same way. But the Justice Department did not win. Nor did it lose—not on the merits. (There is no way to look at U.F. in those years and see anything but a monopoly.) The Supreme Court instead decided—it was a huge decision, rife with unintended consequences—that it did not have the authority to judge, as most of the actions under review had occurred overseas. According to Oliver Wendell Holmes Jr., who wrote the majority opinion, "A conspiracy in this country to do acts in another jurisdiction does not draw to itself those acts and make them unlawful, if they are permitted by the local law."

By growing its product there and selling it here, U.F. had stumbled on the greatest tax-saving, law-avoiding scheme of all time. With this decision, Justice Holmes cleared the way for that crucial player of the modern age: the global corporation that exists both inside and outside American law, that is everywhere and nowhere, and never dies.

7

New Orleans

When Sam Zemurray moved to New Orleans circa 1905, it was for the same reason the striver always moves to the big town: for the action.

The city was at its maximum glory. The people-jammed streets were covered in the smog of industry, the Mississippi crowded with freighters and side-wheel steamers. The wharves were divided into sections: those dedicated to grain and cotton, the outgoing harvest of the plantations; those dedicated to bananas, the incoming harvest of the tropics. As the WPA *New Orleans City Guide (1938)* described it, "All day long the groaning conveyors lift bunches of bananas from the hold of the ship, and all day long men continue to move in a line carrying them. Darkness falls and the lights flash on; there are long swaying shadows, and the fruit is doubly green in the artificial light."

Zemurray lived near the docks. No one could tell me the exact address. Some building in the French Quarter, perhaps a wreck with cracks in the walls and a sloped ceiling, and the heat goes out and the fog comes in. When his business grew, he moved uptown, following the wealth of the city, which had been fleeing the French Quarter for decades. At twenty-nine, he was rich, a well-known figure in a steamy paradise, tall with deep black eyes and a hawkish profile. A devotee of fads, a nut about his weight, he experimented with diets, now swearing off meat, now swearing off everything but meat, now eating only bananas, now eating everything but bananas. He spent fifteen minutes after each meal standing on his head, which he read was good for digestion. His friends were associates, his mentors and enemies the same. He was a bachelor and alone but not lonely. He was on a mission, after all, in quest of the American dream, and was circumspect and deliberate as a result. He never sent letters or took notes, preferring to speak in person or by phone. He was described as shy, but I think his actions are more accurately characterized as careful—he did not want to leave a record or draw attention. His early life in Russia would have taught him that a Jew in the paper is a Jew in trouble.

The office of Hubbard-Zemurray—it was already being called Cuyamel Fruit—was at 21 Camp Street, in a neighborhood of fine houses, deeper than broad, three steps to the porch. Cuyamel was operating as an importer, not growing bananas, but buying them from Central American farmers. Zemurray's worries were about supply, setting a good price, working out deals with exporters. The firm was grossing several hundred thousand dollars a year, most of which went to pay farmers and sailors and local officials, who had to be bribed. When not traveling, he spent the entire day on the phone, shouting or being shouted at, then walked home. If he was in a bad mood, he might continue past his house. There were nights, before wife and children and the accompanying heartache and disaster of family, that he traversed the city from St. Peter Street to Audubon Park then out to the levee where the steamships threw sparks on the river. And the foghorn! And the trade wind! And the stink of the tide! If you looked into his eyes, you would see the machinery turning—that's what Frank Brogan told me. "It's just the sort of person he was," explained Brogan, who worked for Zemurray in South America. "He was one of those guys, part of him is always figuring. You listen to a man like that. He knows something that can't be taught."

It was not easy for Zemurray to find his place in the city, which was dominated by an ancient class-conscious, status-obsessed aristocracy. He had money, was smart and not terribly ugly, but everything else was against him. He was a foreigner—a *fucking* foreigner, as they said on the docks. A stranger, a flea, a Russian from the Pale. New Orleans was not a bad place to be from elsewhere. Jews had prospered in the city from its earliest days. It had been home to some of the big Hebrews of America: Judah Touro and Judah Benjamin, the secretary of state of the Confederacy, and Daniel Warburg, the first member of the banking family to settle in the United States. But Touro and Benjamin were Sephardic Jews (Warburg was German), a breed apart from the Eastern Europeans who arrived in the late nineteenth century. Erudite and refined, assimilated to the point of being unrecognizable, they formed a closed society that traced its roots in the city back a hundred years or more. These men were protective of their position, which, many feared, would be jeopardized by men like Zemurray. In this way, Sam was doubly rejected: turned away from the clubs of the German Jews just as decisively as he was turned away from the clubs of the Catholics and Protestants.

When I talked to Thomas Lemann about Zemurray's rejection in New Orleans—at eighty-six, Mr. Lemann is the patriarch of one of the oldest and most prominent German-Jewish families in the South; he worked for Zemurray, as did his father, Monte Lemann—he scoffed and said, "It might bother you if you're the sort of person who's bothered by such things, but I don't think Mr. Zemurray was that sort of person."

But who's to say? Thomas Lemann, whose family has been important in the South since the middle of the nineteenth century? Thomas Lemann, who graduated from Tulane and Harvard Law School?

I believe Zemurray was less the sort of man who didn't care than the sort of man who could make you believe he didn't care. He was a human being, wasn't he? He must have wanted status and acceptance, these being basic human desires. When he couldn't get acceptance, he sought status; when he couldn't get status, he sought power. He was a quiet man, did not complain, had no giveaways or tells, which does not mean he was not furious inside. He wanted and wanted, which is why he fought so hard for so long, why he pinned his enemies to the wall and studied them with a cool eye.

Zemurray joined Temple Sinai on St. Charles Avenue, though he did not strike acquaintances there as particularly observant or engaged in spiritual affairs. He was sunk deep in the here and now. If he was religious, it was in the modern American way, a private business free of mysticism. He was one of those men who turn up in the back of temple on the High Holidays but are otherwise absent, making amends with generous contributions.

His true religion was the waterfront, warehouses and loading bays, iron rails and boxcars—that's where he found refuge, knew just who he was and exactly what to do. He stood in the sheds in his overcoat, long and narrow, built like a candlestick, shouting orders. By the early 1900s, the port of New Orleans had become an industrial affair, with ninety steamship lines, two barge lines, and nine railroads. There were three main banana wharves: Erato, Desire, and Pauline Street, with fourteen automatic unloaders that carried twenty-five hundred bananas an hour. Twenty-three million stems moved through the city every year. U.F. had private facilities at Thalia Street. New Orleans was a working city then, just as great as Chicago or Philadelphia. The modern town is a husk of its old self, which died on its feet but freakishly still stands. I say this to give you a better picture of Zemurray. He was not a big man in a tourist destination. He was an ambitious man trying to become big in the greatest port in the American South.

When he was in town, he was on the docks, trading, questioning, comparing manifests to cargoes, making sure he wasn't getting ripped off. If some streets were closed, if some houses were for sale but not to him—there was always the river. He knew everyone by name there but paid special attention to the old-timers who had been in the trade since the days of wind power. Grizzled and tobacco stained, in flop-brim hats, as sunburned as pirates, they were former big-timers now just trying to survive.

The most colorful of them was probably Jacob Weinberger, known to everyone as Jake the Parrot King. Jake emigrated from Hungary around 1845, settling in Galveston, Texas, then a barrier island newly acquired from Mexico. He had been traveling to the isthmus since the early 1850s. He would sail a rented sloop into tiny port towns on the Atlantic coast, where he was swarmed by children and merchants. Tall and gaunt when he was young, big and fat when he was old, Weinberger was greeted as a curiosity in the South. He carried knickknacks, kerchiefs, plastic horns, mouth harps, toys, shoes, cotton, whatever he might trade for the local wares—crafts, clothes, coconuts. He brought the first shipment of bananas to Texas in the 1860s. For a time, he dealt exclusively in parrots and macaws, tropical birds picked up for nothing that he sold to the owners of general stores and pet shops. Some of the birds still spoke the filthy slang picked up from Caribbean pirates ("Crack the Jenny's daughter"). This is how Jake made his fortune—or first fortune, anyway. The fact is, Jake Weinberger won and lost many large sums but did not seem to care. He was in it for the travel, the exotic ports of call, the experience, the fun. In *Empire of Green and Gold*, Charles Morrow Wilson described Jake as "an affable Southerner, who gambled wildly for the love of gambling, and mixed an excited English and dog Spanish with violent gestures in a highly original language."

Jake had friends in every country in the isthmus, knew the people who ran the towns and governments, understood how the deals got done. He moved to Nicaragua in 1870 to found the Bluefields Banana Company, where he gave himself the title of president and resident tropical manager. "In sultry, mosquito-harried Bluefields, Jake Weinberger took over in the manner of a white-skinned Emperor Jones," Wilson continued. "He liked the Nicaraguans, treated them hospitably and generously, gave the children candy and dolls and the men stiff drinks. It was not strange that the Nicaraguans liked 'Hacob,' worked for him, grew and harvested bananas for him, and helped him turn hot and swampy wastelands into productive fields."

In its best year, Bluefields shipped a million bananas. Jake was then dividing his time among Mobile, New Orleans, Galveston, and Nicaragua. He had become a wise man of the industry, a wizard who could turn a stretch of jungle into a plantation just like that. He was one of the banana men Andrew Preston enlisted in Mobile, when he was swapping shares of United Fruit. But he was a relic when Zemurray met him in New Orleans, an ancient gunslinger kept around less for prowess than for color and knowledge. Sam hired him as a troubleshooter, a sort of banana man–at–large. Though past his prime, he knew the terrain and was on speaking terms with every honcho on the isthmus.

That's not all Jake had to offer: he had a daughter, too, a beautiful woman named Sarah. Zemurray probably met her at Jake's house, as the men did business over coffee—Sam listening to Jake but thinking of the woman reading a book on the porch. I have seen three pictures of Sarah when she was young, one of them on a passport that carries her vital statistics:

Birth Date: 13, December, 1883
Birth Place: Galveston, Texas
Father's Birth Place: Hungary
Mother's Birth Place: Mexico

I would like to cue the orchestra, swell the music, and picture hearts orbiting Zemurray's head. I would like to show this man, who had been occupied by nothing but work from the age of fourteen, falling in love, but I can't. There is no evidence it happened that way. Was there a moment of hand-holding and nervous talk? I doubt it. The relationship had the markings of an arrangement. Zemurray was thirty-one, successful but alone. He needed a wife. Sarah was beautiful but twenty-five, no longer young by the standards of the day. She needed a future, which meant a good match. A businessman marrying the daughter of a colleague has the added benefit of strengthening ties all around. That's what people mean when they call marriage an institution.

Samuel Zemurray and Sarah Weinberger were married in May 1908. The couple moved into a house near the new campus of Tulane. Their first child, Doris, was born on November 19, 1909. Becoming a father changes the nature of the future. What had been half believed becomes real. The inner voice begins to ask serious questions: *How much do I need? What will it take to keep her safe?* It was after the birth of Doris that Sam Zemurray decided he needed to get bigger and make more. The only way to do this was to expand. And the only way to do *this* was to plant his own bananas. It was a realization that sent Zemurray down the path he would follow for the rest of his life, a tortured path that led south into the jungle.

Yellow

8

The Isthmus

Zemurray traveled to Honduras in the early weeks of 1910. He'd been there previously, but it was his first extensive tour of the country that would eventually become his home. He went with Ashbell Hubbard and Jake Weinberger. He was looking to buy land. He learned to speak Spanish imperfectly in the cantinas and dives. No matter how long he lived in the South, Zemurray could never rise above street Spanish overlaid by his American accent, overlaid by his Russian accent. He was all overlay—identity stacked on identity, life stacked on life.

They landed in Puerto Cortés, a low-slung cinder-block town on the sea. The streets followed the curve of the bay, then vanished into hills where colonial mansions commanded the horizon. The mountains were green in the distance but terrible wilderness up close. Everything—the stores, the palm-choked alleys—felt insubstantial. Though Puerto Cortés is one of the old places of the hemisphere—inhabited for six hundred years—it seems provisional. When Zemurray arrived, it was a kind of frontier town, untouched by government or law—less Bogotá or Quito than Dodge City or Tombstone. There was gunplay every night, the streets awash in liquor and gold. Ten feet from the dance hall, the music faded and there was only the ridgeline, the sound of the waves, the stars. It was a wicked place, small and large, unimportant and critical.

Because Honduras had no extradition treaty with the United States, Puerto Cortés had become a criminal refuge, filled with Americans on the lam. Frank Brown, known as "Cashier Brown," who absconded from a bank in Newport, Kentucky, with $195,000 in 1900, turned up in Puerto Cortés. Alex Odendahl, a New Orleans grain merchant who lit out with $200,000 around the same time, turned up in Puerto Cortés with a full beard and a suit of white duck, calling himself Señor Harris. Alcee Leblanc, an ex–deputy United States marshal from New Orleans, absconded, lit out, turned up. Ditto Edward Burke, who had been state treasurer of Louisiana. (He became a mining tycoon, trailed by mercenaries.) According to an article in *The New York Times*, under the headline "A Colony of Defaulters," "no less than seven bank wreckers, some of them of National fame, are secreted and exiled in that tiny little republic. In fact, the country has become the home of a picturesque population, voluntary exiles, who do not dare return to their native soil, and watch each outgoing steamer with wistful eyes until it rounds the point."

William Sydney Porter arrived in Puerto Cortés a few years before Zemurray. A part-time Texas newspaperman, he stole several thousand dollars from a bank in Austin, where he was a teller, then hid out in the bars on Primera Avenue, soaking up the talk of revolutionaries and banana cowboys, which he turned into the book *Cabbages and Kings*, published in 1913 under the name O. Henry. It was O. Henry who coined the term "banana republic." These pages, which remind me of watercolor paintings on the walls of Florida motels, capture the country as it was first experienced by Zemurray. "That segment of the continent washed by the tempestuous Caribbean, and presenting to the sea a formidable border of tropical jungle topped by the overweening Cordilleras, is still begirt by mystery and romance," O. Henry wrote. "In past times, buccaneers and revolutionists roused the echoes of its cliffs, and the condor wheeled perpetually above where, in the green groves, they made food for him with their matchlocks and toledos. Taken and retaken by sea rovers, by adverse powers and by sudden uprising of rebellious factions, this historic 300 miles of adventurous coast has scarcely known for hundreds of years whom rightly to call its master. Pizarro, Balboa, Sir Francis Drake, and Bolivar did what they could to make it a part of Christendom. Sir John Morgan, Lafitte and other eminent swashbucklers bombarded and pounded it. . . . The game still goes on."

Zemurray and his companions stayed in the city a few nights, taking rooms in the only hotel, then rode out. It was winter, the best season on the isthmus—after the rains and before the rains. They visited the banana lands along the north coast, stopping in tiny Caribbean villages, each different, each the same. The world reverted to wilderness between the towns, the swamps east of Eden. The trees were teeming with parakeets, the underbrush filled with monkeys and tapirs. They heard stories of oso caballo, the Central American bigfoot. They slept in hotels, in the guest rooms of local traders, or wrapped in blankets on the beach. Now and then, they traveled by car, but this was the horse-powered age and the men crossed most of the country by mule. The mules of Honduras were notorious bucktoothed animals with twitchy ears and black eyes, in constant battle with their riders. His first time on, Zemurray was thrown to the ground. The second time, the animal bit his toe. The third time, the mule dropped and rolled. The fifth time, the mule carried Zemurray to the middle of a river and left him. It remained a point of pride for Zemurray—he eventually licked the famously sour mules of Honduras. As the old banana cowboys liked to say, "You will never understand the banana business until you understand the banana mule, and you can never understand a banana mule."

Zemurray was a habitual limit crasher. He loved feats of endurance, proving himself by watching companions flag, throw up their hands, and say, "Cerveza, señor, it's time for cerveza." He crossed Honduras on muleback so he could learn the country, meet its people, scout its property, but also so, years later, a person like me would sit and write "the gringo who crossed the country on a mule."

Honduras is the size of Pennsylvania, with Guatemala on its northern border, El Salvador to the west, and Nicaragua to the south. It's two hundred miles from the Atlantic to the Pacific at the narrowest point. When Zemurray arrived, there were a half million people in the country, the majority of them poor mestizos, that is, half-breeds. It was a divided nation, with the Atlantic lowlands more properly Caribbean than Central American—seaside, frond filled, populated by the descendants of African slaves—and the highlands reminiscent of the ancient Mayan landscape known to the conquistadores.

The country was visited by Columbus in 1502. Following the coast, he sailed past the future sites of Omoa (Cuyamel Fruit), Tela (United Fruit), and La Ceiba (Standard Fruit). He named the country Honduras, which means the depths, though the coastal bays are quite shallow, which is why, in the early days of the trade, before the piers had been built, the cargo ships had to sit a half mile offshore waiting for rafts to ferry out the bananas. In other words, the name "Honduras" was false advertising.

Columbus landed at the future site of Trujillo. In a letter to Queen Isabella of Spain, he described it as a "verdant and beautiful [land with] many pines, oaks, seven kinds of palms, and myrobalans like those in Hispaniola called hobi. They have an abundance of pumas, deer and gazelles." He came across Jicaque Indians, who wore quilted jerkins. He was a man reaching out to touch a picture ever so gently. When he asked about cities of gold, the Indians motioned south, just beyond the next hill, just beyond the horizon. (El Dorado recedes before you.) He continued down the coast to the Torrid Zone, believing he was in the Far East, in the country described by Marco Polo, a ten-day walk from the Ganges River. Most European officials had already realized Columbus was not in Japan or India but somewhere strange and new; Columbus, however, was confused.

He spent two months in Honduras, then set sail. A dozen miles off shore, he was caught in a storm, the tempest that sits at the bottom of our hemispheric memory. "Rain, thunder, and lightning were so continuous that it seemed the end of the world," Columbus wrote. "This intolerable storm continued in such a way that we saw neither the sun nor the stars as a guide. The ships were lying open to the skies, the sails broken, the anchors and shrouds lost, as were the cables . . . and many supplies went overboard; the crews were all sick and all were repenting their sins and turning to God. Everyone made vows and promised to make pilgrimages if they were saved from death, and, very often, men went so far as to confess to each other." Historians say the storm lasted twenty-eight days, but Columbus said it lasted one hundred, which might be his way of saying it seemed to last forever. This is a wild country— that was the message of the storm—ringed by sea serpents and monsters.

Honduras was settled twenty years after Columbus by Hernando Cortés and the conquistadores from Spain, fresh from their conquest of Mexico. Cortés was born in western Spain, in Extremadura, where so many of the Spanish explorers came from. My Honduran guide, Mike Valledares, said, "Cortés was a pig farmer. His father raised pigs, and so did he."

Neither Cortés nor his father raised pigs, but Mike's point seemed clear: the men who destroyed the Aztec Empire were not fit for decent company.

The Central American isthmus is 350 miles wide at its widest point and 34 miles at its narrowest in Panama. It's cleaved by the Cordillera, a narrow range of mountains, rocky heights, waterfalls, cliffs, and canyons. If I have used the word "Cordillera" a lot, it's because I think it's the most beautiful word in the language, summoning images of one-lane roads, switchbacks, and coffee plantations at the top of the world. The highest peak on the isthmus is approximately fourteen thousand feet. This is less landmass than hallway, bottleneck, cloverleaf onto the highway, passage from here to there, forever in-between, forever on the way. If you want to drive the isthmus lengthwise, down the gullet, Mexico to Colombia, where the land broadens and South America begins, your best bet is the Pan-American Highway, which starts in Alaska and continues thirty thousand miles to the bottom of the world. It's a network of roads each charted by a conquistador or strongman. It's disappointing in many places, rutted and small, climbing and descending, battling the jungle and mountains, then ending abruptly in the rain forest of Panama. It's as if the road itself, defeated by nature, walked away muttering. It starts again sixty-five miles hence, on the other side of a chasm. This is called the Darién Gap. It symbolizes the incomplete nature of Central America, the IN PROGRESS sign that seems to hang over everything. Russia is the Trans-Siberian Railroad. Germany is the Autobahn. The United States is Route 66. Central America is the Darién Gap.

It's always been that way on the isthmus—many projects started, few brought to completion; many beginnings, few endings; each boom followed by a tremendous bust. The first came with the conquistadores: all that killing had a trickle-down effect of money and jobs. But the big bonanza came with the European discovery of Peru a generation after Cortés: palaces and mines, ribbons of silver and gold. When the jackpot was gathered up and carried off, the isthmus served as the transit point, the cut-through, the shortest walk from Pacific to Atlantic. Every doubloon was humped across that narrow neck of land. It took three weeks to haul a treasure from Veracruz on the Pacific coast of

Colombia to Porto Bello on the Atlantic, where the sailors drank rum as pirates watched and waited. Witnesses described the port towns as a delirium of hustlers and con men, brass bands, horn players barefoot in the dust. In *A Brief History of Central America*, Hector Perez-Brignoli called the isthmus of those years "a chimerical fantasy."

The boom lasted for two hundred years, from the age of Balboa to the rise of North America, when the mines of Peru were finally exhausted. After the last Spanish fleet sailed from Porto Bello in 1739, the isthmus fell into a deep slumber, a sleep of centuries. With the silver went the pirates and their dreams of El Dorado. The region fell off the map, forgotten and forlorn. The population dwindled, villages were abandoned. Now and then, an entire year went by without a ship arriving from Europe. More than a century elapsed between the departure of that last silver fleet and the arrival of the first banana man. By then, the nations of Central America had broken away from Spain. Mexico, Guatemala, the others. Honduras declared independence in 1821.

In *One Hundred Years of Solitude*, Gabriel García Márquez describes the coming of the new age as the arrival of a single entrepreneur from the North:

> . . . there arrived in Macondo on one of so many Wednesdays the chubby and smiling Mr. Herbert, who ate at the house.
>
> No one had noticed him at the table until the first bunch of bananas had been eaten. Aureliano had come across him by chance as he protested in broken Spanish because there were no rooms at the Hotel Jacob, and as he frequently did with strangers, he took him home. He was in the captive-balloon business, which had taken him halfway around the world with excellent profits, but he had not succeeded in taking anyone up in Macondo because they considered that invention backward after having seen the gypsies' flying carpets. He was leaving, therefore, on the next train. When they brought to the table the tiger-striped bunch of bananas that they were accustomed to hang in the dining room during lunch, he picked the first piece of fruit without great enthusiasm. But he kept on eating as he spoke, tasting, chewing, more with the distraction of a wise man than with the delight of a good eater, and when he finished the first bunch he asked them to bring him another. Then he took a small case with optical

instruments out of the toolbox he always carried with him. With the suspicious attention of a diamond merchant he examined the banana meticulously, dissecting it with a special scalpel, weighing the pieces on a pharmacist's scale, and calculating its breadth with a gunsmith's calipers. Then he took a series of instruments out of the chest with which he measured the temperature, the level of humidity in the atmosphere, and the intensity of the light. It was such an intriguing ceremony that no one could eat in peace as everybody waited for Mr. Herbert to pass a final and revealing judgment, but he did not say anything that allowed anyone to guess his intentions.

Mr. Herbert was Samuel Zemurray, a fruit jobber, a hustler, a man who sees not a nation with a history but a mine ribboned with silver and gold. He arrived with schemes and a bag filled with the tools of the diamond trade. (He kept quiet as he tasted because talking only drives up the price.) The original sin of the industry touched everyone: the way the banana men viewed the people and the land of the isthmus as no more than a resource, not very different from the rhizomes, soil, sun, or rain. A source of cheap labor, local color. One definition of evil is to fail to recognize the humanity in the other: to see a person as an object or tool, something to be put to use. The spirit of colonialism infected the trade from the start.

Zemurray bought his first parcel of land on the edge of Omoa, an old colonial town on the north coast of Honduras. Much of the property ran along the southern bank of the Cuyamel River, where the country is hilly and fine, a thousand shades of green. This was long considered junk land, neither valued nor tended. For $2,000, all of it borrowed, he got five thousand acres. He was soon back in New Orleans, wondering if five thousand was enough. Would it give him the supply he needed to compete with United Fruit? *It does not matter if you think it's enough*, Ashbell Hubbard told him. *We're out of money.* There are times when certain cards sit unclaimed in the common pile, when certain properties become available that will never be available again. A good businessman feels these moments like a fall in the barometric pressure. A great businessman is dumb enough to act on them even when he cannot afford to.

9

To the Collins

Zemurray returned to Honduras in the spring of 1910 with a plan, achingly simple, beautifully effective: head north beyond the last paved road, into the delta of the Cuyamel River, flash the roll, and buy as much land as he could until his cash ran out. He was playing with borrowed money. Having tapped out every line of credit in New Orleans and Mobile, he had gone on to banks in New York and Boston. Whoever was lending, he was accepting. He was out there, overextended, vulnerable. He must have worried about the risk but had to know this was his moment: the land would not be this cheap forever. You see him in the cantinas of Omoa, the big Russian in the doorway, buying drinks for everyone. Unlike most banana executives, Zemurray was comfortable with the people of the isthmus. "Sam adapted himself to the ways of life of those he contacted," *Fortune* reported. "He cultivated friendship, and did not scorn to take a drink with the peasants. He acquired a wonderful command of their language [*sic*], including swear words, which he didn't hesitate to employ. He became a Hondureño." Zemurray told the locals he would bring them wealth and good jobs. When it came time to hire, he offered a wage ten times the going rate, which angered other employers. In the course of a few months, he accumulated the uncleared acres that would constitute his first plantation.

In setting a price for the property, Zemurray took advantage of the local landowners. He had superior information, understood something important lost on the Hondurans. To the peasants, the land was swamp and disease, nothing that will still be nothing in a hundred years. Sam knew better. Because he was raised on a farm, he realized the meaning of all that black soil beneath the weeds. Because he worked as a jobber, he realized the worth of the fruit that would thrive in that soil. This land, picked up for a song, was in fact the most valuable banana country in the world. The crop wants lowland forest—bananas will not thrive above three thousand feet—and the kind of soil known as loam, as well as good drainage and eighty to two hundred inches of rain a year. Honduras has all that. "The Caribbean lowlands, which were supposed to be worthless and in which no white man could live, were discovered to be splendid soil for the growing of bananas," Samuel Crowther wrote in *Romance and Rise of the American Tropics.*

Zemurray then went all across Honduras, meeting government officials. He sat with the emissaries of Miguel Dávila, the president of the country. He was seeking sweetheart deals that would exempt his company from taxes and duties. Such corrupt understandings were common enough in the business to have a name: concessions, unofficial arrangements without which no banana man could succeed. The trade depended on cheap fruit, necessitating cheap labor, cheap land, and no extra fees. The smallest additional cost—a penny per bunch, say—would drive the price above the market rate set by United Fruit. Though the Dávila government was not the most pliable, Zemurray did eventually secure his concessions (by kickback, by bribe). In Honduras, Cuyamel would be exempted from import duties on all equipment, such as freight engines, train tracks, railroad ties, steam shovels, machetes; exempted, too, from paying property, labor, and export tax. Zemurray's bananas would arrive in the United States unencumbered by such fees—this meant he could sell his product just as cheaply as United Fruit. Later concessions would entitle him to clear jungle and build wharves, railroads, and bridges, all of which would be privately owned by Zemurray.

If asked to sum up Sam in these early days, when he was building his first plantation, I would use the word "drive": it was drive, ambition, moxie, guts, or whatever you want to call it that pushed him from Selma to New Orleans, then on to the jungle towns of the isthmus, where the genie was loosed and the man went wild. Drive to make money, leave a mark, climb the pyramid, beat the bastards who gave him the high hat. Why bananas? Because it was the nearest product at hand. The Southern markets reeked of them. If he had settled in Chicago, it would have been beef; if Pittsburgh, steel; if L.A., movies. In the end, it does not matter what you're stocking—selling is the thing. Who knows where such ambition came from? Maybe it was the pent-up energy of dozens of thwarted Jewish generations confined to the ghettos of Europe. Maybe it was the result of some forgotten childhood trauma. Maybe it was evidence of a defect or lack, a missing thing that Sam found in competition. (It's the neediest among us who go the farthest.) Or maybe it was already with him in the cradle, the intangible thing that made him go.

In the fall of 1910, Zemurray opened an office in Omoa, eight miles up the coast from Puerto Cortés. The office has been preserved as a museum: a shack with a desk and a window looking out on low hills to the west. The plantation was fifteen miles inland, on the Atlantic slope. In the autumn, when the rains came, he moved to a bungalow in the fields to oversee the workers—most of them Jamaicans—as they cleared the jungle and planted the first bananas.

The process of building a banana plantation—of replacing the chaos of weeds and vines with neat rows, fences, and shacks—was a science by then, a matter of following specific steps.

The best guide was a book published by United Fruit. Having purchased enough land for a plantation, you were instructed to send engineers into the overgrowth with field glasses, notebooks, and pencils to map every inch of every acre, every dip and rise, every gulley where the fog pooled, every course where the water flowed on its way to the sea. Using these maps, the property was divided into relatively flat plots, thirty square acres apiece, or as close as the terrain allowed. Teams of workers walked the fields, marking boundaries with string, then cleared the brush. This was sometimes done by fire, the black clouds visible as far as the coast, the burning wood redolent in the tropical air. More often it was done by hand, the machetes rising and falling—*thwick, thwack, thwick*. It took several weeks. In the end, the jungle was cut to stubble, nothing spared but the big trees, prehistoric monsters that reached hundreds of feet. There was the guanacaste tree, which blossoms into a canopy, or the ceiba, which rises like a column of marble, its bark mottled with spikes. The ceiba was holy to the Mayans. They considered it a portal to the underworld. A ceiba towering above a lonely stretch of countryside is an awesome sight.

After the undergrowth had been cleared, workers marked off rows in the fields. Then two men came along: the first dug a twelve-inch hole every three feet, the second dropped in a banana rhizome. The big trees were then cut down Montana-style, West Indians pushing and pulling a massive two-man saw until the tree sways and someone yells and here comes the ancient ceiba, holy, holy, holy, falling with a rush of leaves, exploding as the trunk hits the ground. The felled trees were the best fertilizer—hundreds of years of nutrients leaked into the soil as they decomposed. A day after a big tree went down, the ground was a mess of branches and leaves. In a few months, the trunk was gone, consumed by the jungle. The workers had been through the fields dozens of times by then, calling across the crop rows as they cleared the weeds with machetes.

This is easy for me to write, of course, sitting at my desk, looking at the winter landscape out my window, repairing to the kitchen now and then for a cup of coffee, but it was the hardest work in the world. If this is the kind of book I want it to be, it will leave you with a sense of the fields, the heat and fear, the snakes in the brush that have to be killed with a single blow, the sting of the poison that makes you want to lie down, just for a minute, in the shade of the ceiba tree, the scorpions that drop into your shirt in search of exposed skin, the mosquito swarms that portend yellow fever, the malarial dreams, the swampland and broken tools and arsenic tree; the way your health is destroyed, your hands blistered, your back ruined; the way the world appears when you have forgotten to drink enough water, a tiny image seen through the wrong end of a telescope.

Zemurray employed hundreds of workers on the north coast. In the first weeks, they lived in tents, then moved into cabins, barracks, and bungalows. They worked from four a.m. till noon, after which it was too hot to linger outdoors. They wore sandals when they worked, shirts opened to the belly, straw hats, and pants with a machete hooked to the waist. The most popular machete, made in Connecticut, was a six-inch crescent-shaped blade embossed near the wood handle with the name of the maker: COLLINS. Now and then, when two or more workers got into a fight, someone would flash a machete and say, "I'll stick you all the way to the Collins." Over time, this phrase "to the Collins" came to stand for every kind of death that awaited a man in the Torrid Zone.

Three weeks after sowing, the shoots would break through the soil. A few days later, the fields were covered with banana plants. The machete men went through the rows, cutting away the weeds that were forever returning. On a banana plantation, clearing weeds is breathing. Without it, the plantation dies.

Once the plants had reached the height of small children—fourth graders, say, green and promising—the engineers would go back to work, mapping out the train tracks that would wander through the rows, so the fruit, when harvested, could be carried to the warehouse, selected, counted, and stacked into boxcars. The railroads were simple, with grass growing between the ties. ("From the day I was born I had heard it said, over and over again, that the rail lines and camps of the United Fruit Company had been built at night because during the day the sun made the tools too hot to pick up," García Márquez wrote in *Living to Tell the Tale*.) The tracks were indeed laid in the cool before dawn. It took a few weeks, no more. The rails were torn up and reused if a particular field went feral or fallow. You can still see the remnants of many such lines in Honduras: an overgrown field in the Sula Valley, a storybook jungle of snakes and macaws, a glint of iron beneath the tall grass.

Zemurray worked in the fields beside his engineers, planters, and machete men. He was deep in the muck, sweat covered, swinging a blade. He helped map the plantations, plant the rhizomes, clear the weeds, lay the track. He was a proficient snake killer. Taller than most of his workers, as strong and thin as a railroad spike, he shouted orders in dog Spanish. He believed in the transcendent power of physical labor—that a man can free his soul only by exhausting his body. A life in an office, deskbound, was for the feeble and weak who cut themselves off from the actual. He ate outside—shark's fin soup, plantains, crab gumbo, sour wine. His years in the jungle gave him experience rare in the trade. Unlike most of his competitors, he understood every part of the business, from the executive suite where the stock was manipulated to the ripening room where the green fruit turned yellow. He was contemptuous of banana men who spent their lives in the North, far from the plantations. *Those schmucks, what do they know? They're there, we're here!*

After the fields had been planted, the plantation town was built. Most of these were like small American villages sunk in the isthmian wilderness: a crossroads, a steeple, a green; a hospital, a grocery, a five-and-dime. There was a club for top executives with a polished bar and dance floor; a club for employees of the midrank, with pool and poker tables; a club for workers with kegs of beer, whiskey, and fights. Zemurray imported boa constrictors to keep violence in check, believing the presence of the snakes would force his men to stay sober.

He eventually built many banana towns, each laid out in the same basic pattern: the houses of the executives on a hill, the more important the executive, the higher up the hill. The manager's house was at the peak. If the plantation had been laid on flat ground, a hill was constructed. In this way, the landscape was made to reflect the hierarchy of the company. "I noticed that the railroad depots in cowboy movies looked like our train stations," wrote García Márquez.

> Later, when I began to read Faulkner, the small towns in his novels seemed like ours, too. And it was not surprising, for they had been built under the messianic inspiration of the United Fruit Company and in the same provisional style of a temporary camp. I remembered them all, with the church on the square and little fairy-tale houses painted in primary colors. I remembered the gangs of black laborers singing at twilight, the shanties on the estates where the field hands sat to rest and watch freight trains go by, the ditches where the morning found the cutters whose heads had been hacked off in the drunken Saturday-night brawls. I remembered the private cities of the gringos in Aracataca and Sevilla, on the other side of the railroad tracks, surrounded, like enormous electrified chicken yards, by metal fences that on cool summer dawns were black with charred swallows. I remembered their slow blue lawns with peacocks and quail, the residences with red roofs and wire grating on the windows and little round tables with folding chairs for eating on the terraces among palm trees and dusty rosebushes. Sometimes, through the wire fence, you could see the beautiful languid women in muslin dresses and wide gauze hats cutting the flowers in their gardens with golden scissors.

Zemurray reaped his first harvest in 1910, soon after he arrived in the country. A banner crop, cut and stacked, carted out of the rows, counted and loaded onto straw-filled boxcars. The door is shut with a clang. A crewman gives a thumbs-up, the engineer nods, the train moves into open country with a shriek, slow at first, then gaining speed, the wheels seen close up, spinning into a void. The train snakes out of the hills, breaking through the jungle, appearing on the outskirts of the old colonial towns, rattling past alleys and back doors where chicken bones are piled and stray dogs roam. There were a half dozen cars on the early trains, jammed with bananas, thousands of hands reeking in the heat. A team of men worked each run, the conductor in the engine room, the foreman in the caboose, guards on the roof with rifles on the lookout for hijackers. This was wild country, the banana frontier. If Zemurray was not on the plantation or riding the train, he was looking out the window of his office as the railroad sped through Omoa on its way to the harbor.

The first shipment was followed by a second, a third, a fifth, a fifteenth. It's one of the great things about bananas—unlike corn or cotton or tobacco, they have no season, or one season that lasts forever, an endless summer broken now and then by hurricane or drought. The winter, the frost, the early darkness and first flurries—that's another world, banished. Planted correctly, a banana plantation is a never-ending bounty.

Zemurray began scouting for still more property, which would mean more rails, workers, and houses, which would require more money. But he was already overextended. He had taken loans from banks across America. When he realized no creditor would lend him another dime, he went in search of other sources. If you were Zemurray, an entrepreneur at the key moment, when you knew, just knew, you had to risk everything, that this was your shot, but the banks had turned you down and your money was on the table and you had neither wealthy uncles nor elite contacts, where would you go? The history books and articles say he secured the needed funds from unorthodox sources, borrowed on stringent terms, at rates approaching 50 percent. Which of course means gangsters, wiseguys in flashy suits on the corner of St. Claude and Dumaine.

Ashbell Hubbard had agreed to the first round of bank loans and land purchases, and had agreed to the second, if less enthusiastically. But this was too much. Whereas Zemurray thought everything should be risked now, while the opportunity presented itself, Hubbard believed the business should be given time to become established. First plant the land we've acquired, pay off some loans, then we can think about acquiring more acres. But Zemurray must have realized the business had to get big to survive. Go all in, or get out. Sam was young and wanted to bet everything: great fortunes come from big plays. Hubbard did not have the fortitude for such risks. He had become a nervous partner who considered the actions of the Russian with alarm. Asked to describe Zemurray by a New Orleans newspaper reporter, the best Hubbard could say was, *He's a man with big ideas.*

When Hubbard couldn't take it anymore, Zemurray agreed to buy out his share of the company—a 45 percent stake in Cuyamel Fruit. This left Zemurray with 90 percent of the company and United Fruit with the remaining 10 percent. The terms of the deal were never reported, but the company was valued at $400,000, meaning Zemurray paid something like $160,000, money that he surely borrowed from the same nefarious characters who lent him all the other money.

What was Sam thinking, piling debt on debt, risk on risk? By buying out Hubbard, he was taking it all on his own shoulders. But what did it matter? If he failed by himself, he would lose the exact same amount as if he failed with a partner: everything.

10

Revolutin'!

A businessman can live with a certain amount of corruption. Maybe he prefers it. If he's paying off an official, kicking a percentage back to a bureaucrat who landed him a concession, at least he knows where he stands. In New York, they call it honest graft. In Chicago, they call it the Machine. A deal is a deal. Paid for is owned. But if a bribed official refuses to deliver, or if a bought politician suddenly becomes unbought, how can a man do business? This is the other kind of corruption, the corrupt kind, and it leads to bankruptcy and ruin. It's not a question of right versus wrong, it's a question of ethics. If you buy a man, you have a right to expect him to stay bought.

And yet before he had even established himself as a grower, Zemurray began to hear whispers: all the deals he had made in Honduras, or was hoping to make (the Dávila government was not the most pliable), were in jeopardy. Honduras owed millions to bankers in London, far more than it could ever repay. The debt had been outstanding since the 1860s, when the government took out four loans, issued as bonds, with British banks to finance a national railroad. The story of the Honduran railroad epitomizes life on the isthmus. In 1870, the government hired an engineer named John C. Trautwine to lay track from Puerto Cortés on the Atlantic to the Bay of Fonseca on the Pacific, passing through Tegucigalpa, but made the mistake of paying him by the mile. When the project went bust in 1880, Honduras was left with sixty miles of track that wandered aimlessly here and there through the lowlands. (Tegucigalpa remains the only national capital without train service.) In 1900, the amount owed the bondholders, principal plus forty years of compounded interest, had reached $100 million. The bankers demanded settlement, ominously suggesting the issue might be resolved by the British navy. In 1894, British marines had in fact landed in Puerto Corinto, on the Pacific coast of Nicaragua, to collect a debt of just £74,000.

President William Howard Taft was concerned. Anything that resulted in European military action in the Western Hemisphere challenged the Monroe Doctrine. Philander Knox, the secretary of state, devised a plan. He recruited J. Pierpont Morgan, the most powerful banker in America, to buy all of the outstanding Honduran railroad bonds, satisfying the British banks. Morgan would then refinance the debt, issuing $5 million in new loans to the government of President Miguel Dávila. Morgan agreed under the following condition: in return for money and services, officials from the Morgan bank would be seated in the customshouse in Puerto Cortés, where they would collect a duty on all imports. After taking the bank's percentage, the officers would forward the balance to the Honduran government. Morgan insisted that these terms be written in a treaty and ratified by the congress in Tegucigalpa. This infuriated many Hondurans, who considered the terms a forfeit of national sovereignty.

The Knox plan satisfied the British bankers, who agreed to sell their railroad bonds, which had a face value of $500, for $75 apiece. It satisfied President Dávila, who believed it would protect him. If Morgan bank officers were working in Honduras, the American navy would be obliged to defend them, protecting the Honduran government from revolutionaries. The Knox plan was good for everyone, in fact, except the people of Honduras and Samuel Zemurray, whose business could not function without the concessions and sweetheart deals that would be forbidden by Morgan. The Knox plan, in fact, depended on men like Zemurray paying in every way possible. If enacted, it would add as much as a penny per bunch to cost, driving Cuyamel out of business.

Zemurray went to work as soon as he learned the terms of the Knox plan. His goal was simple: undermine, overturn, undo. Kill it dead. In the beginning, he went after this the traditional way, hiring lobbyists who buttonholed congressmen, urging them to pressure the White House. This business of meddling in the affairs of foreign nations had to stop. As the campaign gained momentum—newspaper articles, editorials—Knox became alarmed and inquired after the source of the opposition. *Where's this coming from? Who's behind it?* He soon discovered that the lobbyists were paying for neither their own meals nor hotel rooms. All bills had been charged to a Mr. S. Zemurray of New Orleans, Louisiana.

In the summer of 1910, on what must have been one of the strangest days of his life, Zemurray received a message from Washington, D.C. He was to report to the office of the United States secretary of state. He had been in America less than a generation, and here he was embroiled at the highest levels of national affairs. A Jew from the shtetl off for an audience with the czar. He arrived in the capital early in the morning, left the train station in the dark, rode through the streets at first light. He stopped at the hotel, then went to the Old Executive Office Building, a beautiful chaos of columns, dormered windows, and chimneys. He met first with Alvey Adee, special assistant to the secretary. Adee, a patrician with a gray goatee and steel blue eyes, was an old government hand, having served as the acting secretary of state during the Spanish-American War. He questioned Zemurray, then brought him into Secretary Knox's office, which was wood and brass, globes, books, oil paintings. In photos, Knox looks big, soft, and round, with the commanding nose characteristic of his old Philadelphia family; his eyes were sleepy and sad. His girlish chin staged rearguard action against the bulk of his neck. Zemurray was taller than Knox, long and lean, with a shrewd face that changed when he smiled.

The details of this meeting were reported by Zemurray to friends and a few journalists, who wrote them up and retold them. Over time, it grew into a legend. In my mind, Zemurray sits patiently as Knox explains the history of the isthmus as you might explain it to a child, the instability of the Latin nations and the Latin character, the fiasco of the Honduran railroad and the resulting debt, the danger of foreign encroachment, the issue of prestige. He speaks of Mr. Morgan's role, the good it will do Honduras.

Yes, yes, fine, says Zemurray, but what about the interests of a businessman who invested with certain expectations? Are previous commitments to be simply discarded?

Knox is vague. Zemurray presses for answers. The resulting exchange, which I've pieced together from various sources, went something like this:

—You've not been brought here to haggle, sir.

—Then why have I been brought here? To be told I'm finished?

—That's not my concern.

—Look, Mr. Secretary, if a few simple accommodations could be worked out . . .

—I'm not discussing it, Mr. Zemurray. I'm not bargaining. I'm telling you the policy of the United States. Now that you know that policy, I am advising you, as nicely as I can, to go home and stay out of it. Don't meddle in Honduras. It's not your concern.

—But it is my concern, Mr. Secretary. The treaty will mean the end of my business.

—That's unfortunate, Mr. Zemurray, but my purview is larger than your banana business.

—But what would be the harm if concessions were honored?

If you have a particular concern, I suggest you bring it up with Mr. Morgan.

—"Mr. Secretary, I'm no favorite grandson of Mr. Morgan's. Mr. Morgan never heard of me."

—That's not my concern, sir.

"I was doing a small business buying fruit from independent planters, but I wanted to expand," Zemurray told *The American Magazine*. "I wanted to build railroads and raise my own fruit. The duty on railroad equipment was prohibitive—a cent a pound—and so I had to have concessions that would enable me to import that stuff duty free. If the banks were running Honduras and collecting their loans from customs duties, how far would I have gotten?"

When Zemurray stood to leave, Knox warned him a second time: Don't meddle! Keep your head down! Stay out of it! I better not hear you've got yourself mixed up in the politics of Honduras!

Zemurray nodded and seemed to agree, but Secretary Knox was not so sure.

Though he tried to put people at ease, Zemurray often struck those in power as a man who could not be controlled. If you want to know what he's going to do, forget what he seems to agree to and figure out what's in his interest. (Sure, sure, you won't *hear* I've gotten mixed up in Honduras.) As soon as Zemurray was gone, Knox made some calls, gave some orders. He told officials from the Department of the Treasury to put together a Secret Service team in New Orleans. He wanted the Banana Man monitored. He was not to leave the country, nor were any of his cohorts.

Pretend you're Samuel Zemurray. You're thirty-two. You've been in America less than twenty years. You lived in Russia before that, in a poor farming town filled with rabbis. Now you're here, an entrepreneur of considerable means, but still, somewhere in your mind, the little Jew who snuck in the back door. You're a husband and father, with a young daughter and another child on the way. You've been summoned to Washington, called to account by the secretary of state, warned. What do you do? Put your head down, shut up? Sit in a corner and thank God for your good fortune? Well, maybe that's what you would do, but not Sam Zemurray. He muttered all the way back to New Orleans: these momzers! Don't get involved? How about I overthrow the fucking government? Is that too involved? You made a deal with the president of Honduras, Miguel Dávila? Well, what if Señor Dávila wasn't president no more?

Consider the audacity!

In defying Philander Knox and J. Pierpont Morgan, Sam Zemurray was challenging two of the most powerful men in America.

Zemurray's scheme can be described as a coup disguised as a revolution. (It would not be hard to stir popular anger in the country, since most Hondurans hated the Knox plan.) Dávila would be driven out and a new president put in his place. General Manuel Bonilla, who had been president of Honduras until he was deposed in 1907, was cast in the role of insurgent leader for several reasons: because he was living in New Orleans; because he was known in Honduras; because he was trusted by Honduran businessmen; because Sam knew and liked Bonilla, whom he called *Mi General*; because Bonilla knew and liked Sam, having described him on one occasion as "an angel sent from heaven"; because he had allies in the region who would fight by his side; because he was dark skinned and broad nosed, features described by diplomats as Indian in a way that would give the operation the aura of popular revolt.

Zemurray worked out the arrangements with Bonilla and Lee Christmas, who was the president's right hand. In social situations it was Christmas who did the talking. He was better with English and also something of a public personality. Zemurray would have found the men in the Carousel Bar in the Hotel Monteleone in the French Quarter, a haunt of exiled Latin American leaders and North American filibusters, mercenaries forever in search of a job, a government to overthrow.

Bonilla was picturesque, a tiny man who now and then turned up in the uniform of a cavalry officer: riding boots and whip. Surrounded by followers, he made big promises to return to Tegucigalpa in triumph but was in fact down to his last dollar when Zemurray contacted him, living rent check to rent check in a cold-water flat on Royal Street. (William Merry, of the U.S. State Department, described Bonilla as a "half Indian and half Negro, uneducated and without much ability.") At the moment, his interests were perfectly aligned with those of Zemurray. Sam had money, ships, guns. Bonilla had legitimacy, motivation, and that fine Indian face.

In the summer of 1910, Lee Christmas began recruiting Bonilla's army of liberation, tapping men in the bordellos and dives of the French Quarter, importing others from the port cities on the Gulf. He did this as discreetly as possible but was being watched—through a window, across the street—by Treasury agents reporting to Knox. It seemed as though everyone in town knew what Christmas was up to. According to an article in *The New York Times* (it described New Orleans as "the hotbed of revolution and the Mecca of filibusters"), "Never before perhaps have there been so many people of known revolutionary designs in New Orleans as there are now, and they are leading a score of secret service agents of this and other countries on a merry chase."

The idea of Christmas doing anything in secret was a joke. He was an incorrigible attention getter, gruff and boisterous, a figure from a Saturday-afternoon serial come to life. Like most storied mercenaries, he was less soldier than showman, a pop star playing a role for mild-mannered America. He had a fair complexion, a walrus mustache, and the pretty blue eyes of a Romeo. If circumstances allowed, he wore a military uniform, double-breasted, brass buttoned, with piping and braid, which was tailor-made in a costume shop in Paris. On occasion, he carried a sword. He was a modern hybrid: real and fake, deadly serious and having a laugh. He'd fought in several wars, had been shot more than a few times, but was a clown, too, playing to the crowd. Born on a cotton plantation in Livingston Parish, Louisiana, in 1863, he had refused to play a bit part in life and went adventuring instead. Between 1890 and 1925, he was a featured player in the comic opera of Central American politics.

Christmas had first arrived in Puerto Cortés in 1893. Within a decade, he was a star, having seen action in various battles, having conquered and killed. He was said to be the model for Richard Harding Davis's protagonist in the bestselling novel *Soldiers of Fortune*. He fashioned a pact with General Bonilla soon after they met in the early 1900s. First they were allies, then friends, then brothers. Christmas risked his life for Bonilla's cause in 1907, when the general, his soldiers defeated in battle, was driven into exile.

Christmas was trapped with a few hundred men in the hills outside Tegucigalpa. Realizing their position was hopeless, he ordered his men to surrender, while he made a run for it. According to *The Incredible Yanqui* by Hermann Deutsch, Christmas told his men, "I'm going out. There'll be seven cartridges in my gun and each of the first six will get me one of those rawhides. The last will be for me, in case they nip me on the road. But I guarantee they'll never drag me out in front of a mob and make a show of killing me."

A handful of men volunteered to ride with Christmas. They went at dawn, each with pistol and machete. They burst across the defensive line in a group, riding hard. Three of these men—Ted Reyes, Francis Barahona, Fred Mills—were shot and killed. Christmas rode toward the trees across the clearing. He was almost there, almost there, almost there . . . *wham!* His horse was shot out from under him. The falling went on forever. He was pinned beneath the animal, one leg badly broken. Enemy soldiers ran toward him. He aimed his gun, a German Luger. He believed he had three bullets left—he shot twice, then put the gun in his mouth and pulled the trigger. *Click.* Pulled it again. *Click.*

He never was good at math. He was surrounded, supine in his dirty uniform, the faces staring down, the sky, the peaks—a legendary scene in the life of Lee Christmas.

"Goddamned you all to Hell!" he shouted. "Shoot me now if you've got the guts. Shoot me you miserable heathens. Shoot me and be done with me but don't bury me. Leave me on the ground to rot."

"Don't bury you? But why Señor General?"

Then came the words that Christmas either wrote in advance, made up afterward, or actually spoke—words that attached themselves to his story like a tagline, in the nature of "Do you feel lucky, punk?"

"Because I want the buzzards to eat me, and fly over you afterward, and scatter white shit all over your God-damned black faces."

Christmas said he expected this to infuriate the soldiers: he was trying to provoke them into killing him, but it only made them laugh. "You're a brave man, Jefe," the enemy commander told Christmas. "For this, you will not be executed at all."

A stretcher was made out of branches and saplings. Christmas was carried over the mountains to Tegucigalpa, where his leg was rebroken and set. Once recovered, he was expelled from Honduras, eventually making his way, via mail ship, to New Orleans, where the newspapers, relying on secondhand accounts, had reported his death. In *The New York Times*, the story ran under the headline "Daredevil American Cut to Pieces by Nicaraguan Soldiers." When he turned up in the Carousel Bar as if at his own funeral, his legend was assured.

Here are some of the men Lee Christmas recruited for the army of Manuel Bonilla:

Tracy Custer Richardson of Broken Bow, Nebraska. Like the hero of a folk song, he'd been a rambler and a gambler, a steamship roustabout and oil field fitter before seeing combat in the Nicaraguan civil war. He served in the Mexican border wars, on the Western Front during the First World War, as a member of Wild Bill Donovan's OSS during the Second World War. With Richardson, as with most New Orleans mercenaries, it was impossible to untangle fact from legend. No matter how deep you dig, you never hit bedrock—it's just story on story, tale on tale. In the end, he was the greatest singer of his own song, which he told and retold in novels and penny-a-word true crime pulps. When Christmas found Richardson, he was just another kid getting wasted on Bourbon Street.

Sam "the Fighting Jew" Dreben, who enlisted in the U.S. Army soon after he arrived from Russia. In the Philippines, Dreben participated in America's first war of counterinsurgency, a precursor to Vietnam and Afghanistan. He learned to ambush, booby-trap, track, and kill at close quarters, skills well suited to the isthmus. His manic ferocity came to the attention of General Black Jack Pershing, who decorated Dreben "an outstanding hero of the American Expeditionary Forces." Back in New York, on the Lower East Side, he was a magnet for newspaper hacks. To them, he seemed an oddity—a Jew who loved fighting as other Jews supposedly loved stitching and accumulating. Whenever he appeared in print, it was in the guise of the hapless Yid, the vaudeville act. According to an appreciation that ran in *The New Yorker* in 1925 after Dreben's death, "He looked like an emotional button-hole worker, but he fought like a calm fiend. The unexpected quality of his conduct under fire immediately won him high unofficial rank with his outfit, and for the first time in his life Sam Dreben, the harried, cringing Russian Jew immigrant, tasted the flavor of respect."

Guy Molony, who ran away from New Orleans at sixteen to fight in the Boer War. It was the era of romantic soldiering, when boys heeded the call of Rudyard Kipling ("Ship me somewheres east of Suez, where the best is like the worst, / Where there aren't no Ten Commandments an' a man can raise a thirst," he wrote in "Mandalay"). By twenty, Molony was a man of the world, having fought in South Africa and the Philippines, where he mastered the machine gun. He was the epitome of the modern soldier, less concerned with style than with his glorious weapon. He returned to New Orleans, where he worked as a cop, but longed for his footloose days. He joined Christmas at the suggestion of Sam Dreben, who had moved to New Orleans and become a habitué of the Carousel Bar. "They're getting set to knock off Dávila," Dreben told Guy Molony. "How about it? Want to sit in?"

Dreben gave Molony a note of introduction, which he carried to a house uptown, where he was given another note, which he carried to another house, where he was handed a ticket. He met Christmas on a ship off the coast of Belize. Christmas dumped the pieces of a machine gun at Molony's feet and said, "Put it together." Molony finished in no time. "That's fine," said Christmas. "You're in."

Zemurray's mercenary army would have perhaps one hundred soldiers, a ragtag band of guns for hire, a pirate gang in cast-off clothes, every shape and color, every weapon and motivation. This group was supplemented by recruits from the isthmus. According to *The New York Times*, "Manuel Bonilla is now in New Orleans, preparing for the departure of himself and a few companions for the Atlantic coast of Honduras. There he expects to place himself at the head of a force, already organized and equipped, and raise again the flag of revolution."

The first attempt on Honduras failed "farcically," as it was then described. Bonilla feared his patron's reaction, but Zemurray could not afford to withdraw his support. Having staked everything on the general, he decided instead to figure out what went wrong and fix it. (This is how Zemurray regarded most things in his life: as problems to be solved.) Though not a military man, Sam was a fine tactician who understood the flow of men and machines. He quickly recognized reasons for the fiasco: first, the political moment had not been ripe, the people of Honduras not sufficiently alarmed by the Knox plan. (Friendly newspapermen would soon change that.) Second, the insurgents had been outclassed at sea, where they had just one ship, an old tub that was no match for the Honduran navy. Zemurray corrected the imbalance, procuring, through a third party, a 160-foot warship that could reach fifteen knots an hour, faster than anything in Miguel Dávila's fleet. Called the *Hornet*, the ship had been part of the American naval fleet, seeing action in Manzanillo harbor in Cuba during the Spanish-American War. The government had sold it for $5,100 to a merchant, who then sold it to an agent secretly representing Zemurray. Secretary Knox must have received news of this sale with a string of expletives.

There was not much that could be legally done. Zemurray had covered his tracks so thoroughly that his ownership of the *Hornet* was hard to prove. As far as Port of New Orleans officials were concerned, the ship was the property of a legitimate trader who intended to use it on trips across the Caribbean. If deployed in battle, the owner of the ship would be in breach of the Neutrality Act, but property could not be seized for what *might* happen in the future. Dávila was certain the purchase meant that war was coming. As soon he got the news, he ordered his army to dig trenches around the port cities on the Atlantic, then sent spies to New Orleans, but these men were easily identified in the lobby of the St. Charles Hotel by their phony gringo wear: blue jeans, cowboy boots, tall hats.

The *Hornet* was anchored at Algiers Point, across from Jackson Square, where it was routinely boarded and searched by Treasury agents—early in the morning when the city was gray in the distance, late at night when the streetlights were yellow, in midafternoon when the river was drowsy and the decks smelled like varnish. Nothing was found: not a map, not a knife, not a document, not a bullet.

On December 15, 1910, Charley Johnson, the captain of the *Hornet*, asked permission to sail from New Orleans. There was no reason to hold him. He was a merchant seaman leaving on what appeared a legitimate run to Nicaragua, where he'd arranged a purchase of iron ore. This fictitious trip was to take seventeen days: six days down, three days in harbor, eight days back. It seemed straightforward. What's more, the men Secretary Knox told the agents to watch—Zemurray, Bonilla, Christmas—had never been near the *Hornet*.

When the *Hornet* sailed on December 22, three Treasury agents rode on its deck for seventy miles below New Orleans—just to make sure no filibusters snuck aboard at a country landing. These men disembarked at a river station near the mouth of the Mississippi. Captain Johnson steered the *Hornet* past the customshouse and into the Gulf. He killed the engines beyond the horizon, then drifted like a cork. He headed east when the signal came, sailing through the islands of the Mississippi Sound. He dropped anchor and waited. It was a cold, gloomy time of year. Captain Johnson finally spotted Zemurray's sleek little boat, where the mercenaries were playing poker in the cabin below. It was speeding toward the *Hornet*, getting more distinct as it came. It tied up alongside, then a man, tall and lean in a long overcoat, climbed aboard.

Any trouble getting out? he asked.

No, sir.

Good, said Zemurray. *I'm going to bring the others over now.*

A few minutes later, Bonilla, Christmas, and Molony were on the *Hornet*, helping stack weapons—rifles, bullets, grenades, a machine gun. The newspapers took notice of the sudden disappearance of Zemurray's men. On December 24, *The New York Times* reported that "coincident with the departure late yesterday of the steamer *Hornet*, Gen. Manuel Bonilla, ex-President of Honduras; Gen. Lee Christmas, soldier of fortune, and one of the leaders of the alleged revolutionary expedition against President Davila of Honduras, and several Americans who have seen service in Central American wars disappeared from this city."

As Zemurray stood on deck, he noticed Bonilla shivering. "Jesus Christ, what's wrong with you, Manny?"

"Just a chill, amigo."

Zemurray took off his coat and draped it across the general's narrow shoulders. "I shot the roll on you," he said, "and I might as well shoot the coat, too."

Zemurray climbed down to his boat when the *Hornet* was ready to sail.

It was a five-day journey to Honduras, hours of tedium and small talk, poker and rum, the world filling with color as the ship went south. For Christmas, it was a kind of homecoming. He had been driven out of Honduras. He would fight his way back in, returning to the towns and taverns where he'd spent his best days. As he sat on the deck of the *Hornet*, watching the Gulf coast of Mexico unwind, perhaps he recalled the scenes of his own life.

As a boy, Christmas dreamed of working as an engineer on the railroad. It might sound modest, but in the 1890s the train was the fastest thing going. (A daredevil segment will always be attracted by speed.) At eighteen, he was hired as a fireman on the Great Jackson Railroad, which traveled from New Orleans to Chicago. By twenty-two, he was an engineer on the Illinois Central based in New Orleans. Late one night in 1897, he turned up in a barroom after a fifty-four-hour shift and commenced drinking. An official from the Illinois Central came looking for him at four a.m., by which time Christmas could barely stand. It did not matter to the official; Christmas was needed to run bananas to Baton Rogue. If the cargo went punk, it would become the property of Sam the Banana Man.

Christmas later said he had been too drunk to object, that the railroad official dragged him to the freight yard and put him in the engine room. The sun was rising. A great train of boxcars stretched behind. Christmas's father-in-law showed up with coffee. "Drink it," he said. The switchman signaled, Christmas hit the throttle, and off he went through the city and its outskirts. From the point of view of the drunken engineer, the journey was a montage: a building blurred by speed, iron rails whizzing by, the slum seen at crooked extremes, a dog scurrying from the track, the devil laughing in the window. The train blew through a signal near Metairie, Louisiana, going full steam, sixty miles per hour or more. The brakeman later said he had seen the engineer slumped over the stick, sound asleep.

When Christmas regained consciousness in the hospital, he claimed he remembered nothing: not getting on the train, not drinking the coffee, not pressing the throttle. It was all oblivion. The first thing he recalled was the pain of the steam scalding him in the wreckage. His survival was a miracle. He'd driven off the rails into another train at a bend in the track. The boxcars crumbled into a ball. Smoke hung over the scene. The worst accident in the history of the train company was later written up in the *Illinois Central* magazine.

[Christmas] had been 54 hours on duty and then had been ordered back to his run without a rest; as a result, he went by a station asleep, and had a disastrous collision with another train. In the wreck, Engineer Christmas was seriously scalded and his right eye was knocked out—but that eye is still in use, although he says it has been knocked out three times, the first time when he was in a fight as a boy.

Lee Christmas was fired by the Illinois Central, then blackballed by every other railroad. He was one of that breed of men who had everything and lost it. He spent three years in a drunken haze, stumbling here to there, telling his story to anyone who would listen. His occasional employment included stints at a lumberyard in Natchez and at a railroad hotel in Memphis. He cleaned sewers in New Orleans, lived like a tramp, slept in fields, begged drinks. His fancy clothes turned to rags. Now and then, he was arrested. Now and then, he stole. When his daughter was born, he fell to his knees and promised to change. He met with the night yardmaster of the Illinois Central, the only company in a position to know the true details of the accident. He demanded an investigation and was exonerated. He was offered a job as an engineer on a modest run. He only needed to pass a physical exam.

The doctor listened to his heart, checked his pulse, ears, reflexes, etc., then sat him at a table covered with blocks: red, green, yellow, orange, black, blue. It was a new test for color blindness. In the wake of Christmas's accident, the company had installed electric signals—red, green—at the entrance and exit of every station. The doctor told Christmas to pick up a red block. He picked up a blue block. The doctor told him to pick up a yellow block. He picked up an orange block. When the doctor told him to pick up a green block, he picked up a blue block. He thought he'd scored perfectly but reconsidered when he looked at the doctor, who was shaking his head.

He said, "I'm sorry, Mr. Christmas, but you're color-blind."

"What does that mean?"

"It means you'll never work as an engineer on this railroad again."

Christmas wandered into the hallway, where his friend Boyd Cetti was waiting. "He came up to me dragging his steps, and not the way he used to walk," Cetti told Hermann Deutsch years later. "I asked him what was wrong, wasn't he going to work for us? And he says 'No, because the so-and-so doctor from Chicago tells him he's got the color blind.' He picked up a piece of floss as green as the greenest grass and put it with one that was red as blood and said the color was the same.

"'Lee Christmas,' I said, 'I want you to tell me and tell me straight: do those colors look the same to you?'

"And he looked up like he was kind of puzzled. 'Ain't they the same?' says he.

"'The same!' I yelled. 'Can't you see one of em's greener than the greenest grass and the other is redder than the reddest blood?'"

Christmas went into the street. Then, without realizing where he'd gone, found himself at the river. A steamer was blowing for last passengers. He got on, then, as if in a dream, stayed on deck as the gangplank was rolled away. When the purser asked for his ticket, Christmas handed him $2, all the money he had. "Where are we going?" asked Christmas.

"Puerto Cortés."

"Where's that?"

"Honduras."

That's the legend—the story the mercenary told about himself.

Later, when Christmas became a hero for boys, the story appeared in dime-store novels and newspaper profiles, where it was worked up into a kind of tall tale. It grew with each telling, was fitted with dialogue and turns of phrase. These articles, the tone of them, probably says more about the average wonderstruck newspaper reader than it does about Christmas. The general collected them in a scrapbook that was found beside his bed when he died. In one, which appeared in a newspaper in Toledo, Ohio, on January 29, 1911, Christmas "loafed around the New Orleans harbor for a while. The aroma of bananas caught his nostrils. A steamer from which a cargo of bananas had just been unloaded was preparing to sail. Lee walked aboard and didn't step ashore when the steamer backed away from the wharf. 'Give me a ticket for any old place,' he said when the purser tapped him on the shoulder."

In another, which ran in *The Railroad Man's Magazine* in May 1911, Christmas asked the purser, "Where you headed for?"

"Puerto Cortés is our first stop, sir."

"That's in Honduras, isn't it?"

"Yes, sir."

"Do they have the color test down there?"

"I don't know, sir. The natives are pretty dark, if that's what you mean."

According to *The New Orleans Daily Picayune*, Christmas "wandered to the wharves, boarded a steamer about to sail, and as she went out, stood at the rail, saying good-bye to the scene of his failures, unknowing of the glamour that awaited at the end of his voyage."

He arrived in Puerto Cortés in November 1894 and soon found work with the railroad. There was no color test because there were no lights, and everything was green. He worked out of San Pedro Sula, carrying bananas and ice to the coast. In the spring of 1897, the country was convulsed by civil war. One afternoon, a group of insurgents boarded Christmas's train. He described the scene in his own words, as part of a never-published memoir: "As revolutin broke out on the 13 of April 1897 where I was captured by the Revolutionist and forced to handle the Eng. at the point of a bayonet, I applied for protection of the America counsel which of course I did not get. I was then taken to a drunken general and given to understand that I would be shot. This of course was a bitter pill for me so I said to the general, all right if I have to be made a target, at least give me a gun so I may kill some sons of bitches as I go."

The rebel commander ordered Christmas to take his soldiers to San Pedro Sula, which meant crossing hostile government territory. With this in mind, Christmas made the train into a kind of rolling fort, placing a flatcar in front of the engine and ringing it with sandbags. He put a boiler, with metal an inch thick, at the center of the car as a roost for sharpshooters. Government soldiers stacked blocks of ice on the train tracks outside the town, believing this would slow down or derail the engine. But by the time Christmas arrived, most of the ice had melted and the engine blasted through. The government soldiers opened fire. The rebels returned it. Christmas had been told to lie down in the engine room, but when he heard the battle, he came out firing and soon he was shouting orders to the men. The rebels were forced to retreat, but the myth of the Incredible Yanqui was born. Writing in the third person, Christmas later described himself as an ordinary man "who started in war because he was forced to but stuck around because he liked this new game."

This happened near San Pedro Sula on April 14, 1897, in a narrow place in the hills. Called the battle of Laguna Trestle, it turned Lee Christmas into a celebrity. He was sworn into the rebel army. A few weeks later, he fought again. According to the *New Orleans Statesman*, he "drove the Federales into a mountain gully where they were faced with surrender or death. The Federales surrendered. Christmas dropped his rifle, began mopping his face with the red bandana he brought from the States—a symbol of the railroading he still loved." Christmas was then led to a command post, the article goes on, where he was introduced to "a small vivacious man with heavy mustaches and a gaudy uniform. He was bursting with enthusiasm. 'Great,' 'glorious,' 'genius,' 'warrior supreme'—these were some of the things Lee Christmas heard himself called. He learned his admirer was none other than Manuel Bonilla, the leader of the revolution. 'I'll make you an officer,' Bonilla said. 'A captain in my army. I'll make you rich, give you power once we've taken Tegucigalpa.'"

When the *Hornet* appeared off Roatán, an island near the coast of Honduras, on December 29, 1910, it seemed to materialize out of thin air. Dávila expected an attack on his coastal cities, but Christmas believed the poorly defended bay islands would make a perfect starting place for the war, serving as a base for a broader campaign. The *Hornet* sailed into Roatán harbor at eleven p.m., under a dense fog. The lights of the town could hardly be seen in the gloaming: yellow pinpricks, a line of hills. The shore gun fired but it was useless. The ship sailed unmolested to the wharf. Five minutes later, Christmas was leading a handful of men along an empty road. They reached the old Spanish fort from behind. There was a scuffle, then the rebels were in control of the fort and its big gun. Word was sent to rebel camps across the archipelago and in Guatemala. Soon after, soldiers began to arrive—Manuel Bonilla's rebel army. As rebels celebrated the conquest, the captain of the *Hornet* sat on deck with a man named Florian Davadi. Papers were signed, and everyone shook hands. Having promised to pay $40,000, Davadi had become the owner of the *Hornet*. As the property of a citizen and current resident of Honduras, the ship could take part in the war without violating the U.S. Neutrality Act.

The rebels planned to proceed a few days later to Utila, an island six miles across the bay. There was a government outpost there, a house on a hill where an official lived. But that night at three in the morning, when the stars were as bright as lanterns, a drunk Lee Christmas decided there was no need to wait—accompanied by a few men, he could conquer Utila now. He hired a fisherman to take them across, five men in a skiff. They hit the beach running, laughing, shouting, shooting in the air. The harbor guards dropped their weapons and surrendered. Within a few minutes, they'd been sworn into Bonilla's army. Christmas continued uphill to the manor house and banged on the door. The comandante of Utila came out in his underwear. Christmas demanded the surrender of the island. The comandante agreed. Christmas told the man that he, too, had to surrender. He agreed. Still not satisfied, Christmas ordered the comandante to run around the house, shouting *Viva Bonilla, Viva Bonilla, Viva Bonilla!*

Miguel Dávila commanded from his official residence in Tegucigalpa. He told his generals to fortify the harbors and establish checkpoints, then sent an armored truck to Puerto Cortés, where the Honduran government stored its financial reserves. At his order, $55,000 in silver bars was moved to La Ceiba, a city many military experts believed impregnable. The myth of La Ceiba's invincibility made it a target: its loss would come as a blow. Such a defeat can end a regime. That's how it was with the banana wars: the enemy wins a battle or two, then everyone switches uniforms.

The *Hornet* was involved in a successful attack on Trujillo on January 9. Less than two weeks later, the ship was seized by the U.S. gunboat *Tacoma* for violating the U.S. Neutrality Act. After dismissing Bonilla's protest regarding ownership, the navy towed the *Hornet* to New Orleans to be held as evidence in a criminal investigation. In a strange way, the seizure, which would have been helpful to President Dávila a week earlier, hurt him now. Having established a base in Trujillo, the insurgents no longer needed the *Hornet*. But its seizure made it look to Hondurans like the United States was intervening in a civil war on the side of the government. It was a feat of propaganda: Bonilla and Christmas, working with Zemurray, were able to frame the war as an insurgency, the people rising up against a government selling the nation to gringos and Yankee bankers, whereas what you really had was more sinister and interesting—a battle waged by a private American citizen, a corporate chief, against a debt-ridden but sovereign nation.

The big attack came the morning of January 25, 1911. A group of rebels approached La Ceiba from the ocean side, drawing fire from the government's Krupp mountain gun, but this was a feint. The real attack came along the supposedly impassable beach road. Christmas's strategy was surprise by force of will, by doing what others considered impossible. The road descended into marsh, dissolved into weeds. The rebels hacked, waded, and climbed for hours, reaching the fort with the Krupp gun—really a small cannon—at the hottest time of the day. They lay in the tall grass, riddling the fort with bullets. The government's return fire slackened, then stopped. Finally, an opening. The men broke cover, dashed across the fields, raced up the ancient stairs of the fort, and burst into the plaza. They expected to fight hand to hand, but found nothing but corpses. Molony's machine gun had breached the walls. The survivors had fled, leaving their equipment behind. The Krupp gun had been pushed into the sea. (Christmas salvaged it and used it for the rest of the war.) The insurgents gave chase, following the government forces into the center of La Ceiba, a beautiful town of pink stone, promenades, and hotels facing the Caribbean.

There was a skirmish in the main square. Most government forces surrendered. General Francisco "Chico" Guerrero, assigned to defend the city, sat astride a white mule, waving a machete, urging his men to fight. He called them cowards, sons of whores. Turning to face the enemy, he drew his pistol and shouted, "I will show you bastards how a man fights!" He whipped his mule into a dash but did not get ten yards before he had been shot a dozen times. From there, his story forks into legends. In one, General Guerrero spurs his animal to the office of the British consulate, where he expires in the arms of the ambassador, crying, "I have died for my nation." In another, the mule races through the city in a panic, dragging the general's dead body behind it. According to *The New York Times*, "Guerrero . . . defended the town heroically, and at the time he was shot [he] was trying to force his men to attack the revolutionists. The men deserted and left him alone on his mule, waving his revolver. He started to fire, but before he could do so fifty insurgents in the trenches opened fire on him with rifles. His mule ran back to the British Consulate. There the General, in a dying condition, dropped from the animal's back."

Christmas sent a note to the U.S. naval commander. He said rebel reinforcements were on the way—Dávila must surrender before the battle turned into a massacre. It was a bluff. There were no reinforcements. But it worked. The Americans carried the message to Dávila and urged him to give up the city. By sundown, La Ceiba was in rebel hands, along with the silver bars of the state treasury.

Several small battles followed, fights best imagined as sepia-tone snapshots in the scrapbook of the dying mercenary. Christmas handing out uniforms to turncoats in an alley in a colonial city; rifles piled in the sand outside of Dantillo, where insurgents have stripped off their clothes and run into the sea; the field where Christmas has defeated Pedro Díaz, the general who once captured the rebel commander, burned his feet, and made him walk barefoot in the streets of Tegucigalpa; Guy Molony behind his machine gun where the jungle gives way to tall grass. He hears a battle cry, then the enemy breaks cover, hundreds of Indians with swords. He waits and waits. Then: *rat-a-tat-tat, rat-a-tat-tat*. His machine gun sings, the men fall. More come, more fall, until the field is littered with bodies.

While working on this book, I spoke to Frank Brogan, the last of the banana cowboys. He's an old man, living in Covington, Louisiana, across Lake Pontchartrain from New Orleans. When I asked if he knew Zemurray, Frank said—he spoke just the way you'd want him to, deep and gravelly—"Sure I knew the old man. He taught me how to dynamite fish." I'll say more about Frank later, as he worked for Zemurray for years, but I introduce him here as it was he who explained the 1911 war not as a legend but as something I could understand—a nasty piece of corporate business. Brogan got the story from Molony, whom Brogan knew in New Orleans. "Goddamn, Guy was older then than me now," Frank told me. "He'd been chief of police but was retired when I knew him. We sat on his porch and drank and talked about olden times. His stories about Bonilla's war were terrible. He told me how he set up his gun in the field and waited until these Indians came running. Then he starts shooting, and shoots and shoots, until the bodies were piled like leaves. And it kept on like that until the field was covered with them, and finally them Indians get the idea and give up."

Puerto Cortés surrendered without a fight. The insurgency was in control of the ports and the treasury. Christmas moved into the Hotel Lafebre. He drank in the bar every evening, happy to talk to anyone who would listen. He made fantastic newspaper copy, which is one reason his fame dwindled soon after his death. Without Christmas to sell his own story, there was little to sustain the legend. "The revolution is won," he told a reporter from New Orleans. "The evacuation of

Puerto Cortes . . . was better than a victory by attack. It shows that President Dávila realizes the sentiment of the people. The last stand of the government forces will be at the capital. We can surround Tegucigalpa and starve them out. There need be no more bloodshed."

President Dávila had shut himself in the palace in Tegucigalpa. At fifty-four years old, he had entered the twilight of defeated Spanish monarchs. In the end, all stories become one story by García Márquez, the general in the labyrinth of his own making. Dávila wore a military uniform, saber at his side. He had a single path to salvation: get his congress to ratify the so-called Morgan treaty. If the treaty was signed, the United States, Dávila believed, would come into the war on his side. He argued his case before the Honduran congress on February 8, 1911. He talked of honor, tradition, faith—the pillars of the conservative creed. Speaking of the Morgan treaty, he said, "Providence . . . offered Honduras this opportunity to secure the help of the United States." There was no applause when he finished, nor boos. It was worse: dead silence. The treaty was defeated thirty-two to four.

The U.S. ambassador let it be known that the United States could work with Bonilla. In other words, Philander Knox had switched sides. The secretary still wanted what he had always wanted: a Honduran government strong enough to deal with its debt and keep the British marines off the isthmus. If Dávila could not deliver it, perhaps Bonilla could. On February 9, after meeting with the American ambassador, Dávila agreed to a cease-fire and announced his decision to begin peace talks. Negotiations were held on the deck of the USS *Tacoma*— the gunboat that had seized the *Hornet*—a mile off Puerto Cortés. The talks dragged on. According to *The New York Times*, "Dávila, who is willing to resign his office to secure peace to his country, refuses to accept Bonilla as a substitute President for the very good reason that he is an agent of an American fruit trust."

In the end, Dávila conceded power to a Honduran functionary named Francisco Bertrand, who would serve only until a presidential election could be held. A few months later, Bonilla won office in a landslide. He was inaugurated in Tegucigalpa on February 1, 1912. "Bonilla did not forget his benefactor," reported *Life*. "One of his first official acts was to have congress give Zemurray concessions covering the next 25 years."

Zemurray's settlement included permission to import any and all equipment duty-free; to build any and all railroads, highways, and other infrastructure he might need; a $500,000 loan to repay "all expenses incurred while funding the revolution"; as well as an additional 24,700 acres on the north coast of Honduras to be claimed at a later date. No taxes, no duties, free land—these were the conditions that would let Sam Zemurray take on United Fruit.

"Deposing [José Santos] Zelaya's government in Nicaragua [in 1909] had required the combined efforts of the [American] State Department, the navy, the marines, and President Taft," wrote Stephen Kinzer in *Overthrow*. "In Honduras, Zemurray . . . [did] the job himself."

By financing the overthrow of Dávila, Zemurray did more than relieve himself of taxes and duties: he entered his name in the black book of Latin American history. He had taken ownership of a nation, whether he realized it or not. As Kinzer explained, "No American businessman ever held a foreign nation's destiny so completely in his hands." Over time, Zemurray would become more powerful than even the government of Honduras. When that happened, the people would begin to look to him to supply the sort of services usually supplied by the state: water, health, security, etc., things it would prove impossible to deliver. Every great victory carries the seed of ultimate defeat.

As for the issue that caused the war in the first place: Zemurray tried to refinance the national debt of Honduras himself, working with banks in New Orleans and Mobile to buy out British bondholders. In the end, he was able to chip away at the fringes, but the bulk remained and grew, accumulating interest. As of 1926, Honduras still owed $135 million on the railroad that went nowhere.

Manuel Bonilla did not serve his full term in office. Having contracted a strange tropical disease, he turned power back to Francisco Bertrand, fell into a fever, and died on March 21, 1913. Lee Christmas was at Bonilla's side, weeping and holding his hand.

Christmas, who'd risen to great power in Honduras, lost his influence when Bonilla expired. Christmas was fifty years old, living in the

Palm Hotel in Puerto Cortés. His peak moment had been the surrender of that city. From there, every step was a station on the way to Calvary: government postings, marriages, divorces, gunfights, brawls. He split with Zemurray in 1916. No one knows the exact details. There was an argument, curses, threats. Christmas stormed out of the office in Omoa. Maybe he'd come for money, maybe a job. Zemurray probably told him his services were no longer wanted. (Why hire mercenaries when you own the army?) Because they're impossible to control, men like Lee Christmas are a threat to business. If you want to survive, you must drive them from the country. Perhaps Christmas felt he could intimidate Zemurray as he had intimidated everyone else in his world. But Zemurray was younger than Christmas, bigger and nervier. He was not the sort of person you can intimidate.

Christmas returned to New Orleans to volunteer for the U.S. Army during the First World War. He thought he would be sworn in as an officer, his experience on the isthmus being a boon, but was rejected as too old. He went to Washington, D.C., where, because he was famous, he was able to make his case to President Woodrow Wilson. He then returned to New Orleans and again tried to enlist. After being rejected a second time, Christmas issued a public challenge, calling out any man forty years of age, the army's cutoff, who wanted to fight. *Let them show themselves, and let them be thrashed!* He moved to Guatemala, then back to New Orleans, where he became an inventor, securing patents on a rattrap that worked without bait and a railroad safety device that shut down the engine the moment the engineer took his hand off the throttle, which must've been inspired by his own terrible accident. In 1921, he sued *Encyclopædia Britannica* for libel, citing an article on Central America that said Christmas had been killed in the battle of Maraita in 1907. He asked for $100,000 in damages. The publisher corrected the text but paid no money. He moved to Nicaragua, where he invested in oil wells (they went dry) and home remedies, the last of his money going for shark oil, which he considered an elixir. This venture ended when dozens of sharks, which he was holding in a pen off Puerto Cortés, escaped in a storm and terrorized the coast.

He fell ill in 1922. It started as a vague listlessness, ennui, but turned into fever. He was misdiagnosed, wrongly prescribed. In New Orleans, a doctor told him he had tropical sprue, a blood disease that would steadily weaken him. He collapsed in New York, where he had gone to meet a potential business investor. He was treated at St. Vincent's hospital but could not pay the bill. Guy Molony, who had become superintendent of the New Orleans city police, wired him money and a train ticket home.

He received a full transfusion of blood, donated by Molony, when he returned. This made headlines around the country and struck people as wonderful. It restored him for a time, but soon he weakened again. There were two more transfusions, each less effective than the last. He got in a fight with his wife near the end and left on a train like the dying Tolstoy. He turned up at the door of a long-lost son in Memphis, who put him back on a train for New Orleans. He was too weak to get off the train by himself and cried when he had to be carried. He cried again when he learned that his wife, who had been among the first ladies of Honduras, had taken a job selling radios on Canal Street. He was admitted to Touro Infirmary in January 1924. "When a man becomes my age in the United States," he told Molony, "he's only good for fertilizer." He died a few weeks later. There was a huge funeral. The pallbearers were aging mercenaries. Minor Keith sent a letter to be read, in which he called Lee Christmas "my ideal of manliness and courage." For the second time in thirty years, *The New York Times* ran his obituary.

11

To the Isthmus and Back

Let me show you a picture of Samuel Zemurray's primary residence circa 1912: a white bungalow with a zinc roof in the shade of a coconut tree on the north coast of Honduras. When a storm blows through, which is most afternoons, the rain drums on the roof and the water hangs like a curtain from a steel awning, beneath which Sam sits reading reports. He's up early each morning and eats a breakfast of raw vegetables and bananas. In other cases, I might not linger on what a man had for breakfast, but such details fascinated and confused Zemurray's competitors. In *Empire in Green and Gold*, Charles Morrow Wilson claimed executives at United Fruit were bewildered by reports of the jungle-dwelling Russian who "had been living for weeks on nothing but figs; or [who] was taking a 'fast cure' for twenty days; or [who] had been seen standing on his head beside a shade tree in the process of proving (or disproving) that inversion benefits the digestion."

As for the reports—sales figures and yields, the length of the average banana, the market rate per stem—Zemurray went through these fast, a scan, a few mental notes, done. He disdained bureaucracy, hated paperwork. "So seldom does he dictate a letter that he requires no full-time secretary," *Life* reported. "He will telephone division managers in half a dozen countries, correlate their reports in his head and reach his decision without touching a pencil." A corporate legend told the Cuyamel executives everything they needed to know about their boss. One morning, as Zemurray was eating breakfast, an apparatchik handed him a thick report, fifty or sixty pages detailing every aspect of the operation. There was a summary on page one, chapter headings, bullet points. Zemurray flipped through the document, frowning, then ripped off the first page and threw away the rest, saying, "Most sensible damn statement I ever saw."

In the years that followed the coup, Sam spent most of his time in Honduras. He had a wife in New Orleans, a daughter and a son, but must have felt he had no choice. Having established his position on the isthmus, it was time to work like a dog: build his business, pay his creditors, accumulate his money. By 1913, he had saved enough to buy back the stake U.F. owned in Cuyamel Fruit, a move that would secure Zemurray's independence.

Selling back these shares was unusual for United Fruit, but the company was forced by outside events. In 1913, Congress proposed a tax on bananas, which had already become the most widely consumed fruit in America, an astonishing fact considering that not a single banana is grown here. Called the Underwood Simmons Tariff Bill, it was usually referred to as "the banana tax." This was during the presidency of Woodrow Wilson, who believed the revenue generated by such a tax would close the gaping hole in the national budget.

Did the leaders of the banana industry raise a stink?

Of course they did.

An army of lobbyists, most of them on the payroll of United Fruit, descended on Washington waving documents, quoting figures, and making their case. The banana tax will ruin the business as it has long been practiced: dirt-cheap bananas sold at tremendous volume, unbelievable prices achieved by concession, cheap land, peasant labor, and NO TAX. An additional five cents per stem would return the banana to its original state, a delicacy for the rich. An industry spokesman accused Congress of attacking "the fruit of the poor."

Probably in response to the ruckus raised by lobbyists, the Justice Department opened its own investigation of United Fruit. The Feds believed that by colluding to fix prices and crush competition, the company was in violation of the Sherman Anti-Trust Act. As the Justice Department pursued the case, U.F. searched for ways to make the company look like anything but what it was: a monopoly. Simply put, United Fruit had to demonstrate there were other firms that could compete, that the field had not been cleared by price war and buyout. It was with this need in mind that Andrew Preston sold Sam Zemurray the shares United Fruit still held in Cuyamel. If Zemurray could be shown to be truly independent, perhaps the charges of antitrust would be disproved and the investigation stymied.

Congress lingered on U.F.'s sale of its Cuyamel shares during hearings before the House Committee of the Merchant Marine and Fisheries. It struck many as an effort to fool the government: a drug dealer tossing a parcel into the bushes as the cops close in.

Preston denied such suggestions. A congressman pressed, demanding the reason for the sale of the Cuyamel shares.

"I think Mr. Zemurray desired it," said Preston. "He is a man of speculative ideas, and he thought he could do better if he had the entire property, and on the recommendations of our people, I think it was sold to him."

Though the Justice Department never filed any charges, the investigation had the desired effect: by forcing Preston to sell his shares in Cuyamel, the government created a competitive market. It did this by assuring Zemurray the freedom to develop into a genuine competitor. In later years, when Zemurray had grown powerful, analysts spoke of the mistake U.F. made: they had underestimated a dangerous rival in Zemurray. In fact, the executives at United Fruit, Preston and Keith first among them, understood the genius of Zemurray from the beginning. They had long been dazzled by his rise from the docks, but it was a matter of triage: cut off the leg to save the body; cut free the Banana Man to save the company.

Zemurray must have been elated to free himself from United Fruit. It meant independence and control. What's more, he believed the association with El Pulpo had damaged his reputation. A few years before, when the Nicaraguan banana growers boycotted U.F. and prevented its ships from sailing down the big rivers, U.F. broke the blockade, not with its own fleet but with Cuyamel ships. Everywhere workers gathered, bloodied by the police, beaten but not defeated, they attached their misery to the name on the side of the boats carrying away the product of their labor: *Cuyamel*. It damaged Sam's name in a country where he'd long been admired as the son-in-law of the beloved Parrot King. Zemurray never forgot the lesson. It does not matter how many bananas you ship: when you lose your reputation, you lose everything.

Sam Zemurray lived in two worlds: the world of family and society in New Orleans, and the jungle world of pure escape, hard work, machete fights, and booze on the isthmus. Some years, he sailed back and forth half a dozen times. He stood on the prow of the ship, thrilled by the first sight of New Orleans, its smokestacks and warehouses appearing around the bend in the river, but was probably more thrilled to leave it behind, to plunge into the primitive South of harbors and coasts, change into his work clothes, and find himself surrounded by roughnecks who had come to the isthmus because it was the last place a man could be free. They called it the Banana Frontier because it recalled America before California had been divided into lots, before the grasslands had been wrested from the cowboys and handed to the merchants.

Central America was a fantasyland where nostalgic North Americans could live their dream of Western wilderness. There were old hands who had been on the isthmus long before the incorporation of the United Fruit Company, men who had come looking for a personal El Dorado and realized too late they were ruined for any other kind of life. There were managers who came to get their cards punched and planned to stay no more than a season or two but got stuck. There were rowdies who had come on a spree, to dress in khaki and carry a gun. There were college men who came for the job but stayed for the stuff, how far the dollar could go, a life of leisure, servants, and clubs. *Unifruco*, the United Fruit magazine, which was as slick as *The New Yorker*, speaks of company men returning to an earlier stage of American history on the isthmus, of living as men used to live before the women took over and softened us with their rules and finery, of confronting nature in the spirit of Davy Crockett or Daniel Boone, of again seeing the forest as primeval, wild, and mysterious.

I know how often Zemurray traveled back and forth because I've seen the manifests filled out at each port, the stack of paper that charts his endless crossing. He was a perfect example of the Wandering Jew, always going but never arriving, living out of a steamer trunk, changing twice before dinner, never settled on any one part of the planet, never living at any one time of the day.

Whenever he arrived in Honduras, word spread through the plantation: *the old man is back!* He was respected because he understood the trade. By the time he was forty, he had served in every position, from fruit jobber to boss. He worked on the docks, on the ships and railroads, in the fields and warehouses. He had ridden the mules. He had managed the fruit and money, the mercenaries and government men. He understood the meaning of every change in the weather, the significance of every date on the calendar. There was not a job he could not do, nor a task he could not accomplish. (He considered it a secret of his success.) He was up every morning at dawn, having breakfast, standing on his head, walking in the fields. As far as possible, he refrained from giving interviews, addressing shareholders, or attending functions, all of which took him away from his work. He was one of those men who toiled all day every day until they had to be rolled away in a chair. When he failed to appear at a reception in Havana, Cuba, which had been thrown in his honor, a lieutenant tracked him down to the wharf, where he was going over manifest documents with a ship's purser.

He was wildly ambitious and innovated like mad. As soon as he had full control of his company, he began to visit boatyards. He wanted to build a fleet so he would never again be dependent on other companies to haul his product. I have a list of the ships he purchased: the *Jamaica*, the *Lempira*, the *Omoa*, the *Maya*, the *Augusta*. He had acquired twenty by 1915. Most of these were steamships, ice sheathed in the harbors of New York and Boston, sweating in the humidity of New Orleans and Puerto Cortés. The decks were fitted with loaders, the holds refrigerated. Soon after being stowed, the bananas were "put to sleep," the temperature never allowed to climb above 56 degrees. Many ships were purchased from rival companies that had discontinued a route. Some were in service with Cuyamel for only a year before an upgrade made them obsolete. In 1921, Zemurray acquired the entire fleet of the Bluefields Fruit Company, the property of his father-in-law. By then, the Cuyamel fleet had become a familiar sight on the New Orleans waterfront, where people referred to it affectionately as the Little Navy.

Around this time, Zemurray moved his headquarters in Honduras from Omoa to Puerto Cortés, where he built a modern pier that went out past the shallows a quarter mile into the sea. The company grew and grew, acquiring more and more land in Honduras but also in Nicaragua and Mexico. Following the example of United Fruit, he began to invest in other crops: coconuts and pineapples, palm oil, cattle, timber, and sugarcane. It was a hedge against hurricane and drought, as well as the ups and downs of the market. It was sugarcane, a staple that sells in quantity regardless of the economy, that got Cuyamel through the First World War, when many of the company's ships were impressed for service in the U.S. Navy.

Of course, the most important tests of leadership are intangible: How do you handle a crisis, sweet-talk a landowner, manage the rough stuff? Can you stand up to the goons, face down the mercenary who overstays his welcome? Can you figure out whom to bribe and make it stick? Can you plunge the machete all the way to the Collins? Zemurray was like a character out of Damon Runyon or Saul Bellow. He could play as dirty as anyone else in the game. (Had he been born in Chicago, they would have called him Nails.) If you saw him talking to a crew boss, sleeves rolled back, black eyes narrowed, neck thick and freckled from the sun, every atom in your body would tell you to stay away. That's why Minor Keith never underestimated Zemurray. He recognized him as one of his own, a throwback to the sort of men who built the industry, who went into the jungle with nothing but trinkets and came out with a million dollars. The banana business might be respectable in the North, but it was rough and lawless in the South.

Like every other enterprise on the isthmus, Cuyamel was built on the kickback, the bribe, the threat delivered in symbols: the photo with a face blacked out, the scythe busted in two. Zemurray often implied that his deals were backed by the U.S. Navy. In other words, he threatened. He did not raise his voice when he made these threats, though he did swear with great exuberance. He whispered so people would have to lean close and concentrate on each word. When he said something was going to happen, it usually did. Even if you were a friend, you would be roughly handled if you got in his way. A State Department document chronicles a conversation a U.S. diplomat had with Zemurray concerning a loan Sam made to the government of Honduras. When Zemurray asked if the U.S. government could help collect, the diplomat spoke vaguely of the Hague Convention, which might technically allow it. "Mr. Zemurray was pleased upon learning of this Hague Convention," the official reported, "and seemed to think it afforded a satisfactory guarantee." It was not American action that Zemurray wanted. It was the credible threat of such action, which might be achieved by the simple spectacle of Sam huddled with a diplomat in the dark corner of the bar.

Zemurray was direct in a way that could come across as ruthless. Speaking of Nicaragua, he notoriously said, "A mule costs more than a deputy." These words have been quoted again and again, in pamphlets, articles, and books—nailed forever to his forehead, thrown around him like a cape. They are said to tell everything you need to know about the Banana Man: the callous indifference, the contempt for life, the sort of corruption that borders on evil. Though Zemurray denied speaking these words—it's the sort of thing that enters the record because it's what people imagine him saying—let's for a moment accept the sentiment as his: A mule costs more than a deputy.

Are these words evil, or are they a simple statement of fact?

If a man wanted to do business in Nicaragua, there were certain things he had to buy—these included banana mules and police deputies. When balancing the books, you could not miss the fact: a mule did indeed cost more than a deputy.

Frank Brogan told me the following story: "Jake Weinberger came out of retirement and got a nice little banana business going with his son Leopold. Not that they grew the fruit: they bought and sold it. But Mr. Zemurray didn't want them competing, particularly in New Orleans and Mobile where Jake was selling at a low price. So he went to his father-in-law and said, 'Look, Jake, I want you out of business. I'm going to give you money so you'll be just fine, but I don't want you fooling with price. I want to set the price.' Jake said, 'I'm not going to give it up. I'm making money.' Sam said, 'Well, Jake, you either get out or I'm going to cut my price and drive you out and you'll be ruined.'"

Thinking about Sam Zemurray's career, I ask myself: Just who was this man and where does he fit in the history of the isthmus? Was he akin to the conquistadores, who came and devastated and set themselves up as aristocrats? Or is this a pirate story? Was he akin to Captain Morgan and Jean Lafitte, arriving with a navy to plunder the Spanish Main? Is he Francis Drake in search of the golden city, for Zemurray, too, sought his fortune in the jungles of the New World? Or is he a Yankee businessman building a multinational company, everywhere and nowhere, whose sins are the sins of capitalism?

I think Zemurray was a transitional figure, a bridge between the world of the privateer and the world of high finance. Cuyamel was not faceless in the way of many modern corporations—Sam's face was, if anything, too much in evidence. The culture of Cuyamel was his personality. That was the company's great achievement and its great failing. Its triumphs and overreaching were the triumphs and overreaching of a single human will. It's why his company was less sinful than many of the other banana companies. Unlike other bosses, Zemurray lived in the jungle with his workers, spoke their language, knew what they wanted and what scared them. (As Zemurray liked to say, "You're there, we're here.") It's why he was hated and why he was loved. Because he was a person and a person you can disagree with and be angry at but still admire, whereas United Fruit was faceless in a way that terrifies. It's why banana workers rallied to the big Russian as their own hedge against El Pulpo. It's why some people in Honduras still speak of Samuel Zemurray with rueful affection.

By 1925, Zemurray had paid off his creditors, was free and clear. He invested most of his profit back in the business. Cuyamel was the rising star of the banana trade, the first company to challenge United Fruit in a generation. It was not about numbers. When it came to market share and volume, U.F. was as dominant as ever. Cuyamel was harvesting eight million bunches a year, United Fruit was harvesting forty million; Cuyamel employed 10,000 workers, United Fruit employed 150,000; Cuyamel had a working capital of $3 million, United Fruit had a working capital of $27 million. It was about profit margin, the efficiency of trade, the morale and skill of the employees. It was increasingly clear: Samuel Zemurray had built the better business.

Cuyamel was superior to United Fruit in a dozen ways that did not show up on a balance sheet. U.F. was a conglomerate, a collection of firms bought up and slapped together. There was a lot of redundancy, duplication of tasks, divisions working against divisions, rivalries, confusing chains of command. Cuyamel Fruit was the Green Bay Packers by comparison. Every decision was made with confidence and authority. Zemurray could move without waiting for permission or a committee report. He could take risks without fear of losing his job. He could hire or fire with surety because he actually lived in Honduras and knew the situation on the ground. It was a contrast of styles: the executives who ran United Fruit had taken over from the founders and were less interested in risking than in preserving. Zemurray *was* the founder, forever on the attack, at work, in progress, growing by trial and error, ready to gamble it all. The difference was best seen on the plantations, where Zemurray was constantly inventing. Most people, looking at a banana, see a delicious fruit. When Zemurray looked at a banana, he saw room for improvement. He innovated banana farming, which had not changed since the first days of the trade, in the following ways:

- **Selective pruning**   His men walked the fields, ripping out runts and dwarfs, which was seen by some as madness.
- **Drainage**   Most banana plantations were built in river valleys, which offered natural drainage. Zemurray augmented this with spillways and canals, making good drainage better.
- **Silting**   United Fruit built levees to prevent its fields from flooding. Zemurray allowed certain fields to be inundated, resulting in an accretion of silt, an excellent fertilizer.
- **Staking**   At Cuyamel, each tree was tied to a length of bamboo, which protected stems against high winds and kept them on the straight and narrow.
- **Overhead irrigation**   Traditional banana men considered watering a waste of resources, since the sky delivered two hundred inches of rain a year. Zemurray argued that, as all that rain was not evenly distributed, with the wet season followed by two months of scorchers, the sky could use some help. He filled fields with overhead sprinklers that mimicked the fall of rain and went on with a click.

The result was banana plants exploding with bunches, each filled with the fattest fingers anyone had ever seen. It was not a matter of measurements: you could tell just by looking.

The most ambitious banana men began to flock to Zemurray. Dozens of them quit United Fruit and caught a ride to Puerto Cortés. Cuyamel was hungry in a way that United Fruit had not been since the retirement of Minor Keith. It was more profitable, too, its share price climbing as the price of U.F. slumped. Zemurray was at first slow to hire these turncoats, suspecting a trick. But when Victor Cutter, who succeeded Andrew Preston as president of United Fruit, denounced the traitors, Zemurray began to actively court U.F.'s top talent. He told a reporter he loved "poking the monster in the knees."

Victor Cutter was driven to distraction by Zemurray. Had he waited all these years to run United Fruit just to be humiliated by a fruit jobber? Cutter bad-mouthed Cuyamel, but nothing stuck. People on the isthmus championed Zemurray as their only protection against El Pulpo. "The press and analysts of economic affairs liked Zemurray," Peter Chapman explains in *Bananas: How the United Fruit Company Shaped the World*. "He didn't seek publicity but, when he got it, it portrayed him in his favored guise as the small guy pitted against unfavorable odds."

Whenever previously challenged, United Fruit had responded in one of two ways: buyout or crush. In 1925, Victor Cutter tried the first option, dispatching Bradley Palmer, a prominent company officer, to talk terms with Zemurray.

Turning down the offer, Zemurray said, "Hell, I'm having so much fun, and I'm a young man. Why should I quit?"

12

The Banana War

A corporation ages like a person. As the years go by and the founders die off, making way for the bureaucrats of the second and third generations, the ecstatic, risk-taking, just-for-the-hell-of-it spirit that built the company gives way to a comfortable middle age. Where the firm had been forward looking and creative, it becomes self-conscious in the way of a man, pestering itself with dozens of questions before it can act. *How will it look? What will they say?* If the business is wealthy and strong, the executives who come to power in these later generations will be characterized by the worst kind of self-confidence: they think the money will always by there because it always has been. They sit in their private clubs and railroad cars, saying, "Everyone knows all the land north of the Utila belongs to the company." Or, "What's that little Russian up to now?"

Victor Cutter was born in 1881. His father owned a grocery store in Dracut, Massachusetts, outside Lowell, which is a suburban wasteland now, an eyesore on distant expressway hills, but was booming a hundred years ago with factories and mills, the money pouring in, the product pouring out. Cutter regaled reporters with stories of his early days working on the horse wagon, hawking beets, carrots, and tomatoes. He was setting himself alongside Sam the Banana Man, as in, *I, too, was a peddler. I, too, came up the hard way. I, too, know what the Russian knows.* But if Cutter ever did work as a peddler, and I have my doubts, he did so in the way of a summer job, as my friend Greg Spitz worked each summer on the line at his father's paper plant. This did not make

Greg Spitz a factory worker any more than working at the grocery store made Victor Cutter a fruit jobber. Cutter's work was done by way of character building, a luxury of the middle class. Zemurray's work was done in order to survive.

You might picture the leaders of the banana trade side by side in 1903: Cutter, six foot something, two hundred–plus, standing with his graduating Dartmouth class, in cap and gown, indistinguishable from the rest; Zemurray, big in another way, all elbows and angles, sinew and bone, racing through the Mississippi delta in a boxcar, the ripes piled behind him like a wall. Cutter studied history as an undergraduate, with a major in Latin America and a minor in Spanish. He was preparing himself for the market that boomed in the Torrid Zone in the wake of the Spanish-American War. He went on to earn a graduate degree from Dartmouth's Tuck School of Administration and Finance. Hired by United Fruit in 1904, he began to climb, helped along by connections made on the golf course and in exclusive societies. Zemurray, who was rejected by even the Jewish clubs, learned to golf only late in life, when he built his own course. *Time*, the conservative fiefdom of Henry Luce, told readers everything they needed to know when it described the course "on which the owner [Zemurray] occasionally breaks 100."

Cutter began as a "timekeeper" for United Fruit, a standard entry-level position for college recruits. Young men were fitted in khaki and pith helmets, then sent to live in modest but comfortable bungalows on banana plantations. The job was a manufactured affair, busywork to give Ivy Leaguers an experience of the South without scaring them away. The day began at dawn, with the timekeeper walking the groves, clipboard in hand, continuing to the warehouse and train depot, stopwatching cutters, packers, loaders, and engineers, searching for inefficiencies. Now and then, he boarded the caboose of a train, drank coffee, and looked out the window as the tracks wandered down to Tela, the Honduran headquarters of United Fruit, where he stood on the docks taking notes as the banana boats were loaded. Each task was timed, the numbers included, along with a report, in the packet carried by courier to Boston.

Cutter was famous for his stories, told in an ironic Dartmouth way. He spoke of escapades on the isthmus, but no one believed him because he had the manner of the office creature. It was not his fault. He'd been born too late—after the wild days. "During the previous generation banana lands had been among the most primitive of American frontiers and, appropriately, many rough and tough men had come to open them," Charles Wilson wrote in *Empire in Green and Gold*. "But by the [time of] Cutter, the primitive simplicity of the banana frontiers had gone." He was well suited for the new corporate habits of the trade and rose quickly through the ranks. In 1924, he became the first president of United Fruit who had not been a founder. This marked a crucial change in the career of the company. Though probably the best of the second generation, Cutter was simply not made of the stuff of the old-time banana men. "During the 1920s, death had taken the two great leaders of the trade, Andrew Preston and Minor Keith, and the new management was relatively inexperienced," Wilson wrote. "A few of the more perceptive students of the trade asserted that the most likely contender for leadership was [not these new U.F. men, but] Sam Zemurray, still being described by [Cutter] as 'that little fellow in Honduras.'"

The isthmus, crossed by the equator, hangs at the center of a balance, day and night in equal proportion, the weather maddeningly moderate, the seasons drifting into years, and the years, without the bone of the seasons, becoming an indistinguishable mass. Even though it might not seem like it, time passes. The years turn into decades. A generation goes by. Then another.

At the start of the Banana War, Samuel Zemurray was forty-nine years old, Cutter forty-three. For a period, the men dwelt on opposite banks of the Utila, a gentle river that meanders from the peaks of the Cordillera to the Atlantic Ocean. Over the millennia, the river has carved the Motagua Valley, the most fertile banana land in the world. It's a beautiful country, fields upon fields, mountains beyond mountains. The Utila roughly follows the Honduras/Guatemala border, itself long in dispute. It also marked the frontier between United Fruit, which followed the northern bank of the Utila, and Cuyamel Fruit, which stood near the southern bank. In the mid-1920s, the border turned hot, as each corporation tried to gobble up the last remaining uncleared acres in the valley. These tensions excited national aspirations. Over time, the rivalry between U.F. and Cuyamel came to be seen as a proxy, with the struggle between the banana companies standing for the struggle between Honduras and Guatemala. In pressing north into the domain of United Fruit, Zemurray seemed to be carrying the banner of Honduras, reclaiming land taken by Guatemala. (Ditto United Fruit and Guatemala's southern border.) In this way, a battle between American corporations threatened to turn into a regional conflict.

Was there an event akin to the assassination of Archduke Franz Ferdinand that sparked the Banana War?

Indeed there was.

Do you remember the promise Manuel Bonilla made when he returned to power in Honduras in 1912? How, in addition to concessions, Sam Zemurray was promised 24,700 acres of land to be given at a future date?

In 1915, Zemurray redeemed that promise, laying claim to a vast tract of territory on the Utila, jungle land that United Fruit considered a buffer between the companies. Left wild, it kept the enemies apart. (Sparks flew wherever they touched.) By destroying this neutral zone, Sam's acquisition of the land changed everything. As far as Cutter was concerned, any agreements, formal or informal, that had regulated the competition were null and void.

The struggle commenced as a war of pranks, with each company taunting and testing its rival. Agents from United Fruit crossed the river at night, cut water lines, tipped over trucks, ripped up train rails. Zemurray sent his own team of brigands across the Utila to retaliate. These were the last of the roughnecks who had wandered away from Texas, riding south as the frontier closed, a brooding tribe out of time, each with a horse and *pistola*, working for next to nothing. I want here to sing an ode to the banana cowboy, that wild, unshaven, hell-raising fighter of yore, terror of the isthmus, hired gun in time of conflict, filibuster in time of revolution, arrived from the streets of New Orleans and San Francisco and Galveston, no good for decent society, spitting tobacco juice and humping extra shells in his saddlebag. These roughnecks found a benefactor in Zemurray, who rode and drank with them. When the Banana War came, they were his avant-garde, crossing the frontier at night, raising hell in the fields.

From the outside, the Banana War seems unfathomable. Zemurray had taken on an enemy of superior resources and size over a few thousand acres that could add only marginally to his wealth. Why did he do it? Why didn't he strike a deal? To understand this, you have to understand Zemurray's personality—personality and style being the great unaccounted factors in history. Strength, charisma, shrewdness, power—his defining characteristics were the sort not recorded in photos or articles, which can make him seem mysterious, strange. What drove him? Didn't he know you can't take it with you in the end? (Yes, but this is not the end.) To colleagues like Frank Brogan who knew Zemurray, his motivation was clear: he wanted to win. And would do whatever it took. Here was a self-made man, filled with the most dangerous kind of confidence: he had done it before and believed he could do it again. This gave him the air of a berserker, who says, If you're going to fight me, you better kill me. If you've ever known such a person, you will recognize the type at once. If he does not say much, it's because he considers small talk a weakness. Wars are not won by running your mouth. I'm describing a once essential American type that has largely vanished. My Grandpa Ben was like that, and so were the tycoons who built Hollywood: studies in sublimation, men who channeled all their love and fear into the business, the factory, the plantation, the shop. Did he love his wife, his children? Of course he did, but he needed the company more. Think of him as a gambler in the midst of a run, whose mind is fixed on the one thing. If he does not look up, it's not because he is shallow or stupid. It's because he knows the moment he looks up, the spell is broken and the game is lost.

By 1917, the Banana War was centered on a single piece of land: five thousand acres on the north bank of the Utila that both companies coveted. United Fruit discovered the problem first. The land, which was on territory claimed by Guatemala *and* Honduras, seemed to have two separate legal owners. I do not know who these two parties were, but let's say one was an old woman in Guatemala City, a widow who, upon the death of her husband, a landowner and livestock breeder, came into possession of a box of certificates, deeds to land scattered across the isthmus, including these five thousand disputed acres. She has not seen the land, does not care much about it, but yes, here's the title and the receipt on taxes, right here. Let's say the second owner was a speculator from Tegucigalpa. For him, the five thousand acres was a bet, made long ago, that with the explosive growth of the banana business, prices in the Motagua Valley would soar.

When this mess of deeds came to light, United Fruit did what big bureaucracy-heavy companies always do: hired lawyers and investigators to search every file for the identity of the true owner. This took months. In the meantime, Zemurray, meeting separately with each claimant, simply bought the land from them both. He bought it twice— paid a little more, yes, but if you factor in the cost of all those lawyers, probably still spent less than U.F. and came away with the prize.

Victor Cutter was infuriated—there was no small degree of humiliation, too. As far as he was concerned, Cuyamel had committed a breach. The north bank of the Utila had always been considered U.F.'s territory. By purchasing the land, Zemurray had crossed a line everyone was supposed to respect.

Respect?

What a stupid word!

Zemurray was in Honduras before U.F., which had previously grown most of its bananas in Costa Rica, Guatemala, and Jamaica. U.F. came to the country only after Sam Zemurray proved it was immensely productive.

United Fruit was determined to strangle Zemurray's new plantation and drive him back across the river.

When Zemurray sent his workers to clear the fields, plant the rhizomes, build the houses, United Fruit filed a complaint with the government of Guatemala, charging Zemurray with violating an international border; Cuyamel was a Honduran company but the territory was claimed by Guatemala. This resulted in an inquiry and a referral to the international court. A hearing was scheduled, ratcheting up tension between the neighboring countries. Guatemala issued belligerent statements. Honduras did the same. The U.S. State Department asked the presidents of the banana companies to cool the rivalry. The United States feared they would plunge the isthmus into war.

Time went by. Zemurray continued to clear fields, plant bananas. United Fruit approached Honduran president Tiburcio Carías, a strongman who came to power in 1924. Carías was a kickback artist with the sort of power mustache favored by junta leaders. Zemurray still received

special consideration in the country, but his influence had waned since
the death of Manuel Bonilla. Carías had, in fact, become increasingly
close to United Fruit. When Cuyamel requested permission to build a
bridge across the Utila—a bridge Zemurray needed to get his bananas
to Puerto Cortés—President Carías turned him down. No bridge, no
train. No train, no bananas.

More time went by. Carías continued to favor United Fruit. How
did Zemurray respond? By making room in his southbound banana
ships, not for produce or seed but for hardware, guns, and bullets that
found their way to the liberal insurgents who had taken to the hills in
Honduras. It was always an option: if the leader is in the pocket of the
other guy, change the leader. The State Department, then run by Frank
B. Kellogg, received reports of smuggled weapons. A Cuyamel boat,
anchored at a Hudson River pier in New York, was searched by the
Port Authority. Fifty thousand dollars' worth of weapons were found.
Another cache was discovered in New Orleans—news of which was
reported on the front page of *The Times-Picayune* on May 4, 1928:

> Rifles, automatic pistols and ammunition regarded as harbingers of
> a new revolution in Central America were seized by detectives and
> government secret service operatives in a double house at 1458–60
> Marais Street Thursday night.

Cuyamel Fruit was charged with violating the Neutrality Act. At
the trial in New Orleans, the company was defended by Joseph Montgomery, who, as the New Orleans district attorney, had previously
prosecuted Cuyamel. This was a preferred Zemurray tactic: if you meet
a truly formidable foe, flip him.

When Zemurray realized he would never get permission to bridge
the Utila, he did what he'd always done: innovated, building surreally
long docks on both sides of the river, then having his engineers design
a temporary bridge, though no one was allowed to call it that. The in-
flatable device could be thrown from extended dock to extended dock
in no time, completing the railroad that ended on one pier and began
again on the other. According to *Life*, "The whole contraption could be
taken up or down in three hours." When United Fruit complained to
Honduran officials, saying Cuyamel had built a bridge without a permit,

Zemurray smiled and said, "Why, that's no bridge. It's just a couple of little old wharfs."

U.F. purchased thousands of acres in the Honduran highlands near La Lima, a mysterious acquisition as the terrain was not suited for bananas. What was Cutter up to? Zemurray soon figured it out, realizing, in one terrible moment, that the land contained the headwaters of the rivers that watered the Sula Valley, where Cuyamel grew most of its fruit. By damming or rerouting those rivers, Cutter could cripple Zemurray. ("Endowed with means that had been reserved for Divine Providence in former times," García Márquez wrote in *One Hundred Years of Solitude*, "[the banana men] changed the pattern of the rains, accelerated the cycle of harvests, and moved the river from where it had always been and put it with its white stones and icy currents on the other side of the town.")

By the autumn of 1928, what began as a corporate rivalry had turned into an open conflict, with soldiers in the field and ships on the sea. If this were a mob movie—and the story of Sam Zemurray was the story of Don Corleone on the isthmus—here would be the part where the capos took to the mattresses and prowled the weeds, searching for the decisive blow.

I've been trying to give the impression of a pot rising to a boil, the tension that began when Zemurray made his first move on the Utila building to a crescendo when he threw his temporary bridge across the river and sent his vaqueros into the field. The region seemed set to explode. Armies were mobilized in Honduras and Guatemala. Soldiers in trucks rushed to the border, the treads of their tires caked in mud. At the last possible moment, the diplomats got involved and a sort of peace conference was convened. In normal cases, this would be the head of the League of Nations calling the presidents of the feuding countries to Vienna or Yalta. In this case, it was officials from the U.S. State Department summoning the bosses of the fruit companies to Washington, D.C. The Banana War threatened American interests, breeding hatred for the United States on the isthmus and posing a danger to a region that included the Panama Canal.

Zemurray made the trip by ship and rail, checked into his hotel, waited. It was the spring of 1929. Several meetings followed, Zemurray across a table from Cutter and his lackeys. The best solution, the only way to end the feud, would be a merger or a buyout. The companies must be forced into a union for the greater good. If there was one company instead of two, if Zemurray and Cutter had the same interests, things might return to normal. Which, of course, raised flags: What about the antitrust laws? Together the companies would control 68 percent of the market (U.F. had a 54 percent share; Cuyamel, 14 percent). Wouldn't such a combination result in prosecution under the Anti-Trust Act? It was the threat of such a prosecution that caused Preston to sell his Cuyamel stake in the first place. Assurances were given. After all, the authorities *wanted* the companies to merge. It's how our government operates, lurching from crisis to crisis, trustbuster to peacemaker: *now there is not enough competition, now the competition is too chaotic and free.*

Once the concept was agreed upon—where there had been two companies, there would be one—it was merely a matter of settling the particulars. Months of negotiations followed, offers pushed back and forth across a table, Zemurray studying the numbers through half-closed eyes. Since God is in the details, that's where he went, adding and multiplying but never subtracting. He fought over each clause and contingency, threatened, complained, and swore in every language he knew. According to friends, Sam was a sharp trader who knew the prize goes to he who does not lose his head or open his mouth too soon. What cannot be accomplished by threats can often be achieved by composure. Sit and stare and let your opponent fill the silence with his own demons.

The word "sellout" is thrown around with gleeful ease in our society. *Did she sell out? You hypocritical sellout!* In most cases, such charges are false, as you actually need something to sell to qualify as a sellout. Sam Zemurray really was a sellout, in the classical sense. He had gathered his winnings in a pile and carried them to the counting room, where he sat across from Cutter, as shadowy figures tallied the skim. He was putting a price on his company, which was more than a company—it was his body and soul, twenty years in the jungle, epic journeys on muleback, Mobile, New Orleans, and Puerto Cortés. Cuyamel Fruit was

Zemurray in the shape of a corporation, his personality made manifest, his home and his love, where he tested his theories and formed his philosophy: *get up first, work harder, get your hands in the dirt and the blood in your eyes*. And here he was preparing to sell it to United Fruit.

Why?

There was the matter of the State Department, of course. The summons to D.C., the demand for a solution. The pressure was intense. But Sam had never been afraid to defy the government, to curse in Spanish and walk away. This was the man who, told by Philander Knox to mind his business, raised an army instead. But that was a different time in the life of the Banana Man. Then he had been a kid, an outsider with nothing to lose. He had since become a man of means. Whereas the young Sam was reckless and immune—from nowhere, with nothing— there were all sorts of ways the middle-aged Sam could be hurt. Success limited his options and made him vulnerable.

There was also the matter of the stock market. One Friday in October, as the men were negotiating, news came of the collapse in New York. In the course of a day, the wealth accumulated over a decade by the blue-chip companies of America vanished. U.F. stock was not greatly affected, not at first, nor was Cuyamel stock, but a tremendous sense of insecurity followed the crash. For a man like Zemurray, who was as sensitive as a weather vane, it must have seemed like a propitious moment to attach his fate to the fortunes of the behemoth. Just ask Christopher Columbus, tossed by wind and rain for one hundred days, what a man needs to survive a tempest: lots of food, lots of money, lots of luck—size, size, size. It must have seemed like the perfect moment to sell. If you deal now, you deal from a position of strength. Who knows what will happen next year?

In the end, after weeks of bargaining, with the threat of a walkout always in the air, the final agreement was worked out in a haphazard, casual way. Bradley Palmer, United Fruit's largest shareholder and a ranking director, tracked Zemurray down to a pub in London, where he was eating alone. Palmer ordered a pint of Bass. Zemurray ordered a pint himself. Twelve pints later, the deal was done. Not a buyout but a merger, with the smaller company becoming a division of the larger. This was the key for Zemurray, not only for reasons of pride but also because it meant none of his workers would be fired, nor any of his plantations shut down. The deal would be structured as a stock swap. When Zemurray brought it to his investors, holders of Cuyamel's stock signed agreements allowing their shares to be exchanged for shares in United Fruit. (Cuyamel was trading at $107; U.F. was trading at $108.50.) Sam would receive three hundred thousand shares of United Fruit for his shares of Cuyamel. His stake, after the merger, would be valued at more than $30 million. A figure worth considering, as it would make Sam Zemurray, who had arrived in Selma with nothing three decades before, one of the richest men in America.

U.F. would take possession of Cuyamel, the best banana company in the world, with thirty-five thousand cultivated acres in Honduras, Nicaragua, and Mexico, fifteen top-of-the-line banana boats, and the capacity to produce and ship six million bunches a year. "It was a marriage of opposites," wrote Thomas McCann, a longtime U.F. employee, in *An American Company.* "Zemurray's personal style, as well as his operating practices, was completely contrary to the traditions of United Fruit. Zemurray had lived in the tropics and had personally pioneered many of the practices in agriculture and engineering which became the standards for the industry. By contrast, the management of the United Fruit Company had been content, for the most part, to sit in Boston and count the money and watch bananas grow with the same detachment with which an actuary watches the growth and death of populations."

As part of the agreement, Zemurray, who would now become the majority owner of United Fruit stock, agreed to retire from the banana trade. United Fruit would be run as it had been: by Victor Cutter and his board of directors in Boston. U.F. management insisted on this. To them, the deal was aimed less at acquiring extra capacity than at driving their greatest competitor from the field. They wanted to get rid of Zemurray, bury him under a pile of stock. Sam agreed to retire, promising to neither work for a rival nor start a new fruit company of his own. A standard noncompete clause. Zemurray was given an honorary title but would really have no more say than any other shareholder: he could attend public meetings and raise his hand.

The deal was approved by U.F. stockholders in December 1929, two months after the stock market crash. It was among the biggest corporate mergers of the era, first reported on the front page of *The New York*

Times on November 26, 1929, with the headline "Cuyamel Accepts United Fruit Offer: Holders Vote for Merger of Companies at Share-for-Share Exchange of Stock." The same news, carried in the United Fruit Annual Report in 1930, ran to two sentences. There was no mention of Zemurray, the Banana War, the banana cowboys, the State Department, or the twelve bottles of ale. It's the sort of description—"In December of last year the directors authorized the purchase of the properties of the Cuyamel Fruit Company. These assets will be added to the inventory of the United Fruit Company"—that attempts to shape history Soviet-style, by exclusion. As far as the executives of United Fruit were concerned, Zemurray would now fade away like the other storied figures of the banana past. If remembered at all, it would be as a folk hero from an antique age, "the *gran hombre* of the Chamelecon-Utila Basin," as Charles Morrow Wilson described him, who "spent sodden weeks and months walking scores of jungle trails from Ceiba Point to Tegucigalpa."

This was the state of affairs circa January 1930, when Sam boarded a steamship in Puerto Cortés to return to New Orleans. In the way of a retiring politician or athlete, he promised to embrace his retirement, spend more time with his loved ones, pursue causes and fancies. For once in his life, which had been nothing but sixteen-hour workdays, he would enjoy his success and be happy. It's possible he believed these things as he said them, but, in truth, Zemurray was not old and was still angry, easy to insult, easy to incense, driven, and restless. Show me a happy man and I will show you a man who is getting nothing accomplished in this world.

Ripe

13

King Fish

Samuel Zemurray returned to New Orleans in the winter of 1930. He was fifty-three years old. Though never handsome, he was one of those powerful men who get more impressive with age. He dressed in the simple way of a mariner home from sea, button-down shirt, linen coat, slacks. He had dark eyes and a high forehead that folded like an accordion when he was concerned. He was rich and famous, a legend of the industry, but people let him believe in his anonymity, that he was coming across as just another fruit jobber, drinking coffee on the wharf, soaking up the gossip of the river trade.

He was experiencing a caesura, a pause between the episodes of his life. For the first time, he seemed inclined to ruminate and consider. I do not know if he was a religious man, if he believed in God or if there was nothing he could hold on to. I do not know if he was scared of death, or if he believed that the soul of a person never perishes. Whenever I reach the borders of Zemurray's story, where the record leaves off and the shadows encroach, I come across the same word, assembled in pickets, marking where I can and cannot go: UNKNOWN, UNKNOWN, UNKNOWN. After all, some of the most profound moments of any life are lived between three and four in the morning, when you stare at the ceiling as the silence roars.

New Orleans was a great city in 1930, blocks and blocks of streets lit by yellow lights, storefronts aglow in the evening, tobacco shops, coffeehouses, newsstands, hotels and taverns, the storied restaurants, Antoine's, Galatoire's, Arnaud's, the antiquated hitching posts of the French Quarter, wrought-iron balconies, the clang of the streetcar. Zemurray was living in the house at 2 Audubon Place that for many remains the most famous thing about him. It's tied to him as Monticello is to Thomas Jefferson, as Graceland is to Elvis Presley.

Built in the early 1900s for a lumber tycoon, the house was a redbrick Beaux Arts mansion shaped like a cross, with columns, porches, porticoes, overhangs, and grand front steps. The sitting rooms and libraries, the staircase that ascends like a helix, were made from Louisiana pine and Virginia cypress. Zemurray purchased the house for $60,000 in 1917. Tulane University had recently moved into its new uptown campus, which began a few hundred feet from Sam's lawn. Though the address is Audubon Place—a gated street favored by the elite of the city—the front door opens on St. Charles Avenue across from Audubon Park.

Rebuilding the house was a project of Zemurray's retirement. He installed dumbwaiters and elevators, added rooms. By 1931, it looked like it does today: a white mansion in the Antebellum style. On the third floor, he built a ballroom with a parquet floor lit by a crystal chandelier. A handmade organ piped music throughout the house. An intercom connected the rooms. Now and then, you might hear the voice of the Banana Man booming through the halls: *Sarah! Where are you? Sarah Zemurray! Please come upstairs! Sarah! . . . Sarah?* There was an office on the second floor with a mahogany desk where Zemurray rested his feet as he read the paper. The master bedroom looked out on St. Charles. There was a screened sleeping porch where the family slept on hot nights. There was a kind of crow's nest on the top floor of the house, windows with views, where Zemurray paced as he talked on the phone. It was his favorite room. He often had breakfast on the porch, where there was always a stem of bananas hanging from a hook. Now and then, he pulled down a finger or bunch. He might consume five bananas at a sitting. No. 2 Audubon remains perhaps the most fashionable address in New Orleans. In this city, people tell you it's the most beautiful house in America. When Zemurray died, he left it to Tulane. It's been the official residence of the university president since the 1970s, a place of fund-raisers and galas. But an inspection of its rooms is still a tour through the mind of the Banana Man. The house is rooted in an antique age. Its façade is Sam's face, how he wanted to be seen by the world.

Zemurray bought a twenty-five-thousand-acre plantation near Hammond, Louisiana, fifty-eight miles north of New Orleans, where he could repair in the worst of the summer heat. It had been the property of a lumber company. Zemurray knocked down the old woodworks, built a house, planted flowers and trees. It was his retreat, the place he could reconnect to the essential things: dirt instead of concrete, paths instead of roads, fields instead of markets. He built a golf course, a hunting lodge, a game park stocked with exotic fauna. He planted orchards, harvested crops, crossbred, experimented. "All my life I've wanted to be a real season-to-season farmer," he explained. "I've been wanting a farm of my own since I was a little boy looking at the tall wheat fields back in the old country."

The plantation became very special for Zemurray. It's where he took associates when a deal had to get done, where he went with family when he needed to impart and explain. His thoughts turned increasingly to the next generation, to his daughter, Doris, whom he loved, and to his son, Sam Jr., whom he loved in a different way. It was Sam Jr. who would carry on the name. Everything that was being accumulated was, in a sense, being accumulated with him in mind. Passing on the Jewish traditions was clearly not that important to Sam. If it had been, he would not have given his son his own name—it's a very un-Ashkenazi thing to do. But legacy did matter. He wanted to teach his son everything he knew so his son could improve the life and status of the family in the next generation. In this way, Zemurray replaced tradition with progress and Zion with America.

Sam found the only check on his power in his wife, Sarah Weinberger, the daughter of the Parrot King. *Life* described her as "a quiet, plainly dressed, self-effacing woman, who practices housekeeping as a fine art." Sarah did indeed see herself as a maestro of the near-at-hand. She stayed at home when Sam traveled, raised the family when he was gone. If she suffered, she suffered quietly. Like a range of distant hills, she was the background against which the action is staged—a member of the last generation of American women to take their domestic role so seriously that they have vanished.

Sarah Weinberger-Zemurray wrote a handful of books on the

domestic arts—*One Hundred Unusual Dinners and How to Prepare Them*, for example—which, considering the place her husband occupied in the dream life of banana land, stand as a counterpoint to *One Hundred Years of Solitude*. As García Márquez was imagining a tempest that would clear the landscape of plantations and gringos, Sarah was imagining Shad-Roe and Asparagus Soup (Menu 38): "Beat the cream stiff and put 1 tablespoonful in each serving"; Giblet Gumbo (Menu 21): "Use feet (skinned and toenails chopped off). Cut feet in half, skin the gizzards"; Consommé with Avocado Balls (Menu 77): "Mash avocado with salt and pepper to taste, shape into balls."

One Hundred Unusual Dinners was published in 1938 by the Thomas Todd Company of Boston. It's a cookbook, but most of the recipes would torment a professional chef. Imprecise and vague, they read less like directions than like visions of archetypes. Here's the light: you build the tunnel. The meals themselves speak of an indulgent time, when everything was jellied, fried, and covered in cream. The menus might explain Sam Zemurray's tortured relationship with food, his diets, vegetarianism and constant swearing off. Reading the details of his cures—only bananas and water; only figs; only lettuce and toast—alongside his wife's calendar of smothered entrées is like catching an echo of an old argument. Here you have not just two menus but two ways of life: the calorie-rich, cream-heavy indulgence of the domestic world versus the spare manner of the banana cowboy.

According to articles and photos, Sarah Weinberger was a stout matron, a paragon of the Jewish South. She wore dun-colored dresses that swept the floor and big-soled shoes that could be heard at a distance. Her hair was usually pinned into a bun, a cushion that, one afternoon, a million years before, on a beach on Padre Island, Texas, say, when her shoulders were tanned to freckles, a boy might have described as spun gold, but had since faded to ash. She was young, but only for a minute. On formal occasions, she was the woman in back of the family photograph. To people of that vintage, the camera was an untrusted mechanism that required utter stillness. In my mind, Sarah, seen only at full length, is a stand-in for every Jewish grandmother of three or four generations back, a product of old America, with a keen sense of propriety and undying faith in progress, suggested every time she looked at her son and said, "Sam! My God, he's taller than you!"

While Sam was raising bananas, Sarah was raising human beings. Doris, born in 1909, crossed the Gulf of Mexico with her father several times when she was a girl. To most children, this would be a trip through the wardrobe: on this side, the austere rooms of 2 Audubon Place; on that side, the banana frontier, where vaqueros drink rum beneath the tin roof of the shanty. Staying on the isthmus, in the house of the boss, behind electrified wire, might make some children haughty, but it fascinated Doris. She wanted to know everything about Honduras, its people and politics, the story of it lost civilizations—subjects that would become the great passions of her life.

Sam Jr., remembered mostly as a physical presence, was a young man written in all capitals. Born in 1913, he became everything a father could want: handsome, smart, admired. Five feet tall in the fifth grade, six foot one in the tenth grade, he just kept growing. Sam Jr. was six foot six when he entered Tulane. He played on the school's football team, which was among the best in the nation. He was captain of the boxing team. His friends called him Pig Iron. His great love was airplanes. He would sit on the edge of the runway and watch the Curtiss Carrier Pigeons and Ford Tri-Motors take off. He earned his pilot license when he was really still a boy. His father bought him a prop plane that sounded like a buzz saw. Sam Jr. would fly to the plantation, where the old man, sitting on the porch, would watch the plane cross the sky and land on the strip behind the pine trees. While studying for a business degree at Harvard, Sam Jr. met Margaret Thurston Pickering, a member of a prominent family. She was the granddaughter of William Henry Pickering, an astronomer who predicted the possibility of flying machines (correct), the presence of a ninth planet (correct), the presence of vegetation on the moon (incorrect). They were married on June 25, 1936, in the Harvard Memorial Chapel by C. Leslie Glenn, a Presbyterian minister. They settled in New York.

Sam Jr. was the world to his father, the point of all the work and the gift he would leave behind when he was gone. He was the future. He was America. Tolstoy described a child as a sphere of vulnerability, another place the world can hurt you. It's possible that Zemurray loved his son too much.

As the occupant of the grandest house in New Orleans, Zemurray had obligations, a role to play. He had given to charity as soon as he had money, but now is when his real career in philanthropy began. For a man like Zemurray, this was less a matter of warmhearted sympathy than an aspect of the complete life: a requirement. In some ways, the world was better back then. It did not matter if you were kind or as mean as a snake—you were supposed to give, so you gave. That's all.

Though apparently not religious, Zemurray was, in important ways, as Jewish as can be. His philanthropy was an example: it was not how much he gave, it was the way he gave. He seemed to be aware of the concept of *tzedakah*, the obligation to give as spelled out in Deuteronomy and explained in the Deuteronomic Code—a man needs a code or else lives willy-nilly, like an animal—which requires *tzedakah* from every Jew, even the struggling. If you have a little more than nothing, divide that little more into ten parts and give one away. For a righteous life, *tzedakah* is more important than prayer or trips to Jerusalem or professions of faith. Don't tell me how you feel; show me what you've done. In the Bible, the guidelines are explained in reference to agriculture: if you have one hundred vineyards, leave ten unharvested for the poor; if you have ten olive trees, leave one unbeaten for the poor. This would have spoken to Zemurray, a man who considered himself a farmer first and last.

Among the highest forms of *tzedakah* is to give anonymously, in a way that does not disgrace the person in need. Whenever possible, Sam gave without affixing his signature: neither press conference nor public announcement nor strings attached. A private man who shunned publicity, he believed charity was sacred but that those things that often surround it—newspaper pomp, ribbon cutting—were tawdry. I don't know whether Zemurray read the Bible or knew the code, only that he'd clearly been affected by the folk wisdom, what his father told his mother over the dinner table in Russia: that giving with display is not giving, but trading. I give you money, you give me prestige. Philanthropy that does not degrade is done so quietly not even the rescued learns the name of his rescuer. For this reason, we'll never know how much Zemurray gave, or to whom. *Life* said, "Zemurray has given millions for philanthropic purposes—usually in secrecy." We know of only the public projects and causes, those that could not be advanced without attracting a crowd.

There was, for example, Tulane, which Zemurray was determined to turn into one of the world's great universities. He made his first gift in 1911, when he donated $32,000 to the school to fund a department of hygiene and tropical medicine. He wanted to help cure the Torrid Zone diseases that now and then devastated New Orleans. The population of the city had been punished by yellow fever in 1905. You could not go ten minutes that summer without hearing horns and drums as the funeral processions went through the streets to the cemetery beyond the old city ramparts. In 1925, Zemurray made another contribution, building a dormitory for girls that is still in heavy use today. Named for Zemurray's daughter, it's called Doris Hall. As in, *I'll meet you inside Doris.* He put up $40,000 for a girls' gymnasium in 1932, when Sam Jr. was a student, then kicked in another half a million for projects various and sundry. He sat on the school's board for years and was involved in key decisions, some good, some terrible. (In the 1950s, he opposed a plan to desegregate the university.) In other words, in addition to money, he gave expertise, time. When I was a student at Tulane, it seemed half the school was named for members of his family. Two buildings named for his daughter, New Doris Hall and Old Doris Hall; a complex for his son-in-law, the Stone Center; a dorm for the patriarch himself, Zemurray Hall. Walking through the campus was like wandering though a family album, though most of the students hardly noticed. People accept the world as they find it. For them, Zemurray was not a man on a mule. He was a building where you got so drunk you wondered if you were actually living this life or were just a figment in another person's dream. All this nameplating might seem contrary to the ideal of anonymous giving, but most of the titles were affixed after the Banana Man died. I think he would have hated it.

More charity:

Zemurray gave money to establish a clinic for troubled children in New Orleans, funded the city's first hospital for "Negro" women, and, at the urging of his daughter, made a $250,000 gift to Radcliffe College to endow a professorship at Harvard, an endowment that resulted in the first woman professor on the Arts and Sciences Faculty of the university. It's called the Samuel Zemurray Jr. and Doris Zemurray Stone

Radcliffe Professor of the History of Science. He gave vast amounts to *The Nation* magazine, which had fallen on hard times, and more to found the Zamorano, the Panamerican Agricultural School, which is a short drive from Tegucigalpa. Still considered among the best schools of its kind in Central America, the Zamorano was tuition free. Graduates were discouraged from taking jobs in the banana industry. Zemurray wanted to build an educated Central American class independent of the trade; the overreliance of the people on the fruit companies had become a problem for everyone. He had a passion for giving money on the isthmus. His charity in Central America included hospitals, highways, power grids, seawalls, levees, orphanages, and schools. There was a saying in New Orleans: "If you want something from Sam Zemurray, ask for it in Spanish."

Perhaps most significant, he helped create the Middle American Research Institute (MARI) at Tulane, a center with origins in Omoa, where a plantation manager set a grinning little idol on Zemurray's desk.

What the fuck is it? asked Zemurray.

I don't know, said the manager, *but we keep finding them in the fields.*

Tell you what, said Sam. *I'll give you a dollar for every one you bring in here.*

In this way, Zemurray amassed one of the most important collections of Mayan artifacts in the world: idols, statues, dinnerware, and hundreds of tchotchkes boxed and sent to New Orleans, where they were among the founding treasures of MARI. Several years after Sam funded the center—now called the Roger Thayer Stone Center for Latin American Studies—the WPA guide described him as "an interested man of wealth who preferred to remain anonymous."

In the 1930s, Zemurray was increasingly drawn, against his will, kicking and screaming, onto the public stage. His wealth and position seemed to demand it. Though he long steered clear of American politics—he had the foreigner's dread of drawing attention—he was a vocal supporter of Franklin D. Roosevelt and the New Deal, which he criticized only for not going far enough, fast enough.

To Zemurray, who spent his formative years in Russia, awash in ideology, who followed from afar the triumph of Mussolini and Stalin and was mesmerized by the rise of Hitler, America did not seem immune. In the first years of the Great Depression, he must have sensed the same dark mood that was spreading across Europe: in the eyes of the crowds, in the grumbling on the bread lines, in the temper of the vagabond armies that haunted the docks. Something had to be done to help these people, work had to be found, or who knows what might happen. Zemurray was a member of the last generation of American tycoons that identified less with Republicans than with Democrats, less with capital than with workingmen. Hence his contributions to *The Nation*. Hence his involvement with the New Deal. He traveled back and forth to Washington, D.C., sat through government meetings, served on federal commissions. It was not that, looking at the crowds, he thought "That could be me"; it was that he realized "That *is* me"—if the dice took one more turn, if the switchman slept though the morning call and the ripes turned brown. He helped write the codes enforced by FDR's Agricultural Adjustment Administration, which paid American farmers to leave fields fallow. He served on the Board of Economic Welfare and advised Henry Wallace, the secretary of agriculture. On occasion, he met with the president himself. He was one of the unofficial advisers some people had in mind when they referred to the commander in chief as President Rosenfelt.

But Zemurray's most notorious struggle was waged at home, against the governor of Louisiana, Huey Long, the plump, red-cheeked country boy in overalls, with colic and grin, the scourge of fat-cat businessmen who promised to burn it all down and take it all away.

Huey Long grew up in Winnfield, Louisiana. His father was a farmer, as was *his* father, as was *his* father. He won a scholarship to Louisiana State University but could not afford the textbooks so went on the road instead, working, variously, as a salesman of canned goods, a hawker of elixir medicine, and an auctioneer. He had a wonderful voice, a beautiful way of phrasing. He entered politics in 1918 as an elected member of the Louisiana Railroad Commission, where he made his name in fiery public hearings. By twenty-five, he was the dreaded foe of Standard Oil. He had the advantage of being underestimated, condescended to, and dismissed as a buffoon, all the while amassing a huge popular following. A. J. Liebling described him as "a chubby man

[with] ginger hair and tight skin that was the color of a sunburn coming on. It was an uneasy color combination, like an orange tie on a pink shirt. His face faintly suggested mumps." He broadened his attack from Standard Oil to corporations in general; from corporations in general to the corporatist mentality; from the corporatist mentality to the handful of oligarchs and politicians who were remorseless and cunning in their control of our markets and lives. He referred to them as the "Old Regulars" or "the Ring." When Long ran for governor, he promised to kick out the bosses and soak the rich, the parasites, relieve them of their ill-gotten gains and remind them of the people on the farms and in the small towns who one day, and that day is coming, brother, will shake off the old regulars like so many fleas. He campaigned under the slogan "Every man a king, but no one wears a crown."

"How many men ever went to a barbecue," he asked in a speech, "and would let one man take off the table what's intended for nine-tenths of the people to eat? The only way you'll ever be able to feed the balance of the people is to make that man come back and bring back some of that grub that he ain't got no business with!"

It's not just what Long said, but also how he said it. His face was expressive in a way unimaginable in the pallid politics of today. He spoke with his hands, got his whole body into it. Goofy yet strong, he seemed like he was having a great time. Here's the crucial quality often overlooked by historians of the era: Huey Long was funny; comedy was a big part of his appeal from the beginning. He delivered his kickers not to shouts but to laughter. The man who wanted to make the bastards pay was the scariest thing of all: an evil clown.

Huey Long was elected governor of Louisiana in 1928. He had been prominent in the state for years, but the Depression turned him into a star. With a quarter of the American people out of work, his talk of upending the establishment, of making the whalelike corporations disgorge bellyfuls of fish, rang like a bell. He shouted, cajoled, threatened, becoming a national figure in the process. In the 1930s, after many years as a Roosevelt man, he began to distance himself from the Democratic Party. He hinted at making his own presidential run. To some, Long was the best hope for a more equitable distribution of wealth. And yet, even at the height of his power, he remained small-town, fixated on Louisiana. Though he served in the U.S. Senate, his internal map of the world, the friends and foes who really mattered, the secret hierarchy that controlled everything, was focused on a handful of clubs in New Orleans. To Long, "the people" meant the farmers of Louisiana, and "the establishment" meant a dozen or so machine politicians who had sworn to defeat not just Long but Long-ism, that terrible uprising of the rabble-rousing trash.

Long was truly hated by his opponents. It had less to do with policy than with taste. To them, Huey stood for everything crass. "They despised him," John Barry wrote in *Rising Tide: The Great Mississippi Flood of 1927 and How It Changed America*. "In the evenings they literally sat around their drawing rooms discussing ways to murder him."

By 1930, Long was preparing to run for the U.S. Senate, challenging the incumbent Joseph Ransdell for the Democratic nomination. In the course of this campaign, Long believed he uncovered the shadow force bankrolling all his enemies. "Our opposition undertook to form a coalition of practically every political element in the City of New Orleans to overcome whatever lead I might have in the country outside that city," Long wrote in *Every Man a King*, his autobiography. "The opposition was well on its way toward effecting such alignment, when I discovered the power behind the throne."

Long identified this power as Sam Zemurray, a friend and ally of Senator Ransdell. Long then spent several weeks crossing Louisiana, denouncing the Banana Man—parasite of parasites, the worst offender in a den of thieves. He did this from the stage and he did it from sound trucks, driven in and out of towns in northern Louisiana, along the Gulf Coast beaches, through the parking lot of LSU stadium. Long's organization printed two million copies of a circular—it appeared as a bulletin from *The Louisiana Progress*, a newspaper owned by Long—which was plastered to every telephone pole and tree in the state, stuffed into every mailbox and beneath the wiper on every windshield.

WHY THE ZEMURRAY MILLIONS
SUPPORT THE RING—
THE BLOOD OF AMERICAN SOLDIERS THAT IS SPILLED
FOR ZEMURRAY—

HIS REASON FOR BACKING RANSDELL—
WHY RANSDELL FOUGHT HIS PEOPLE ON FLOOD
CONTROL—
THE BARTER OF THE JUDICIARY AND SEATS IN
CONGRESS—

It is not a matter of very common knowledge, but it is nevertheless a fact, that the United States has kept a standing army down in Central America to fight for certain interests "making investments" in such countries as Nicaragua and Honduras. The story runs that, when one of these large American interests is not pleased with what he can get at the hands of the Central American governments, they "change the government."

Among the men who have made millions in Central America out of the work of the soldiers of this country is one Sam Zemurray of New Orleans. He has many concessions in the Central American countries. Time after time, except for the blood of the soldiers of this country, his "concessions" would have gone up in smoke. Wherever he drove down his stob and laid claim to a few hundred miles of property, no matter what side of a revolution he bought it from, he was able to make good his claim by the fact that the United States would send soldiers there to back him up.

It took influence to have the army of the United States in a constant war to make money for Zemurray. There was no war declared, and yet the U.S. soldiers spent their blood for the cause of the financial gain of Mr. Zemurray, just the same as if war had been declared. Why? Mr. Zemurray took in as an associate, we find, a nephew of Senator Joe Ransdell, Joe Montgomery, and this Zemurray and Ransdell's kinfolks' combination made millions on top of millions that anybody else could have made if they had only been furnished with the United States army to back them up in their concessions and grants, in the revolutions of Central America.

Many a mother's son lies in an unmarked grave in the tropics for the cause of Zemurray's millions.

It must have been a nightmare for Zemurray, a private man who disdained publicity, to be dragged out into the spotlight where the multitudes gawk, the sort of thing that got him cursing and threatening that miserable, rotten, no-good son of a bitch.

Long turned paranoid. He began to speak of himself as a target of assassins. He was especially fearful of the former New Orleans police official Guy Molony, who turned up in the city in 1934 after a lengthy stay in Honduras. Long believed that Molony had returned at the request of an anonymous third party to lead a mercenary army to overthrow Long and replace him with T. Semmes Walmsley, the mayor of New Orleans. When questioned about this at a public hearing, Molony laughed as he denied the charges. There is no such plot, said Molony, but he would be happy to participate if one was organized.

Long began to travel amid a phalanx of bodyguards, Louisiana state troopers in squeaky black boots and mirror shades. He investigated his enemies, had their tax returns scutinized, desks rifled, comings and goings monitored.

At first glance, Zemurray and Long seemed to have had a lot in common: both were self-made men who grew up on farms; both were seen as interlopers, shut out of the best clubs; both were Democrats with a similar critique of the New Deal—neither far enough nor fast enough. But unlike Zemurray, who wanted to reform the system to save it, Long wanted to tear it down. In him, Zemurray would have recognized an old foe: the charlatan, the snake-oil salesman, the Cossack. When Huey said, "Let's soak the rich," Sam heard, "Let's soak Zemurray." When Huey said, "Let's crush the Ring," Sam heard, "Let's crush Zemurray." To Long, Zemurray represented everything that was wrong in America: the fat cat who had taken more than his share, the tycoon whose fortune was built on the backs of the poor. His brain is money; his teeth are rifle shells; his eyes are the stolen jade of the Mayan highlands; his fingers are ripes; his diet is human misery and human blood. On foreign policy, Long seemed to have just one concern: he did not want U.S. troops sent to the isthmus, where, Long claimed, they would protect the interests of Zemurray, whom Long denounced on the floor of the U.S. Senate.

It seemed the conflict would turn into something truly ugly. Then it didn't. Or maybe it did. On September 8, 1935, at 9:20 p.m., Senator Long, who had returned to Baton Rogue to attend to legislative business, was approached by a man in the hall of the Capitol building, Dr. Carl Weiss, the son-in-law of a Louisiana judge. Weiss shot Long in the chest, then struggled with his bodyguards, who knocked the assassin to the ground and shot him thirty times. As for Long, after he was hit, wrote A. J. Liebling, he "spun around, made one whoop, and ran down the hall like a hit deer." He was taken to a hospital, where he died two days later. He was forty-two years old.

I'm not saying Zemurray was behind the Huey Long assassination, though skeptics still contest the official version of the killing: Dr. Weiss, acting on a mad impulse of his own, sneaks into the statehouse and fixes Huey good. There was enough doubt to warrant a full-scale investigation by the Justice Department in the fall of 1935. I once knew one of the investigators, Morris Leibman, who had worked for the Justice Department when he was a young attorney. When I asked him about the killing, he said, "Louisiana—you never know." Later evidence suggested the bullet that killed Long came from a .38-caliber or .45-caliber pistol. Dr. Weiss owned a gun, but it was a .32-caliber. In fact, the bullet that killed Huey Long matched the guns carried by his own bodyguards. And we know for certain they fired their weapons that night, a number of times. Some people suggest Long's death was a tragic accident: a jumpy bodyguard set off another jumpy bodyguard, until the air was full of lead; others suggest Dr. Weiss fired and missed, but Long was accidentally shot in the ensuing melee. In either scenario, Dr. Weiss is framed by the bodyguards, wishing to avoid a scandal. Others suggest a darker conspiracy, a collusion of interests determined to prevent Long from challenging Roosevelt in the upcoming presidential election, in which case Dr. Weiss was the patsy. Or perhaps the assassination was the Ring settling a score. In this scenario, the bodyguards were paid off, corrupted. ("In the evenings they literally sat around their drawing rooms discussing ways to murder him.") So, no, I'm not saying Zemurray was behind the assassination of Huey Long, knew about it in advance, or did anything other than mourn when he got the news. But the fact is, the few men stupid enough to outrage Sam Zemurray, to challenge him, or disrespect him, or get in his way, from Miguel Dávila to Huey Long, had a habit of coming to a bad end.

14

The Fish That Ate the Whale

One morning in 1931, Zemurray woke early, had a breakfast of figs and water, stood on his head for fifteen minutes, went through his front door, crossed St. Charles Avenue, and headed downtown. This was Sam in early retirement, unable to keep away from the wharves, the ships, the machinery. He followed Calhoun Street to Magazine, which is curio shops and storefronts, then turned onto Nashville. The streets run down as you approach the river. The potholes fill with oily water and truck drivers grip their wheels tight as if bouncing across the face of the moon. Zemurray took a right on Annunciation Street, which is as sleepy and small as a street in the hills above Cannery Row—it being understood, I hope, that I'm re-creating a typical walk, not saying this is the route he followed every day. He cut down Octavia and turned left on Tchoupitoulas, then crossed the overpass that carried him above the railroad tracks to the Mississippi.

He walked along the river most mornings, now and then following it for miles. Did Sam miss the jungle? Did he long for the isthmus, where he could get out of these itchy clothes and away from this polite society? He lingered on the Erato Wharf, the Desire Wharf, the Pauline Wharf, where twenty-five hundred bunches of bananas were unloaded every hour. He liked the smell of the river and the ships covered in produce, the fishermen in the rigging. He liked the shop talk of sea captains. He liked the fruit piled on the railroad sidings, greens and ripes and browns. But the morning I speak of he would have seen something terrible and new, a feature that appeared on the river as if overnight: a shantytown built by the homeless. In New York City, the

Hoovervilles were built in Central and Riverside parks, great agglomerations of lean-tos ands tents. In New Orleans, the Hooverville was like Venice, built on the water with rafts and barges. It was a mirror of the city laid out by the French, a prophecy of what that city would become in the time of the Flood. Most of the structures were made of driftwood that came down the river. Hoboes fished out the scrap and lashed it into shelters. It grew by accretion, a monument of ingenuity, a chaos of rafts and skiffs that lined the river from Thalia Street all the way to Carrollton. This picturesque slum must have impressed Zemurray in a way he would never be impressed by statistics or employment rolls. It was the future if nothing was done.

Zemurray had become increasingly aware of the direness of the situation. America teetered on the edge of an abyss. He would see it in the collapse of the national economy, in the army of men who had taken to the roads, in the shuttered factories. He would hear it in the hush that settled on the docks, where only half the shipping lines were running and the stevedores had little to do. He would recognize it most clearly in his own dividend checks and the reports that came from the Boston headquarters of United Fruit. The company, which had weathered the stock market collapse of 1929, was being crushed by the economic depression that followed. As one of the world's first truly global corporations, United Fruit—its entire product line grown overseas, most of its market domestic—was uniquely vulnerable. In 1930 and 1931, the company diminished in ways that would have stunned Preston and Keith. Collapse of demand, labor unrest, deflation—there was serious trouble. In 1928, U.F. had made $45 million in profit. In 1932, it made just $6 million, an 85 percent decline. This meant fewer workers employed, fewer fields planted, fewer bananas grown, which meant even lower profits, which meant still fewer fields planted and fewer bananas grown. The less we produce, the less we profit; the less we profit, the less we produce. The company was caught in a death spiral.

For Zemurray, the collapse of United Fruit would have been devastating. Most of his net worth was tied up in U.F. stock. The more the company struggled, the bleaker his prospects became. When Sam merged with United Fruit, its stock was trading at just over $100 a share. Two years later, the same shares were going for $10.25. The Zemurray fortune, once figured at $30 million, was valued at less than $3 million by 1932. Whether he was sitting on his porch or walking on the docks, Sam was watching it all go away.

The greatness of Zemurray lies in the fact that he never lost faith in his ability to salvage a situation. Bad things happened to him as bad things happen to everyone, but unlike so many he was never tempted by failure. He never felt powerless or trapped. He was, as I said, an optimist. He stood in constant defiance. When the secretary of state teamed up with J. P. Morgan and the Honduran government in a way contrary to Zemurray's interests, he simply changed the Honduran government. When United Fruit drew a line at the Utila River and said, "You shall not cross," he crossed anyway. When he was forbidden to build a bridge, he built a bridge but called it something else. For every move, there is a countermove. For every disaster, there is a recovery. He never lost faith in his own agency. With his fortune fast diminishing, it was time to act.

He started by asking two questions. First: Are the challenges facing United Fruit part of the systemic failure of the global economy, meaning there's nothing to do but hope and pray? Second: If the answer to the first question is no, what can be done to move the product, increase profits, resuscitate the company? How can U.F. be saved?

Where did Zemurray go for answers? Did he meet with economic experts and college professors? Did he call Daniel Wing, the chairman of U.F.'s board, and Victor Cutter, its president, and ask, "Do you have a plan?" And even if they did have a plan, so what? These were the same men who had run the company into a ditch. He went to the docks instead, where he spent the winter of 1932 walking through warehouses and standing on the decks of banana boats, talking to fruit peddlers and captains, loaders and stevedores—the people who really knew. (It was the end of his retirement, though few realized it at the time.) He peppered them with questions. He wanted to know specifics, the mood on the isthmus, the color and size of the latest harvest, the speed of the crossing. How fast is the captain running her? Is he letting out all the stops? In this way, he learned, among other things, that the banana captains were on orders from Boston to lay off the throttle and cross the Gulf at paddle speed, thus saving gasoline. But a man focused on the near horizon of cost can lose sight of the far horizon of potential windfall. By quick calculation, Sam realized that whatever money was being saved on fuel was being lost on the high percentage of fruit that ripened during the extra days on the water. *The schmucks! They're losing more than they're saving.*

Zemurray wrote his findings in a letter—unusual for him, as he liked to leave no record—which he sent to Boston. He pointed out obvious problems, then went on to paint a troubled big picture pieced together from details picked up on the docks: banana boats running half speed, half full, ripes dumped into the sea, fields of undernourished stems, labor unrest in banana towns where the company had stopped spending. He included suggestions, ideas. Repurpose the boats, fallow the fields, control supply.

The members of the United Fruit board, the financial elite of Boston, were not interested in the ravings of the Russian. They had, in fact, taken over Cuyamel with the purpose of keeping him out of the conversation. Having been well paid for his silence, he was supposed to stay away and shut up. The letter went unanswered. There must have been a moment when Zemurray felt that the sale of his company to these fools had been the mistake of his life. He was like the gambler who had won all night, only to lose everything on the last hand. His concerns, which had been those of an investor—three hundred thousand shares!—grew into something deeper. More than anger, it was the rage of the self-made man who's been treated like something he used to be: the fruit peddler, the immigrant, the schnorrer.

In June 1932, Zemurray traveled to Boston to attend a meeting of the board of directors. The details were reported in *The American Magazine* and *The Wall Street Journal*: Zemurray sat quietly as a secretary read through minutes and notes, reports from various tropical divisions. The corporate officers then discussed a request from a plantation manager, who wanted $10,000 to build an irrigation ditch in Guatemala. The executives called on experts, who detailed the costs and benefits of the project. Zemurray grew restless. To him, such a debate was symptomatic of a greater problem. The executives running United Fruit did not understand their role, what they could and could not do. He raised his hand, stood to speak. "This man in Guatemala, he's your manager, isn't he?" Zemurray asked.

Yes.

"Then listen to what the man is telling you. You're here, he's there," said Zemurray. "If you trust him, trust him. If you don't trust him, fire him and get a man you do trust in the job."

Zemurray went on to explain his frustration with how the company was being run, then offered a few ideas. He had some experience. He wanted to help. His offer was rejected at the meeting, rejected again later by Victor Cutter, who dismissed Zemurray's complaints as the griping of a man who did not comprehend the business cycle.

"I became worried," Zemurray told a reporter. "I attended a directors' meeting and told the management I was not satisfied. I could see that most of the others also weren't satisfied. I had previously worked hard and had built up a big company into excellent shape. I knew that I could render great service to United Fruit, if given the opportunity. But the directors turned me down."

My mother says, "Don't go away mad, just go away."

Zemurray went away mad. He was not used to being slighted, condescended to, rebuffed, ignored. He spent the following weeks on the road, traveling from city to city, sitting in the offices and living rooms of shareholders. He made the same case over and over. The current management is not up to the task. Don't believe me? Just look at the most recent quarterly report. The board must change course, follow the plan I have outlined or something similar. If allowed to continue on its current path, the value of the stock—then selling at $10 a share—will dwindle away to nothing. The company will become a relic: overgrown fields, ships sold for junk. Within five years, United Fruit will be a story of the once-upon-a-time variety.

When Zemurray spoke to the board again several months later, he had with him a bagful of proxies, the voting rights turned over to him by other stockholders. Along with his own shares, these proxies could give Zemurray control of the company, though he kept their existence a secret—for the moment, anyway. The best tycoons are like magicians; they know when to share information and when to withhold.

The meeting took place on the tenth floor of the United Fruit Building at 1 Federal Street in Boston on a January morning in 1933. It was an iconic corporate showdown of the era, remembered and discussed to this day. The outsider finds himself in a room of sneering insiders, the board of United Fruit being made up of the elite as it existed before the levees broke and the Catholics and Jews flooded in: Thomas Jefferson Coolidge, a descendant of two presidents; Channing H. Cox, the former governor of Massachusetts; Bradley Palmer, the company officer who negotiated the buyout of Cuyamel—one of the few people in the room sympathetic to Zemurray; Francis Hart, the oldest son of an original investor in Boston Fruit. A former division head, Hart had published three books on Caribbean life. He was famed for his planter's punch. To such men, Zemurray, with his diets and love of the vernacular, was comical, offensive, crude. This meeting epitomizes the moment the establishment began to give way to the strivers.

The chairman of the board was Daniel Gould Wing, who descended from an old New England family. The president of the First National Bank of Boston, Wing looked askance at uncredentialed, ill-bred strangers who wandered in off the street. To him, Zemurray was still Sam the Banana Man, the fruit jobber from the docks. He already knew what Sam could teach him about the business: nothing.

Wing welcomed Zemurray without looking up, greeting him, as Thomas McCann characterized it, "frostily at best." Zemurray waited as the board went through its tasks. When it was finally his turn to speak, he chose each word carefully, explaining his ideas in the thick Russian accent that he never could shed. It was the accent of neither the Russian bourgeois nor the peasant; neither the voice of Tolstoy nor the voice of Khrushchev. It was the voice of the Jewish Pale of Settlement, the Yiddish-inflected voice of our grandparents, the fruit peddler, the street haggler, the Yid.

When Zemurray finished, Wing smiled and said, "Unfortunately, Mr. Zemurray, I can't understand a word of what you say."

The men at the table started to laugh. Zemurray's pupils narrowed to pinpricks, his hands turned into fists. He muttered, then stormed out. Perhaps the board members believed Zemurray had been chased away, was fleeing back to New Orleans. In truth, he had only gone to retrieve his bag of proxies. Returning to the boardroom, he slapped them on the table and said, "You're fired! Can you understand that, Mr. Chairman?"

What followed was the sort of graveyard silence in which each board member recalculated his own prospects.

"You gentlemen have been fucking up this business long enough," Zemurray told them. "I'm going to straighten it out."

Much later, analysts pointed out the flaw in the noncompete clause Zemurray signed at the time of the merger: it barred Zemurray from working for a rival or starting a new fruit company, but it did not foresee the outlandish possibility of Zemurray taking over United Fruit itself. "[I didn't want to watch] the greatest company in the world go to hell in a hand bucket," Zemurray explained.

Victor Cutter was fired. He had run United Fruit for eight years, had served in its ranks for thirty. His earlier triumph over Zemurray had suddenly been revealed as stage one of his eventual defeat. By merging with Cuyamel, he had invited the wolf into the house. Zemurray retained just a few members of the United Fruit board, including T. J. Coolidge, who would become one of Sam's confidants, and Francis Hart, whom Zemurray made president, a figurehead position perfect for Hart, who was a link to the old banana royalty. His presence would reassure certain partners and politicians, as well as more tradition-minded investors. It gave the illusion of continuity, suggesting there had been no radical break. Of course, there had been. The past was dead and gone. All power would now be concentrated in the hands of one man: Samuel Zemurray, who named himself United Fruit's managing director of operations. When Francis Hart died several years later, Zemurray added "President" to his title.

It was in these years that Zemurray became known as the dictator of the banana trade, a man who, with a single phone call, could undermine governments. It was a moment of triumph, a decisive coup d'état in a career that was nothing but coup followed by coup. When Zemurray showed up at the first meeting of the new board, he said, "I'm ready to go to work."

Here's how the above events were reported in *Time* on January 23, 1933:

One day last summer Samuel ("Sam") Zemurray of New Orleans strode belligerently into a room at No. 1 Federal Street, Boston, where the directors of the potent, far-flung United Fruit Co. were holding a meeting. Down on the long table from his old enemy, President Victor

Macomber Cutter, he flung a handful of proxies. Said he: "You've been ——ing up this business long enough. I'm going to straighten it out."

To most of the reporters and stock analysts who covered United Fruit, Zemurray was a mystery. *The New York Times* called him "the fish that swallowed the whale." "Except for a comparatively limited circle of friends and acquaintances in Honduras and Louisiana, few people actually knew him," Charles Morrow Wilson wrote in *Empire in Green and Gold*. "Outside of the New Orleans telephone directory, where his residence and office addresses were listed, the new boss's name was not to be found in any widely used directory. For the most part Eastern financiers knew Zemurray only by name, if at all. During his occasional attendance [at] directors' meetings in Boston and New York, United Fruit men knew him only as an extremely tall, rather well-dressed man, who listened thoughtfully, spoke little, rarely wrote letters, occasionally argued vehemently and asked questions of devastating directness, then lapsed into deeply reflective silence. Observers also noted that the *hombre* from the far south had an amazingly good memory, that he knew Honduras like the contours of his hands, which he frequently studied thoughtfully while listening to others talk."

Those who did know Zemurray—the veterans of Cuyamel, the roughnecks and banana cowboys—believed the company finally had the right leadership. Many of them also believed it would not matter. When Zemurray took over, United Fruit was plagued by inefficiency, debt, angry workers, low morale. The stock had collapsed. The company was failing. Zemurray might be the best man, but it seemed he'd arrived too late.

15

Los Pericos

Word of Zemurray's takeover went through the isthmus like a jungle fire. In the tin-roof cantinas of Tela and Puerto Cortés, where the men strummed Spanish guitars and the young women cried because they'd been rejected in love, the field hands and the plantation managers raised their glasses of fermented cane to drink one for the Gringo. The return of Zemurray seemed a godsend. For years, the employees of United Fruit had sent their reports to Boston and for years those reports had been rejected or ignored. The company had been governed by missive, edicts issued by a king as he soaked in his tub: *your request for $10,000 for a ditch has been denied for reasons sufficient to Boston.* As a result, many of the company's decisions seemed irrelevant or just plain wrong. In Zemurray, the men in the compounds and banana towns recognized one of their own, the hombre who crossed the country on a mule. United Fruit had not had such a leader since the passing of Minor Keith.

Zemurray wanted to reassure the workers from the start, change their mood by showing them things would be different. There is the substance of what you do, then there is the style, the subtext of your story told not in words but in how you go about your business. Unlike other incoming chiefs—here I'm thinking of CEOs who take over bureaucracy-heavy companies in trouble—Zemurray did not begin his work at company headquarters. He did not spend his first days with accountants, nor coop himself up with reports, nor shout his head off at meetings. He went out on the road, announcing straightaway that he would begin his tenure with a six-week tour of the banana lands. He wanted to visit every country where United Fruit owned plantations, ports, railroads. He wanted to talk to the men in the fields. He wanted to see for himself.

He boarded a ship at Thalia Street Wharf, in New Orleans, say, where the city is fog shrouded and blue with rain. It was his first trip to the isthmus in some time. He had left as an ambitious player who had cashed in his chips. He was returning as the man who had won the casino itself, who, in the way of Kublai Khan, possessed everything as far as the eye could see. United Fruit had over a million acres under cultivation, owned hospitals and schools, thousands of miles of highway and railroad, piers, warehouses. Zemurray visited as much of it as possible, stopping in Honduras, Guatemala, Colombia, Panama, Nicaragua, Costa Rica, Mexico, Cuba. He walked in the heat, stood in the fields, strolled through the towns, drank in the bars, laughed with the vaqueros. His manner was as informal as can be, just another banana man in mud-caked boots and khaki pants, tall and friendly, standing in the shade of the great fronds, watching the cutters cut and the loaders load, examining the straw-filled boxcars, lingering in the dives where men got drunk and spoke the truth, now and then asking a seemingly simple question: Have you considered combining the sugar and the fruit in one haul?

For Zemurray, it must have been a second youth. Once again he had a job and knew just what to do. He overlooked nothing. Not the traffic of the Great White Fleet (many of the ships were leaving the isthmus half full). Not the confused looks on the faces of the plantation managers, some of whom had risen through the ranks merely because they had never defied Boston. Wherever he found a man who could not act or was slow to decide, he replaced him with a veteran of Cuyamel. He was putting his own team in position, remaking the behemoth in the shape of his old company. "I realized that the greatest mistake the United Fruit management had made was to assume it could run its activities in many tropical countries from an office on the 10th floor of a Boston office building," Zemurray told *Fortune*. "The management had tried to tell every executive in every country exactly what he must do and how he must do it. Executives on the spot were treated like messenger boys. I completely reversed that policy. I laid down what might be called a constitution for the company. This constitution provided for a maximum of home rule in the field. It was established as a fixed policy that if [a plantation manager] could not handle his difficulties reasonably satisfactorily, we would appoint some man who could."

Thus began the "Zemurray era" of United Fruit. He fired thousands of employees, the deadwood and wishy-washy. Legend later had him discarding a full 25 percent of the workforce, but Sam denied this, saying he replaced only those who failed. He solved the problem of half-empty ships, selling some, mothballing some, renting out space in others. A United Fruit ship did not leave port until it was packed. The Great White Fleet, which had been costing the company to operate, began to earn. He had U.F.'s holdings reappraised—the value of the machines and land had collapsed during the Depression—saving millions in taxes. He canceled stipends paid to independent growers who had been augmenting the company's banana supply. He left fields fallow, further decreasing banana supply, controlling market price. On some plantations, he replaced bananas with sugarcane, a staple always in demand. Realizing the company had become overly dependent on a single product, he looked for other crops to plant: coconuts, pineapples, quinine trees. "From Boston to Bogotá, he weeded out superfluous employees until one of every four was gone," reported *The Wall Street Journal*. "In place of managers he did not like, he put in veterans of his Cuyamel organization and ordered them to whittle down 5,000,000 in loans that had been made to independent planters. He pushed through a re-evaluation of properties at 50,000,000 below their previous figure of nearly 250,000,000, thereby saving some 4,000,000 a year in depreciation charges."

It was not these policies alone that turned things around; it was also the energy behind the policies: the six-week tour, the firing and hiring, the tough decisions made about the fleet and the fields. A light was burning in the pilothouse, a firm hand had taken hold of the tiller. United Fruit's stock price stabilized, then began to climb. It doubled in the first two weeks of Zemurray's reign, reaching $26 a share by the fall of 1933. This had less to do with tangible results—it was too early for that—than the confidence of investors. If you looked in the newspaper, you would see the new head of the company landing his plane on a strip in the jungle, anchoring his boat on the north coast of Honduras, going here and there, working, working, working. In a time of crisis, the mere evidence of activity can be enough to get things moving. Though Zemurray would stay at the helm for another twenty years, United Fruit was saved in his first sixty days.

Over time, Zemurray realized the company faced a problem bigger than half-empty ships or weak managers, a problem that could be solved neither by smart hires nor by the recovery of markets. The product itself—the Big Mike, the only banana that most Americans had ever tasted—was shadowed by ecological calamity.

Sigatoka disease appeared in the South Pacific in the 1900s, specifically on the banks of the Sigatoka River in Fiji, where the palm trees danced in the evening breeze. It was initially reported by fishermen who forded the river, old-timers who remarked on the pestilence that had beset the banana plants, darkening their leaves to the ground. It looked like the trees had burned. Within a year, great stretches of jungle had turned black. Walking the country was like entering a haunted wood. It was spooky, uncanny, ominous, disturbing, strange. It was the rustle of dead fronds on dead stems.

Sigatoka is a fungus that sweeps through banana country, killing around half the plants. For a time, Preston, Keith, and the other banana men simply hoped it would stay in Fiji. It did not. The disease spread by boat, train, plane, in the black mud on the migrant's boot. In 1930, it was spotted in Colombia. A leaf turned black, then a stem, than a field. Dismay filled the offices of the banana companies. Without a cure, Sigatoka would be the end of the Big Mike.

Bananas are especially vulnerable. Because they have no seeds. Because each stem is a cutting, a rhizome hacked off another rhizome, which was hacked off another. When you look at a banana, you're looking at every banana, an infinite regression. There are no mutts, only the first fruit of a particular species and billions of copies. Every banana is a clone, in other words, a replica of an ur-banana that weighed on its stalk the first morning of man. This has been the strength of the industry, and its weakness. The strength because *talk about quality control*! The weakness because the lack of diversity puts each banana species at risk. Given the opportunity, a disease that kills one Big Mike is going to kill them all.

Zemurray fought Sigatoka the way empires have always fought barbarians: by quarantine, lockdown, inspection, wall. Each plantation was surrounded by a fence. On entering the fields, farmhands walked across serrated grates, which scraped microbe-carrying mud off their boots. Being modern, Zemurray knew these were only temporary measures. The long-term solution would have to be supplied by chemistry. Zemurray had scientists at work in jungle labs, concocting and applying potions. In the mid-1930s, one of them came up with the first effective poison, a compound made of copper sulfate and lime powder. He called it the Bordeaux mixture. When the first test results were reported at headquarters, Zemurray said, "You put the medicine on the leaves and that cures the disease?"

"It's not that simple," said the scientist. "Sigatoka is an airborne spore. We think the Bordeaux mixture—"

"Please, Sport, don't confuse me. You put the medicine on the leaves—"

"It's only an experiment."

"We'll spray five thousand acres," Zemurray said.

The poison was applied by overhead irrigation and airplane. Soon, this was being done on an industrial scale, the sprinklers going on with a click, the crop dusters appearing in the west, the roar of the engines, the faces of the pilots, the copper sulfate falling like rain. When the wind blew, the mixture carried into the banana towns. The dinner jackets of the honchos turned turquoise. The dirt turned blue in the groves, the fruit the same.

Starting around 1936, U.F. bananas were rinsed in a solution that turned blue bananas green again. For the best results, men had to walk the fields as the mixture was applied, making sure the poison dispersed evenly. Over time, these workers began to experience certain abnormalities. They lost their olfactory sense and their appetite. Everything from shrimp to beans tasted like paste. After a month, they could not keep down food. They wasted away but kept volunteering for the hazard pay. After two months, the men began to turn color. After three months, they were blue. On the plantations, they were referred to as *Los Pericos*, the Parakeets.

Los Pericos constitute a subchapter in the history of Zemurray and United Fruit. The outcasts of the trade, these men swapped taste and smell for money. In this, they represent the isthmus as a whole, simultaneously enriched and destroyed. Some *Pericos* recovered. Some survived but could never again enjoy food. Some died. Perhaps hundreds, perhaps a thousand. These men became part of the lore, the hymn of *Los Pericos*, blue in the morning, blue in the evening, the blue heart of a blue business, the victims without whom there'd be no sliced banana on the cornflakes in the sunny American kitchen nook.

After Sigatoka was curbed, an even worse pestilence threatened the industry. Unlike Sigatoka, which destroyed plants, Panama disease destroyed earth, rendering vast stretches of jungle a ruinous waste for bananas. It lived in the soil, attacking the roots of the plant, then the rhizome. The leaves withered to a husk, the tree fell on its face. The disease was spread by the banana men themselves, carried on clothes and equipment. They sowed it with the rhizomes in each plantation. It remained asymptomatic for years, not attacking for a decade or more, then striking everywhere, wiping out acres of plants in the course of a season. After that, the plantation itself was diseased and had to be abandoned.

Panama disease reached the Isthmus from Southeast Asia in the early 1900s but did not become a serious problem until the 1920s. Scientists at Imperial College London's Department of Tropical Agriculture began searching for a cure in 1922. United Fruit hired the biologist A. J. Chute to find a banana resistant to the disease the following year. There are thousands of varieties of bananas undiscovered in Asia even today. In the meantime, Zemurray devised a simple solution, rife with unintended consequences. He began buying as much virgin jungle as possible. Not thousands of acres, but hundreds of thousands, most of it left uncultivated, laid in like canned goods. When a plantation fell to disease, he simply reached up for one of the cans on the shelf. In this way, he kept moving from virgin jungle to virgin jungle, forever one step ahead of the disease. U.F. came to possess tremendous stretches of wilderness as a result. By 1940, the company owned 50 percent of all private land in Honduras, but cultivated less than 10 percent of what it owned. The company became a symbol of concentrated wealth in these years, more powerful, in many countries, than the government itself. In its endless quest for disease-free land, United Fruit would become too big for its own good.

———

After Zemurray returned from his tour of the isthmus, he began to settle into the routine he would follow as the head of United Fruit. For part of the year, he would have to live in Boston, where the company was headquartered. He spent an afternoon crossing the city with a real estate agent, walking through houses in Brookline and Back Bay, where many United Fruit executives lived. Though he would stay in the city only a few months a year, the address was important. Choosing a home was making a statement, showing a commitment to the traditions of the fruit company. He walked through brick houses built in the Federal style, through houses that mimicked grand Tudor estates, through Victorian waterfront mansions that were nothing but dormer and gable. From the eastern windows, you could see the ocean, so different here from the ocean in Puerto Cortés, different tints and colors, Jehovah working with a limited palette of muted greens and dirty grays.

Zemurray was no longer young. What's more, he was no longer nearly young or recently young. He was deep in middle age, on the far side of a room that he had been through and explored, having tried out every style, every way of being powerful in the world. He had been loud and voluble, quiet and reserved. His mere presence, size, the ice of his glare, were usually enough to get his way. He wore double-breasted suits and conservative ties. His hair, combed to the side, checked now and then with a broad open hand, had thinned and gone gray.

All this time, he'd been aging. He started as a kid, a set of eyes peering from the steerage deck of an Atlantic steamer. He grew into a young man, a go-getter hauling ripes. He became a hustler, hurrying through the streets of the French Quarter with a pocketful of bills. When he went to the isthmus, he became the Gringo humping over the mountains on a mule, buying and clearing swaths of jungle. Then he was El Amigo, the father of the revolution, a man with nothing to lose. Then he was the little guy at war with the Octopus. Then he was a millionaire, a sellout, a retiree, a battler in a political war, a symbol of everything good and bad about America, the opportunity to rise and the inevitable corruption, the best and worst. He had finally become the boss, the king, one of the most powerful men in America.

And yet . . .

Zemurray made offers on several houses in Boston, but in the end each deal fell through—because there had been a better price, because a seller had suddenly decided to take the property off the market. It was the old problem: no Italians, no Irish, no Jews—regardless of how much money you had. I was told this story by people who knew Zemurray. When I asked if it bothered him, they said no, no, the Banana Man was beyond such petty concerns. They told me he faced it with a smile, as if to say, *You have won the hand, but I will win the game.* "Over the years I have heard many stories about how this treatment [in Boston] galled Zemurray," Thomas McCann wrote, "but in most cases the tellers were Bostonians who had never even met him, and I came to believe that the stories were based on wishful thinking. Zemurray was too big a man to care. *That* must have galled the Brahmins."

After a few days of hunting in vain, Zemurray decided, *Screw it, they don't want to sell, I don't want to buy.* He would keep a suite at the Ritz-Carlton instead, charging the cost to the company. He would never be more than a visitor to Boston as a result, a hotel man who came and went as dictated by his schedule. You can judge a place by how it treated the Banana Man. Rejected by Russia and Boston, accepted by Puerto Cortés and New Orleans.

Zemurray spent the last quarter of his life in transit, traveling from town to town. He was one of those men who seems still in mind only when his body is in motion. His wife grew old, his daughter moved away, his son became a father, pushing Sam one row closer to the abyss in the family photo. He spent every winter on the isthmus, where he lived in a house that a colleague described as "slightly larger than the others, orchids growing in profusion in hanging baskets." Honduras, Guatemala, Costa Rica, Mexico, Colombia, Ecuador—no matter the country, the scene was always the same. The grid of streets, houses and stores, the electrified fences, golf courses, banana fields, bowling alleys, and swimming pools. "There was something at once very exciting, very masculine and very romantic about the company [in those] days," wrote McCann. "It was a mixture of John Wayne movie clichés and the legacy of an incredible period in history: gin and tonics and Dewar's White Label Scotch on tropical verandas; endless miles of private jungle fiefdoms, natives who were variously brooding, surly or submissive; boots, khaki uniforms, horses and pistols; the Great White Fleet that was really the largest private navy in the world (and operated on the open-secret motto 'Every banana a guest, every passenger a pest'); the early morning produce markets and the colorful, crude men who ran them: longshoremen, traders, plantation managers, ambitious men, hard men, lazy men, rich men; and behind it all a tradition of enormous wealth and power and privilege that already was beginning to decay."

By 1940, the network of banana colonies had developed its own society, its own codes, poets, heroes. There was cruelty and racism, the dark-skinned made to scrape and bow, the white man king (the constant mention of skin color, defined to the minutest degree, is perhaps the most miserable relic of that era). There was the sporting life, baseball stars who played for U.F. teams in Ecuador and Cuba, who barnstormed, packing the wooden bleachers. There was *Unifruco*, the company's magazine published with the intent of forging a banana culture. The pages were filled with poems, quizzes, and letters from far-flung divisions. A typical lead: "Puerto Barrios had faded away in a crimson and mauve sunset." More than a hundred thousand people worked for the company at the peak, with alumni scattered across the world: H. L. Mencken, who toiled on a U.F. dock in Baltimore; Lee Harvey Oswald, who unloaded its cargo in New Orleans; Fidel Castro, whose father grew sugarcane for the company in Cuba. Writers employed by the company chronicled its development, the most famous being William McFee, a U.F. sea engineer who wrote stories between trips across the Gulf of Mexico. McFee published many books, the titles of which tell the story of the era: *Letters from an Ocean Tramp, Harbours of Memory, Sunlight in New Granada, Sailors of Fortune, The Beachcomber, Sailor's Wisdom, Ship to Shore, The Law of the Sea.* There was the leisurely tempo of the life, golf tournaments and regattas. "John Wayne . . . often visited the company's Central American plantations," wrote McCann, "anchoring his yacht in a bay protected by United Fruit property, playing cards long into the night with company 'banana cowboys' and living as the company's guest for days at a time."

Zemurray spent more and more time in New York. He stayed in the Roosevelt Hotel on Forty-fifth Street off Madison Avenue. By then, he had traded his cotton pants and work clothes for wool suits. He wore tortoiseshell glasses, which gave him a scholarly air, and combed his hair left to right, covering the smooth bald plain that was his skull. Broad faced with heavy circles under his eyes, he filled out as he aged, got some meat on his bones. His irises were black gems and remained tranquil as his face puffed out, filled with lines, then sagged, losing their mischievous sparkle only at the very end, when they were clouded with cataracts. He was one of those placid men who seem to get wiser as the years pass, and understand more than a person probably has a right to.

Each morning, he took a car to the United Fruit office on Pier 3, which was built on pilings in the Hudson River. The Humphrey Bogart movie *Sabrina* was filmed there. You see it in the climactic scene when Bogie runs after the ship that is carrying away his beloved. Elia Kazan wanted to use the dock in *On the Waterfront*, but the U.F. public relations department refused. The building was a warren of concrete and tin. Zemurray's office was on the south side, with big windows looking out on the Palisades of New Jersey, the ferry sheds of Weehawken, Ellis Island, the Statue of Liberty, the crowded shipping lanes of New York Harbor. It's gone now, ripped out in the early 1970s to make way for the World Trade Center.

16

Bananas Go to War

Hitler ruined everything. He ruined the life of the Jews, he ruined the dream of Europe, he ruined the history of Germany. He ruined the banana business, too, the indolence of the compounds, the excitement of the trading houses. Some of the causes were proximate, having to do with the way the Second World War would discredit all varieties of colonialism; some were direct, a result of the hammer blows that began to fall as soon as the German army crossed the frontier into Poland in September 1939.

A war that fills the oceans with U-boats is bad business for bananas. A pure import, with no real local market, no home country, every stem has to be shipped at great expenditures of manpower and fuel, great risk to vessel and sailor. As soon as the bullets fly, gasoline prices rise and insurance rates spike, and the financial model fails. In 1939, the British government, looking to save money and resources, declared the banana a luxury. All shipments to Britain and its colonies were banned. One day, the British market accounted for 20 percent of United Fruit's profits; the next day, it was gone. For Sam Zemurray, the game was survival.

British-flagged ships of the Great White Fleet were seized soon after, twenty-three banana boats impressed into service in the Royal Navy, most converted into troop carriers. Big and slow, these became a favorite target of German submarines. As the U-boat captains were not especially careful about distinguishing repurposed boats from active members of the U.F. fleet, the life of the banana captain turned hazardous. On June 12, 1942, the *Sixaola*, an iron horse that had been in service with the company almost from its start, was torpedoed off Guatemala. Rescue boats, cutters, and yachts responded to the SOS. Men swung lanterns in pilothouses, called for survivors, sent up flares. Nothing was found but a patch of oil and a few thousand bananas floating in the debris. Twenty-nine people died, the worst tragedy in the history of the Great White Fleet.

Profits tumbled as the ships went down. Zemurray was never heard to bitch or justify. He was a member of a generation that lived by the maxim "Never complain, never explain." Like a lot of business leaders of that era, he probably felt there was something ennobling in the losses, which were not losses in the ordinary sense. It was blood shed in the service of a great cause, and nothing compared to the sacrifices made by the men who were actually fighting. Zemurray was never more engaged than he was in those years. The battles, the headlines—they seemed to wake him from the moneymaking dream of the previous decade. You sense it in his great burst of activity: how he raised money, championed causes, advised politicians. The war brought together the key obsessions of his biography: Sam the Russian, Sam the Jew, Sam the American, Sam the Capitalist. Soon after the Japanese attacked Pearl Harbor, the American War Department followed the British example, limiting the importation of bananas (a quota) and seizing most of the Great White Fleet. (The company was left with only the clunkers.) Though the impressed ships, remade with armor and cannon, had become the property of the U.S. Navy, Sam continued to follow them as you might follow the exploits of a war-fighting son—a terrible premonition. Edward Bernays, the public relations guru who began working with Sam in these years, recalled a meeting at which a secretary handed Zemurray a note every few minutes. Zemurray would glance at the paper, then carry on. Only later did Bernays learn that each note brought news of another banana boat destroyed at sea. U.F. would lose nineteen ships in the course of the war.

Zemurray's business challenge was straightforward. Though his product was as excellent as ever, he did not have the ships to get it to market. Between 1942 and 1944, an average of seventy thousand tons of United Fruit bananas rotted in the fields.

What do you do when your product rots?

Find something else to sell.

United Fruit still had acres of sugarcane scattered across the Caribbean, which continued to be profitable, but it was not nearly enough. Zemurray began to look for other crops he could grow on his plantations, crops that could be classified as necessities (no quota). He sent agents in search of plants and trees that grew in the tropics on other parts of the globe, in the band of sunshine that wraps the earth. The men returned with cuttings, bulbs, seeds. During the war, Zemurray introduced many crops that remain staples in the region, some that had always grown wild on the isthmus but were never farmed, some that were novel: palm oil, quinine, hemp. He was especially interested in plants critical to the war effort but whose import from Asia had been blocked by the Japanese. Hemp for rope, quinine for antimalaria pills, rubber trees for tank treads, boot bottoms, and everything else. He promised to meet the military demand with supplies grown in our own hemisphere, making America more self-sufficient. He explained in an essay:

WAR CROPS

When the Jap blitz cut off rubber, hemp, quinine, and other vital supplies, it opened our eyes to the potential riches of Latin America. Here the head of the world's largest tropical farming organization tells how, with the aid of our Southern neighbors, we are developing the essential products we formerly got from the Far East.

By 1944, Zemurray had thousands of acres bearing strange fruit. As he later told reporters and friends, it was among the proudest achievements of his life. He was a farmer at heart. And here he was behaving like a farmer in the midst of a locust blight, innovating his way out of ruin.

He involved himself in the war effort as much as possible, volunteered, hosted, contributed—did everything but fight, and would have done that, if not for his advancing years. As part of FDR's National War Board, he brought more than twenty thousand men from Jamaica to work in factories in the Midwest—a surreal historical interlude. Sam gave everything he had in the battle against Germany and Japan.

Sam Zemurray Jr. enlisted shortly after the attack on Pearl Harbor. He went into the service in the summer of 1942, was assigned the rank of major and sent to train with the U.S. Army Air Forces—he was already a skilled pilot. He was shipped to North Africa, where he would take part in America's first battles of the Second World War.

In those days, when the fighting started, you went. If you did not go, there was something wrong with you—a defect, a malfunction. What's more, Sam Jr., who was smart and surely understood history, the general history of Europe and the particular history of his father, would have known that this was no ordinary war. It was *the* war, the sons of darkness against the sons of light.

Sam Jr. was attached to the Western Desert Air Force, which consisted of British, South African, Canadian, and American fliers. There were fighter wings, bomber wings, reconnaissance wings. P-51 Mustangs and Hawker Hurricanes stood tail to nose on the runways. It was extremely dangerous work. The German antiaircraft guns were only part of the problem; the real challenge was the landscape, the fog that settled on the desert floor, the hills that rose up from nowhere. Show me a picture of Allied pilots from the North African campaign—tanned, dark eyed, happy—and I will show you young men who did not survive.

Here's a photo of Sam Jr. taken in the fall of 1943. He's broad shouldered and handsome in his flight suit, aviator's cap, goggles pushed back on his head, hands in his pockets, smiling as the landing strip behind him swarms with vehicles. He was assigned a P-51 modified for photo reconnaissance. He flew dozens of missions, the desert falling away, the sky filling with stars. He flew over the German lines into enemy territory. He photographed military camps, ridges, beaches, artillery positions, and guns, the hazards Allied infantry would have to face. He was transferred to a base in Algeria, where the mess hall buzzed with men from a half dozen nations. He was probably happiest in the sky, when the world was a pattern of lights. He set out again and again, his plane creeping to the end of the runway, the go signal, the rush of speed, the hills suddenly far below. Recon pilots in the Desert

Air Force had to fly dangerously low to get their pictures, brush the rooftops of towns, swing out over the sea to escape.

Sam Jr. took off at sundown on January 7, 1943. The ground crew would see him closed in his helmet, closed in his head. Then he was a star on the horizon, fading as it goes away. He vanished over the hills or into the sea. No one is sure exactly what happened—it's a puzzle without a solution. The best guess: Major Samuel Zemurray Jr., thirty-one, having lost his way in heavy fog, flew his P-51 into a mountain. There was a flash when the fuel tanks ignited, then darkness. I don't know when Zemurray Sr. got the news. There was often a delay of days or even weeks before word made it back to the family. It's impossible to express the horror he must have felt: one moment there was a world full of people and markets, the next moment there was nothing.

The story was reported in *The New York Times* on February 4, 1943.

NEW YORK MAJOR KILLED
Samuel Zemurray Jr. Loses Life
in Plane Crash in Africa

Major Samuel Zemurray Jr., son of Samuel Zemurray, president of the United Fruit Company, was killed Jan. 7 when his plane struck a mountainside on a scouting expedition somewhere in Africa, according to word received here yesterday. He was 31 years old. The major left the United States last October for foreign duty. He had seen action in Casablanca and later was assigned to service in Algeria. . . .

A memorial was held at Temple Sinai on St. Charles Avenue in New Orleans. It was the saddest thing of all—a funeral without a body. For a time, Zemurray had clung to the hope that Sam Jr. had escaped the wreck and was still alive, lost and wandering in the desert. The memorial ended such fantasies. The service was led by Rabbi Julian B. Feibelman. Zemurray wept as he chanted the Kaddish, the Jewish prayer for the dead, the rhythms falling on the hushed heads of the congregants: *Yis'ga'dal v'yis'kadash sh'may ra'bbo.* . . . Standing beside Sarah, he suddenly looked very old.

Friends and family gathered at 2 Audubon Place afterward. It was the start of the shiva, the seven-day mourning period that follows a death.

Rabbi Feibelman chronicled these events in his autobiography, *The Making of a Rabbi*, starting with a description of "the banana king," an "innately modest and retiring [man who] wore no conspicuous prominence on his sleeve."

"His son Samuel Jr. was the first casualty in the Second World War among our members," Rabbi Feibelman wrote. "I offered to have a memorial for the family on the Friday evening following the announcement of his death. Mr. Zemurray came, together with his wife and closest friends. After services I went to his home, the imposing, white columned house on the avenue . . . I was told he had gone for a walk in Audubon Park, across the avenue. When he returned, we shook hands and spoke solemnly. He still spoke with an accent, but I was always impressed with his well-chosen words and his unfailing manner of projecting his expressions with precise meaning. 'Rabbi, I never believed my son was dead. I toyed with the idea that he was still alive in spite of contrary reports. But when I listened to you recite the Kaddish . . . then I knew he was dead.'" Zemurray paused, wiped away his tears, then said, "Well, you've opened the wound all over again. But now it can heal."

It was the blackest period in his life. Historic events transpired—the invasion at Normandy, the dropping of the atomic bombs—but he did not notice. All these things (soldiers on the march, men returning from war) were seen as if from a great distance. The war ended on August 14, 1945. V-J Day. In New Orleans, the squares filled with sailors. The men got drunk. The mothers wept with joy. Sam did not know what they were celebrating. The first peacetime shipment of bananas arrived soon after. He did not care. Everyone I spoke to who knew Zemurray—there are fewer each year—told me the death of Sam Jr. was the great tragedy of the old man's life. He came out of it and got back to work, but he was never the same.

17

Israel Is Real

Sam Zemurray needed a project to take him out of his trance, a cause bigger than his own. He would find it in the nascent state of Israel.

Here's how it started:

In 1922, Zemurray was contacted by Chaim Weizmann, who would become the founding president of the Jewish nation. Weizmann had been traveling the United States when he heard his first Banana Man story. "I made an unusual 'find' in New Orleans, where lived a very remarkable personality in American Jewry—Samuel Zemurray, the banana king," Weizmann wrote in his autobiography. "I paid my first visit to New Orleans specially to meet him. He had been told of my arrival and postponed his own planned departure from the city for several days—days which I found not only extremely interesting, but also profitable for the Funds."

The men met several times that year. Their conversations lasted for hours, drifting from English to Russian to Yiddish, whatever language best expressed the thought of the moment: English for money, Russian for struggle, Yiddish for the heartaches faced by a Jew in the world. Weizmann talked about his hometown in Poland, his disappointments and anger, his realization that the Jew will be free only when settled in his own land. Zemurray talked about life on the isthmus, his career in ripes and greens. "Throughout all [his] success Zemurray retained his simplicity, his transparent honesty, his lively interest in people and things, and his desire to serve," Weizmann wrote. "His chosen studies in leisure hours were mathematics and music, and he got a great deal of satisfaction out of them."

In his memoirs, Weizmann took time to chronicle the career of Zemurray. Few Jews of that generation could resist the story, which unfolds like the legend of the Hebrew giant, gloriously free from the constraints of stereotypical Jewish life. For men like Weizmann, Zemurray was the *shtarker*, the tough Jew called on in dark times, the archetype of Willy Loman's Uncle Ben in Arthur Miller's *Death of a Salesman*, who laughs as he says, "Why, boys, when I was seventeen I walked into the jungle and when I was twenty-one I walked out. And by god I was rich!"

Zemurray did not have a strong sense of Jewish identity. It was never how he described himself, his religion being just another detail in his biography: a citizen of New Orleans, a foe of Huey Long, a resident of the isthmus, a trader of bananas, a man of the Hebrew persuasion. The fact that neither of his children married Jews, raised Jewish children, or much cared about Jewish causes tells you that Sam did not dwell on the subject at home, obsess, or fill his children with fear of the goyim. When offered the freedom of America, which is not only freedom here and now, but also freedom from the past, freedom to choose what to remember, he grabbed it.

And yet, like more than a few such men—European-born Jews who shrugged off ethnic identity as soon as they touched American soil—Zemurray became, in late middle age, a champion of Zionism. In part because of the personal connection with Weizmann; in part because of his sympathy for the early Zionists, Eastern European Jews who, like Zemurray himself, seized control of their own destiny. He gave them as much support as he could. "Zemurray was one of the highlights of my visit to the States," Weizmann wrote. "I never missed an opportunity of seeing him on later visits. He did not take a public part in our work; but his interest has been continuous and generous." Zemurray donated half a million dollars to the Jewish Agency in the 1920s, money used to buy land for settlers, build houses, buy farm equipment and seed. He served as director of the Palestine Economic Corporation, which put him in league with Louis Marshall, Felix Warburg, Samuel Untermyer, and Herbert Lehman, among the most powerful Jews in America. In 1926, he gave $700,000 to build a power station in Palestine, a gift reported in *The New York Times*. He met Weizmann again in 1939, soon after the British issued the hated White Paper, which banned immigration to Palestine, closing a last path of escape just as Hitler moved into the most murderous phase of his war on the Jews. Weizmann found Zemurray "depressed, yet hopeful of the ultimate outcome." In the early 1940s, Sam used his influence in the Caribbean to help convince Rafael Trujillo of the Dominican Republic to accept several hundred Jewish refugees from Europe, a harried contingent that settled in Sosúa on the country's northern coast.

Although Zionism was important to him, it was never a primary concern in Zemurray's life. This changed in the last days of the Second World War for two reasons: the death of Sam Jr., which left Sam bereft and in need of a cause; and the death of everything and everyone in the old country. It's hard to explain the effect of the Holocaust on men like Sam Zemurray. Self-made Americans who had always felt secure in their adopted country, they were suddenly reminded, in the middle of life, of the true nature of their condition. No matter his wealth or power, the Hebrew would always be a stranger in a strange land, vulnerable to the slightest shift in the popular mood. If it could happen in Germany, it could happen anywhere.

What's more, as the details emerged—six million—men like Zemurray came to regard themselves as all that remained of a lost world. The Jews of Europe had been a remnant of an ancient kingdom. The Jews of America were thus a remnant of a remnant, invested with special responsibility. *It's up to us to see it never happens again* was the sentiment of the moment. For many, the only solution was the creation of a Jewish state. Not only would it protect the living, providing shelter and a place of refuge, it would redeem the millions who had died.

Shortly after V-J Day, Zemurray received a call from a Zionist operative who had been charged with procuring ships for the Bricha, the secret effort to smuggle Holocaust survivors out of Europe and into Palestine, then under British blockade. His name was Ze'ev Schind. There was a joke going around Tel Aviv: David Ben-Gurion said, "Find me a man who knows everything about ships." But because of his Polish accent, this was written down as "Find me a man who knows everything about sheep." Which is why they recruited Schind, a twenty-five-year-old shepherd from a kibbutz in Palestine.

Of course, Schind was not just a shepherd, he was also a member of the Mossad, the Israeli intelligence agency. (He would take command of the Mossad in 1947.) Weizmann advised Schind to contact Zemurray as soon as he reached the United States. When Schind explained what he needed, Zemurray said, in essence, Not on the phone. Come down to Louisiana. Let's talk.

One morning in 1946, Schind, who worked out of the Jewish Agency at 342 Madison Avenue in New York, caught a plane from Idlewild Airport to New Orleans, then hired a car that took him north to the plantation near Hammond. Twice a year, the grounds bloomed with azaleas. Zemurray opened the door. His back was stooped, his hair was turning white, there was a tremor in his voice, but he was still imposing. His entire life was expressed in each gesture: his handshake, his smile, the flick of his eyes that said, "Follow me." He led Schind to a kind of lodge in back of the house. The men sat by the windows. The country was swampy and green. Beautifully moody. The strip where Sam Jr. used to land his plane had already disappeared beneath choke-berry and sumac,

"What do you need?" asked Zemurray.

Schind explained the situation: There were a million Jews in displaced persons camps in Europe, many of them in Poland, in what had been concentration camps, now being run by American soldiers. These people, who had emerged from the fires of hell, were all that remained of Jewish Europe. America would not take them, France would not have them, the Russians jailed or deported them. The White Paper was still in effect, barring their entry into Palestine. When some tried to return to Poland, they found their houses occupied by people who chased them away, beat them, or killed them. There was a pogrom in Kielce, Poland, in 1946, a town I once saw from the window of a car, its streets ominous and mean. I've mentioned this pogrom in previous books because I find it unbelievable: to kill Jews after the Holocaust, or to survive the death camps only to be murdered when you have finally made it home.

On May 22, 1945, two weeks after Germany surrendered, Weizmann wrote to Prime Minister Winston Churchill and asked him to revoke the White Paper. Churchill told Weizmann such matters would be attended to when "the victorious Allies are definitely seated at the Peace table." This angered Weizmann, who, on June 5, sent a second letter: "I had always understood from our various conversations that our problem would be considered as soon as the German war was over:

but the phrase 'until the victorious Allies are definitely seated at the Peace table' substitutes some indefinite date in the future. I am sure that it cannot have been your intention to postpone the matter indefinitely, because I believe you realize that this would involve very grave hardship to thousands of people at present still lingering in the camps of Buchenwald, Belsen-Bergen etc."

Schind told Zemurray these people could not be left in the camps.

Zemurray agreed, saying something like, Yes, yes, but what do you want from me?

Everything, said Schind. Money, ships, documents, expertise.

Zemurray raised his hand, summoning a servant. He asked for whiskey.

The man returned with a bottle and glasses. Zemurray poured shots, one for himself, one for Schind, drank his, poured another, drank that, then started to talk. Sam did not tell his story often. When asked about his past, he might shrug. "I was there. It happened. What's there to say?" This occasion was different. It was as if, in response to the picture painted by Schind—it spoke to Sam on frequencies the average person might not detect—the story of his life was all he had to offer.

He talked about Selma and Mobile, the strangeness of the delta towns, the first banana, the first ripes. He talked about Puerto Cortés, the vaqueros, the soldiers for hire. He cried when he talked about his son, then chased away his tears with another whiskey. Told this way, the incidents of Zemurray's life, which might otherwise seem disconnected, reveal themselves as a cohesive narrative, an epic, an adventure, the story of a generation and the story of a people. Only at the very end did he speak about Russia, and the fields, green in summer, black in spring, and his father, and the death of his father, and his last view of his first home, a house swallowed in the immensity of the steppe. Everyone has an Eden, a perfect world lost when they were small. For Sam, it was that wheat farm in Russia, and his father was alive. When Sam was finished talking, he sat quietly, the bottle drained, the sun gone, the room dark, then turned to Schind and said, in essence, I cannot help you. Not openly. Nearly half of United Fruit's ships fly British flags and much of our business is done there. A British company cannot run the British blockade. But I will send you to a man who will help. He'll tell you what to do, and give you what you need. If you get stuck, come back.

The Bricha was soon under way. Contacts established, money raised, ships purchased, papers issued—documents that caused the harbormaster to sign the manifest and open the gates. Zionist agents spirited refugees out of the DP camps, leading them over mountain trails to ports in Romania, France, Italy, where ships waited at anchor. Some of these tubs, jammed with poor lost souls, made it through the blockade. Others were stopped by the Royal Navy, boarded, turned back. Every few months, Zemurray received an update, sometimes followed by a meeting at 2 Audubon Place in New Orleans, the Ritz in Boston, the Roosevelt in New York, or the plantation near Hammond. Schind might turn up alone, or he might bring a colleague such as Meyer Weisgal, the executive director of the Jewish Agency. According to Weisgal, Zemurray helped the Bricha in several ways, crucially in the procuring of ships and getting those ships out to sea. He did it by putting Schind together with the men who ran the docks—"[Schind] was always making trips to Boston or New Orleans to see people to whom Zemurray directed him for papers of registry and visas for crews," Gottlieb Hammer, the head of the United Jewish Appeal, wrote—and by pressuring Central American officials to flag Bricha ships as their own. In one case, three ships, refused exit papers from the port of Philadelphia, were released after Zemurray made a few calls. One of them, purchased with money partly donated by Zemurray, was the *Exodus*, the refugee-packed steamer that, in its pitiful, homeless wandering, personified the Jewish people, demonstrating the need for a Jewish state. "Zemurray helped raise the purchase price and pushed through the registration of the *Exodus*, which carried emigrants through the British blockade into the Promised Land," Thomas McCann wrote. The most famous vessel of the Bricha, the *Exodus* is one of the storied ships of Jewish history, right up there with the fishing boat that carried Jonah away from Tarshish.

The British Mandate of Palestine was terminated in May 1948. According to *The Jews' Secret Fleet* by Joseph Hochstein and Murray Greenfield, the Bricha had by then carried thirty-seven thousand Jewish refugees to Palestine—many of them on American ships procured or sped along by Sam Zemurray.

Well, that's the story people tell you in Israel, where the name Zemurray is better known than it is here. The historical record consists of a mere scattering of letters, diary entries, documents. The fact is, Zemurray, always wary of drawing the wrong kind of attention, was, for the most part, able to disassociate his name from the cause. Gottlieb Hammer described him as "an international mystery man" who "made and overturned governments at will according to business needs. He was one of the richest and most powerful men in the United States, yet Zemurray was able to avoid publicity and keep his name out of the newspapers. The only condition he put on his aid to [the Bricha] was that he never be publicly identified and that the entire relationship be treated with the utmost discretion."

For reasons never fully disclosed, Zemurray resigned as president of United Fruit in 1948, turning the office over to his colleague Thomas Cabot. Sam remained the largest stockholder and retained ultimate control, but he relinquished daily operation. Perhaps he did it with his mortality in mind (he was seventy-one). He must have been exhausted. Or perhaps he did it for the Jewish cause in Palestine. With the coming end of the British occupation, the fate of such a state had been turned over to the United Nations, where it would be decided by a vote in the General Assembly. The resolution to divide Palestine into two nations— one Arab, one Jew—needed a two-thirds majority to pass. A season of politicking would begin as soon as that vote was scheduled, a game Zemurray was uniquely positioned to play.

His involvement began in October 1947, when he was approached by Weizmann, who, according to his own writings, told Zemurray, "The situation is such that your help is very much required at this critical stage. Believe me, it's urgent."

Early tallies showed the partition vote lining up this way: the European states, members of the Western Alliance as well as the Soviet bloc, each with its own history in mind, would approve; the countries of the Muslim world, for reasons I don't have to explain, would oppose. This would leave the issue to be settled by unaligned countries that seemingly had no direct interest at stake, several of them, it just so happened, in the Torrid Zone of America where the banana flourished. According to Ignacio Klich, in his article "Latin America, the United States, and the Birth of Israel," the Zionist leadership had neglected the region, believing "Central American support might be won through UFCO's president and largest shareholder Samuel Zemurray." But the politics were complicated by the large Arab populations in several of the Latin American nations.

There were two votes for partition. The first, on November 25, 1947, resulted in a deadlock, the nays and abstentions leaving Resolution 181 just short of passage. A second was scheduled for November 29, four days after the first vote. It was in these days, a crack of light between dispossession and statehood, that Sam Zemurray went to work, calling key players in banana land, wheedling, cajoling, strong-arming. It was the culmination of his career, the hour when Zemurray could finally use everything he had learned to play a secretly decisive role on the world stage. He asked each leader in the region two questions: How do you intend to vote on partition? and Can your vote be changed? Zemurray told Weizmann that every vote from Mexico to Colombia was for sale, but the price was often prohibitively high. Zemurray apparently suggested they focus on just those nations where he carried great influence. The ensuing bribing and lobbying became so intense that President Harry Truman complained to Weizmann of the hardball tactics: Truman found it "unbecoming."

"The pressure was unlike anything that had been seen there before," Truman wrote in his memoirs. "I do not think I ever had as much pressure and propaganda aimed at the White House as I had in this instance. The persistence of a few of the extreme Zionist leaders—actuated by political motives and engaging in political threats—disturbed and annoyed me."

Weizmann promised that no such pressure was coming from the Zionist leadership. "[While] generally accurate in what he said," wrote Ignacio Klich, "Weizmann passed over in silence the more important activities of the supporters of Jewish statehood who were not part of the Jewish Agency leadership, including his own approach to UFCO's Samuel Zemurray."

The president of India, Jawaharlal Nehru, later claimed he'd been offered money, "a bribe of millions," by a powerful businessman associated with the Zionist cause, to vote in favor of partition. (India voted against.)

By the time of the final tally, enough countries had changed their vote—Haiti from no to abstain; Nicaragua from abstain to yes—to pass Resolution 181. Knowing about the work of Zemurray, certain yes votes that might otherwise seem mysterious—Costa Rica, Guatemala, Ecuador, Panama—suddenly make perfect sense. Behind them, behind the creation of the Jewish state, was the Gringo pushing his cart piled high with stinking ripes.

Walking through 2 Audubon Place, Marjorie Cowen, the wife of the president of Tulane, stopped in the window-filled room on the third floor. "This is where Mr. Zemurray made the calls," she told me. "He sat in a chair right here, calling every leader in Central and South America, talking and explaining until he got enough of them to change their vote to make modern Israel a reality."

The vote for partition did not assure the existence of the Jewish state. (As Zemurray knew, you get nothing without fighting for it.) Prime Minister David Ben-Gurion's declaration of independence was in fact followed by calls for war across the Arab world. In the summer of 1949, armies streamed over the Israeli frontiers from Egypt, Jordan, Syria, Iraq, and Lebanon. Israel would be at a huge disadvantage in the coming battle—surrounded, outnumbered, and challenged by an arms embargo that had been declared on the region. No weapons could be sent to any party in the conflict. As the Arab countries were already well armed—the Jordanian army was commanded by British officers—the embargo fell disproportionately on Israel.

You name it, they did not have enough: bullets, rifles, pistols, grenades, trucks, tanks. The Israeli Air Force consisted of a single plane, a decrepit German Messerschmitt. Israel survived on the smuggled weapon, the clandestine arrival, the box hidden behind the false panel on the container ship—it says vegetables, but it smells like gunpowder. In the first days of the war, the majority of these boxes arrived from only three places, sent by three types of interested parties: Czechoslovakia, where Communists shipped trucks, guns, and planes with the consent of the Soviets, who believed a prolonged Middle Eastern conflict would embarrass the British; New York and New Jersey, where, at the urging of Meyer Lansky and Longy Zwillman, dock bosses like Socks Lanza looked the other way as ships bound for Haifa or Tel Aviv were filled with weapons; and Central America, where banana men filled ship after ship with boxes marked FOOD or SUPPLIES, carried weapons to the Israeli Defense Force.

Much help came from Anastasio Somoza García, known as "Tacho," who ruled Nicaragua from 1936 until 1956, when he was assassinated. According to Ignacio Klich, Somoza smuggled weapons to Israel throughout the 1948 war. Years later, when world opinion turned against Somoza's grandson Tachito, who ruled Nicaragua from 1967 until he was assassinated in 1980, only Israel continued to ship arms to the dictator. When asked about this, Prime Minister Menachem Begin spoke of an old debt that needed to be honored.

Israel's War of Independence ended in victory for Israel in January 1949. Sam returned to United Fruit soon after, reclaiming his place at the center of the banana world. He was relatively young when the Second World War began—now he was old. He was already showing signs of the disease that would kill him. Thomas McCann, who was introduced to Zemurray in these years, described the meeting this way: "The old man put out his hand and took mine, and I could feel the tremor of Parkinson's disease, a palsy that seemed to start in his feet or under the ground we stood on."

Zemurray had considered retiring altogether, letting his leave lapse into forever. He was seventy-three, much older than most other top executives in America. A new generation had come to power in the business world, men who had fought in the Second World War. Zemurray was an ancient among them, Methuselah himself, a relic of a time when mercenaries ruled the isthmus. Minor Keith, Lee Christmas, Jake the Parrot King—the pirates were gone, replaced by Ivy League managers. High times had given way to the corporation. In truth, Sam returned only because the future of the company seemed to depend on it. The top job had been given to Thomas Cabot, and Thomas Cabot had failed. The division heads were bickering, the provinces were restive, the leadership was uncertain. Zemurray, who walked the earth when the world was new, was the only man with the requisite authority to make the moves and right the ship. He planned to stay no more than a year or two, just long enough to set things in order, train a successor, move on. But two years turned into five, seven. It's the one problem he could never solve: having designed a uniquely powerful position for himself at the top of the company, tailored to his character and style, Zemurray could not find anyone else to fill it. United Fruit had been on the verge of collapse when he took control in 1932. He gave the company twenty extra years of life, but it was far from clear it could survive his retirement.

18

Operation Success

Back to the isthmus! Back to the sandy loam! Back to the land of United Fruit camps, each with its swimming pool and golf course, each with its Quonset huts and its electric green fields and *Los Pericos* blue from poison! Back to port towns and jungle towns and railroads, where machete men doze in the shade of the ceiba, and the palm trees applaud when the wind blows! Back to the preserve of the banana cowboy, with his mule and pistola! Back to the land dominated by one crop, one corporation, one will! Back to the slender neck of continent south of Mexico and north of Colombia, where you can swim in the Atlantic Ocean in the morning and the Pacific that same afternoon! Back to the Mayan ruins and the Mosquito Coast and the coffee plantations where the pickers make a penny a pound and every meal is beans! Back to the land where the banana is king and the Gringo gives the orders!

The isthmus had changed greatly in the course of the Second World War. There were physical changes, all the exotic crops imported by Zemurray, for example, but there were metaphysical changes, too—the appearance of a new mood characterized by hope. The people of Latin America were profoundly affected by the language America had used during the struggle: the calls to end oppression, colonialism, racism, tyranny. Asked to name a hero, most South American liberals of that era would mention FDR, specifically citing his four freedoms: freedom of expression, freedom of worship, freedom from want, freedom from fear. In short, the Central Americans heard our words and actually believed them.

For those on the isthmus who dreamed of the new world suggested by Franklin Roosevelt, but still lived in the old one ruled by Sam Zemurray, a terrible gap yawned open: between expectation and reality. This is where revolutions are born. The call for increased rights and freedoms was a challenge to United Fruit, which depended on compliant governments and cheap labor. What's more, with the start of the cold war, the struggle on the isthmus got tangled up with the global battle between capitalism and communism, which turned even the smallest feud into a test of ideologies. The region was flooded with fears of implication and precedent. If you wanted to open the gates of hell, all you had to do was point and say, "Communist."

Take Guatemala, where United Fruit prospered, and where the dream of United Fruit would end. The country was perfect for bananas: lush jungle, poor workers, lots of rain, accommodating dictators. General Jorge Ubico, who had assumed power in 1931, was the banana republic strongman in concentrated form, kicking down, kissing up. He looked like Buster Keaton in the silents, dreamily imagining a cavalry charge. Do I need to say he considered himself the reincarnation of Napoleon? Or that he was tiny, with delicate gloved fingers? Or that he carried a sword and wore medals all over his chest? Or that he was obsessed with astrology and bewitched by numbers? Eccentric at the beginning, mad by the end, he had a hatred of Communists so pure it burned blue. The general banned the words "trade union," "strike," "petition," and "worker." There were no workers, he told his people, only employees.

At times, it seemed the general had just one constituent: United Fruit. Peasant workers—excuse me, peasant employees—were required to work a minimum of one hundred days a year for landowners, which usually meant United Fruit. Anyone who failed to follow the order could be legally killed. (Not good for the bargaining position.) United Fruit had acquired an obscene amount of property in the country to stay ahead of Panama disease. By 1942, the company owned 70 percent of all private land in Guatemala, controlled 75 percent of all trade, and owned most of the roads, power stations and phone lines, the only Pacific seaport, and every mile of railroad. The contract that drove people especially crazy, perhaps the most lopsided deal in the history of Guatemala—it gave U.F. unprecedented rights on the Pacific—had been negotiated by John Foster Dulles, then a lawyer with the white-shoe law firm Sullivan & Cromwell.

Anger was the inevitable result, resentment, frustration, rage. The pressure built until the lid was rattling on the pot, the stove was straining against the wall. In 1944, the whole country blew. It started with a massive demonstration. Workers filled the main plaza in Guatemala City, demanding that the dictator step down; they wanted a new system with decent wages and the sort of social security system Franklin Roosevelt had championed in the United States. (Life expectancy in Guatemala was forty-seven years and most people made less than $300 a year.) General Ubico told his army to clear the plaza. Some soldiers opened fire on the demonstrators, but others stripped off their uniforms and joined the crowd, which swelled until it was the only thing that mattered. The masses stormed through the city, looting and burning. They marched to a military base on the outskirts of the capital. There was a brief fight, a civil war, black smoke rising from the slums.

Hundreds of Guatemalans were killed. The general mumbled through a resignation speech, turned control over to his lieutenant, General Federico Ponce, then went into exile. As the first demonstration had been organized by educators, the upheaval came to be known as "The Schoolteachers' Revolt."

General Ponce called for elections. Some of the people who led the revolt invited Juan José Arévalo, a college professor who had spent the previous fourteen years in exile, to return to lead the movement. Arévalo had written essays that inspired the revolution, as well as textbooks standard in the country. Everyone knew his name. He was forty-two when he returned, slender to the point of being sickly, with an intellectual's myopic stare. A crowd met him at the airport. Men and women threw flowers and shouted his name. General Ponce tried to have Arévalo arrested, but a clique of leftist military officers prevented this. I say "prevented" as if it were a simple matter—a traffic cop preventing a car from entering a one-way street—but it was, in fact, bloody. On October 20, 1944, a group of junior officers killed over a hundred of their superiors, securing the revolution.

Juan Arévalo won the presidency with 85 percent of the vote, the first popularly elected leader in the history of Guatemala. He took the oath of office on March 15, 1945, a clear, spring afternoon. He wore a business suit because he was a civilian, not a general. His inaugural address promised a new age. He had three audiences in mind: Guatemalans, the government of the United States, and the president of United Fruit. He spoke of his past—a childhood of poverty. He spoke of the future—a vision of big landowners forced to reform and share. And he spoke of his heroes, Abraham Lincoln and Franklin Roosevelt, who "taught us there is no need to cancel the concept of freedom in the democratic system in order to breathe into it a socialist spirit." He said he would govern by a philosophy of his own invention, which he called "spiritual socialism."

To Zemurray, who had agents scattered in the crowd, every word of the speech would have sounded like a threat. It was Huey Long all over again. The call to strengthen the unions, spread the wealth, break up the large holdings of land. . . . There were some U.F. executives who worried that Guatemala would go Communist from the beginning. Zemurray rejected such talk. He did not believe that the people of Guatemala, most of them poor Indians, were sophisticated enough to embrace an ideology associated with European intellectuals.

Arévalo, a smart man who understood the limits of his power, was exceedingly careful in dealing with United Fruit. Though he passed land reform legislation, he left it unenforced. He focused instead on crowd-pleasing issues that Zemurray could hardly oppose. A forty-hour workweek, social security guarantees, rights of the unions to organize—all based on the New Deal legislation that Zemurray himself championed in the United States. In 1947, the Guatemalan congress enacted the Labor Code, which, for the first time ever, permitted banana workers to join trade unions. In the past, force had been used to break strikes. Labor leaders were now free to organize on U.F. plantations. The company filed protests against the code and even threatened to withdraw from Guatemala altogether. But in the end, business continued as usual.

I'm not saying that it was a frictionless time. (There were twenty-five coup attempts in the Arévalo years.) Nor am I saying Zemurray stood by calmly as this college professor made Guatemala less hospitable to the company. (In 1948, Guatemalan agents discovered grenades and guns hidden in a United Fruit train bound for Puerto Barrios.) I'm just saying, compared to what followed, the Arévalo years were boringly peaceful.

In 1951, Arévalo was succeeded by his vice president, Jacobo Arbenz, one of the young officers who had purged the old regime.

Jacobo Arbenz was born in Quetzaltenango, Guatemala, in 1913, when U.F. was already monstrously powerful. His father was from Switzerland, blond haired, blue eyed, as pale as a stalk of wheat. He stood out amid the dark crowds of Quetzaltenango, which was populated mostly by Indians. Why his father moved to Guatemala, I don't know. He married a Guatemalan of European descent, her skin as white as ivory, hair as black as coal. He settled on the outskirts of the mountainous city and opened an apothecary. He was a licensed pharmacist, a man of prescriptions and containers filled with potions. He did what the kingpin tells the drug dealer he must never do: got high on his own supply. He became addicted first to one kind of pill, then to several kinds, then to narcotics in general. They filled his days with epiphanies: shadows of the trees, hills in the distance, faces in the market—everything became profound, a manifestation of the divine. He made poor decisions under the influence, gave away what he should have kept. To his son, he was a good man broken on the wheel of capitalism. Then the drugs stopped working, or began working in a terrible new way—revealed devils where they had once revealed angels. He turned sullen, depressed. No one could talk to him. One day, he went into the back room of his apothecary and shot himself in the head.

These details were compiled for a CIA file years later, when Jacobo Arbenz was classified an enemy of the United States. E. Howard Hunt, the American spy later famous for his role in the Watergate break-in, elaborated on the death of the elder Arbenz in *Undercover: Memoirs of an American Secret Agent*. According to Hunt, the elder Arbenz, wanting to be certain his suicide was successful, filled his mouth with water before shooting himself, which made his "head explode like a bomb."

The Arbenz family lived a vagabond life after the tragedy. Jacobo, who was still a boy, moved from house to house, uncle to uncle. He grew taciturn and sad. He radiated that peculiar melancholy that comes across as depth. He was as blond as his father, very handsome. Everyone said he looked like Alan Ladd. That does not mean much now, but Alan Ladd was one of the biggest movie stars in the world back then. Alan Ladd played Shane, the gunman who tried to lay down his weapons only to discover a fighter must fight until he dies. At the end of the movie, Shane, shot in the gut, rides into the mountains as if ascending to heaven. When Jacobo was fourteen, his mother sent him to military school, and a good thing she did, because that's where he finally found a sense of belonging. He loved order and rules, knowing who was above him and who was below. He went on to the nation's elite military academy, where he amassed one of the best academic records in the history of the country.

Arbenz was a man when he graduated, tall and elegant, laughing with fellow officers, as enviable as a soldier in a story by Tolstoy, drinking vodka, gambling and whoring, believing this life will last forever. If he had an ideology, it was personal: the world as seen by the young man who believes his father was killed by the system, which is another name for the banana company. The sophisticated ideas that he later expressed in speeches and rants came from his wife, María Cristina Villanova Castro, a Nancy Reagan or Lady Macbeth who recognized in the officer a perfect vehicle. Maria Castro grew up in El Salvador, the daughter of a wealthy coffee grower who claimed she had been turned against her class by Steinbeck, Marx, and Bartolomé de Las Casas. Her father banned her from his library, but she read in secret. He cast her into the outer darkness of children who have disappointed their parents. Ideas for which Jacobo Arbenz was later condemned—redistribution of wealth, seizing the means of production, etc.—came from his wife. Arbenz was more instinctual, with convictions that derived less from books than his own experience. You don't need a book to understand injustice. Just look at the electric fence that surrounds the banana plantation.

When Arévalo formed his cabinet, he named Arbenz minister of defense. He did this to secure the loyalty of the military, where Arbenz was wildly popular. He then tapped Arbenz to succeed him as president, to pursue and complete the goals of the revolution. After winning the election, Arbenz formed a coalition government made of factions, including members of the small Communist Party of Guatemala. (As far as American officials were concerned, the presence of these Communists suggested Arbenz was probably a Communist himself.) He took the oath of office in the spring of 1951, with the departing president at his side. It was the first peaceful transition of power in the history of the country. In his farewell address, Arévalo ominously warned of the power of the banana company. "The revolution will have to be pushed forward," he said, "or it will be lost."

Arbenz was a different sort of president than his predecessor. Arévalo condemned United Fruit but never undermined the company or challenged Zemurray directly. He was cautious, deliberate. Arbenz advanced soldier-style, by quick, decisive strokes. He was a man aware of time, who wanted to push through his program before the weather changed. He did not fear Zemurray. In fact, it seemed he wanted to infuriate the bosses of United Fruit, make a display of his independence and defiance. He wanted to remind the banana moguls who the elected leader of the country really was. In his inaugural speech, Arbenz promised to make Guatemala "a dependent nation with a semicolonial economy, [into] an economically independent country." He said achieving this would mean ridding the nation of the latifundios, large private estates and farms, once and for all.

A new urgency was evident from the first days of his rule. It could be detected in the tone of informal diplomatic dialogue, as well as in the tenor of official communication. Whereas previous Guatemalan leaders seemed to accept U.F.'s view of its history—an enlightened company that had mastered nature (the conquest of the tropics)—the new government sought to undermine the founding myths of El Pulpo. (A company, like a nation, cannot survive without its mythology.) "All the achievements of the Company were made at the expense of the impoverishment of the country and by acquisitive practices," said a government minister, Alfonso Bauer Paiz. "To protect its authority [United Fruit] had recourse to every method: political intervention, economic compulsion, contractual imposition, bribery, [and] tendentious propaganda, as suited its purposes of domination. The United Fruit Company is the principal enemy of progress of Guatemala, of its democracy, and of every effort at its economic liberation."

On June 27, 1952, Arbenz signed Decree 900, which gave the government the right to expropriate uncultivated portions of large plantations. Farms under 223 acres were exempt, as were farms of 223 to 670 acres that were at least two-thirds cultivated. In a speech, Arbenz promised to "put an end to the latifundios and the semi-feudal practices, giving the land to thousands of peasants, raising their purchasing power and creating a great internal market favorable to the developments of domestic industry."

Only one landowner held many great parcels of uncultivated property: United Fruit. It was the company's hedge against the spread of Panama disease (U.F. cultivated only 15 percent of its property in Guatemala). Hundreds of thousands of acres were confiscated from United Fruit, broken into plots, and divided among thousands of peasant farmers. In return, the company was reportedly paid $627,572 in twenty-five-year Guatemalan bonds, which yielded 3 percent interest.

United Fruit officials complained to the Guatemalan government and to the U.S. State Department. Even if the seizure were legal, the price seemed grossly unfair. Auditors valued the land at $16 million. The Guatemalans said their appraisal had been determined by the company itself—from its own tax filings. (Zemurray, who had depreciated the company's holdings after he took over in 1932, was now paying the price.) When a formal complaint was filed in Guatemala City—it said undervaluing for tax purposes was an accepted practice understood by previous governments and irrelevant to the land's actual worth; it demanded full payment of the property's real value—this came not from United Fruit but from the U.S. State Department, a detail Arbenz should have noticed.

Arbenz rejected the complaint and carried on as if no one could stop him. This assertion of authority proved as galvanizing as the seizure itself. By defying El Pulpo, Arbenz became a liberal hero across Latin America. His picture was posted everywhere. Finally, someone with the guts to stand up to the Banana Man. It marked the dawn of a new revolutionary era in the South. Spanish-speaking reformers of every variety—Communists, Socialists, Trotskyites—as well as adventure seekers and people simply curious to taste freedom, set off for Guatemala. By becoming a symbol and a refuge for the disenchanted, the country drew still more attention from the State Department. In the minds of diplomats, Guatemala was turning into a rogues gallery. Each day, more bad actors streamed into the country. Slept in hotels, camped on beaches, filled the coffeehouses with smoke and excited talk. It was the next fifty years in miniature. All the rabble-rousers who would long bedevil the United States seemed to be in Guatemala City, or on their way.

Here's a picture of Che Guevara. He is wearing a beret and dirty fatigues, the uniform of the revolution. His hair is thick and dark, pushed back and tousled, as if blown by unseen winds, messy yet perfectly arranged in a style not unfamiliar to fans of Elvis in the middle years, when his name flashed behind him in lights. Che's eyes, coffee brown, are rolled to the side of their orbs, perhaps spotting something in the periphery, the mobs that will follow him, the bullet that will kill him. It was his eyes, more than his beard, more than his Kalashnikov, that made him a trademark in the way of Chiquita Banana, United Fruit's dancing mascot—the firebrand on the poster in the dorm room, the soldier at war with the stooges of the Banana Man. He's leaning back, as if a battle has been won, as if there is time to enjoy. He smokes a cigar, the product of Cuban factories and fields, the symbol of the farmworker and the capitalist, as if to say, *Look, I am smoking your cigar, my gringo friend.*

Zemurray and Guevara were flip sides of a coin. First the Banana Man, then the revolutionary who fights the Banana Man. They would, in a sense, lead rival corporations: United Fruit and World Revolution, Inc. Two philosophies, two ways of life, the banana compound or the guerrilla camp. They were interdependent, two figures carved in a single block of stone, coiled around and facing each other.

Guevara grew up in Rosario, Argentina, on the Paraná River, in the northeast corner of the country. His given name was Ernesto. His family was Irish/Spanish, part of the elite. They were upper-middle-class liberals. Like Jacobo Arbenz, Guevara listed FDR among his heroes. He excelled at sports yet suffered debilitating asthma. In certain stories, he succumbs to an attack in the midst of battle, wheezing over his gun. Like many sickly children, he became acutely observant. He could see through appearances from the time he was small, recognizing not only the presidents but also the businessmen lurking in the shadows behind the presidents. He rooted against the big corporations the way other kids root against Superman villains. He said he first experienced true hatred while reading about the Braden Copper Company, a subsidiary of Kennecott, the American concern that dominated the South American mining industry. Spruille Braden, the big-faced Montanan who inherited the company, stood for everything Guevara despised.

When Zemurray hired Braden—a member of the Council on Foreign Relations and a State Department employee, he held positions at Standard Oil and W. Averell Harriman Securities—it confirmed Guevara's sense of how the establishment is organized: the American government and the global companies might look like various concerns with varying interests but was in fact a single beast with a million mouths.

Guevara went to college, then medical school. In the summers, he toured South America, sometimes on foot, sometimes by motorcycle. He first came across a United Fruit compound in Costa Rica. He walked for miles through the fields and banana towns, which he described in his diary as "well-defined zones with guards who impede entry, and, of course, the best zone is that of the gringos." Guevara claimed that his philosophy crystallized by a campfire in the highlands, where he stopped after a day of travel. Twenty-five, a doctor with leftist sympathies, he found himself in conversation with an old man, a refugee of Stalin's purges. He had been brutalized but still believed. He told Guevara to embrace his sense of injustice, as it was a finger pointing him in the right direction. "There's a battle waging," the old man said, "and you're on one side or the other, even if you don't know it."

Guevara claimed it was at this moment—by the fire, beneath the pines—that he finally understood the inevitability of the universal struggle. But even if that's true, it's only part of the story. Guevara was an intellectual whose sense of reality came as much from literature as from experience. For him, a moment as clarifying must have come in 1950, when Pablo Neruda published the poem "United Fruit Company":

> *When the trumpet blared everything*
> *on earth was prepared*
> *and Jehova distributed the world*
> *to Coca-Cola Inc., Anaconda,*
> *Ford Motors and other entities:*
> *United Fruit Inc.*
> *reserved for itself the juiciest,*
> *the central seaboard of my land,*
> *America's sweet waist.*
> *It re-baptized its lands*
> *the "Banana Republics,"*

and upon the slumbering corpses,
upon the restless heroes
who conquered renown,
freedom and flags,
it established the comic opera:
it alienated self-destiny,
regaled Caesar's crowns,
unsheathed envy, drew
the dictatorship of flies:
Trujillo flies, Tacho flies,
Carias flies, Martinez flies,
Ubico flies, flies soaked
in humble blood and jam,
drunk flies that drone
over the common graves,
circus flies, clever flies
versed in tyranny.

Among the bloodthirsty flies
The Fruit Co. disembarks,
ravaging coffee and fruits
for its ships that spirit away
our submerged lands' treasures
like serving trays.

Meanwhile, in the seaports'
Sugary abysses,
Indians collapsed, buried
In the morning mist:
a body rolls down, a nameless
thing, a fallen number,
a bunch of lifeless fruit
dumped in the rubbish heap.

(Translated by Jack Schmitt)

In his elegy to William Butler Yeats, W. H. Auden famously wrote that "poetry makes nothing happen." While that might or might not be true in the United States, it was not the case on the isthmus in the twentieth century. Zemurray, who defeated the jungle with the sweat of a hundred thousand workers, amassing a great fortune and empire in the process, was, in part, undone by forty-two lines of poetry. If I exaggerate, it's only a little. In these years, a new Central American narrative was being written, a new foundational myth. United Fruit was going to be the devil in this narrative, the snake in the Garden. Zemurray understood this at some level and tried desperately to forge a new corporate identity. Hence all the money for universities and hospitals. But it was too late. By 1953, when Guevara started his bike and headed north to Guatemala, the basic outlines had been written. "I had the opportunity to pass through the dominions of the United Fruit," Guevara wrote in his diary, "convincing me once again of just how terrible the capitalistic octopuses are. I have sworn before a picture of the old [and mourned] comrade Stalin that I won't rest until I see these capitalist octopuses annihilated. In Guatemala, I will perfect myself and achieve what I need to be an authentic revolutionary."

You might say it was prejudice that left Zemurray unprepared for the furor. As I said, he did not believe the masses of the isthmus, poor, illiterate Indians, could grasp or rally to the cause of the intellectuals. It was only with the execution of Decree 900 that he became first concerned, then alarmed, then determined to fight.

In the old days, he might have simply hired an army of mercenaries, sailed down to the isthmus, and changed the government. But this was during the cold war, when even the smallest thing was about the biggest, and the U.S. government had its snout in every part of the world. A new day called for a new way to solve an old problem.

Zemurray, who tried to retire again a few years before, had returned to handle the Guatemala situation. No one else seemed up to it. He had long been hiring power brokers and lobbyists, men who could help him work the levers of government. Here, for the first time in the story of the banana trade, which began with parrot kings and guns for hire, you recognize the contours of the current system, where the millionaires who run Halliburton field white-collar armies who wreak more havoc than a whole division of Machine Gun Molonys.

Among the most effective of Zemurray's government men was Tommy Corcoran, known in the White House and Congress and every tavern in D.C. as Tommy the Cork: you push him down here, he pops up over there. Corcoran had been one of the deftest operators in FDR's White House, a Harvard graduate and a former clerk for Oliver Wendell Holmes Jr. He worked as a lawyer for FDR's Reconstruction Finance Corporation and drafted much New Deal legislation, helping create, among other things, the Securities and Exchange Commission. He met Zemurray in 1936 while raising money for midterm congressional elections. Zemurray hired the Cork as soon as he left the government to work as a lobbyist. Sam referred to him as *my man in court* and kept him on a $100,000 yearly retainer, though the arrangement was secret. (His counsel to officials regarding bananas would be more trusted if people did not know it was paid for.) Corcoran briefed Zemurray on the thinking of top government officials. For example, under what conditions would President Truman be willing to go to war on the isthmus?

It was the Cork who insisted Zemurray hire Walter Bedell ("Beetle") Smith. The head of the CIA under Truman, Smith became disenchanted when Eisenhower moved him to the State Department. "Right after he became Undersecretary of State, Beetle told me of his desire to assume the presidency of the United Fruit Company," Corcoran wrote. "He told me he always liked to watch those pretty sailing ships on the Atlantic—the Great White Fleet. I took the message to the Fruit Company. I told them: 'You have to have people who can tell you what's going on. He's had a great background with his CIA association.' Their answer was: 'He doesn't know anything about the banana business.' I told them: 'For Chris-sakes, your problem is not bananas, you've got to handle your political problem.'"

To cover the right wing—the Guatemala crisis stretched across the Democratic administration of Truman and the Republican administration of Eisenhower—Zemurray hired John A. Clements, a newspaperman who later launched his own PR firm and did work for the Hearst Corporation for years. Clements, who was pals with Senator Joe McCarthy, connected Zemurray with the red-baiting fringe. Kept on a

$96,000 yearly retainer, he lobbied congressmen and planted stories. When Clements died in December 1974, his correspondence was purchased by Hearst and burned.

The hiring went both ways, with officials leaving the government to join U.F., and U.F. executives taking positions in the government. Ed Whitman, U.F.'s in-house head of public relations, used to tell his employees that whenever people read "United Fruit" in the Communist propaganda, they mentally substituted "United States," the implication being that these people were wrong and needed to be corrected. But looking back, it's not clear who needed to be corrected. By 1954, the network of connections had grown so extensive it was hard to tell where the government ended and the company began. John Moors Cabot, the American assistant secretary of state in charge of Guatemala, was the brother of Thomas Cabot, who had been the president of United Fruit. John Foster Dulles, who represented United Fruit while he was a law partner at Sullivan & Cromwell—he negotiated that crucial U.F. deal with Guatemalan officials in the 1930s—was secretary of state under Eisenhower; his brother Allen, who did legal work for the company and sat on its board of directors, was the head of the CIA under Eisenhower; Henry Cabot Lodge, who was America's ambassador to the UN, was a large owner of United Fruit stock; Ed Whitman, the United Fruit PR man, was married to Ann Whitman, Dwight Eisenhower's personal secretary. You could not see these connections until you could—then you could not stop seeing them.

Where did the interest of United Fruit end and the interest of the United States begin? It was impossible to tell. That was the point of all Sam's hires: If I can perfectly align the interests of my company with the interests of top officials in the U.S. government—not the interests of the country, but the interests of the people in charge of the country—then the United States will secure my needs.

Zemurray's most important hire was Edward Bernays, the man who invented modern public relations. Bernays approached the age of mass media like a scientist in search of general principles, which he recorded in articles and books: *Crystallizing Public Opinion, Propaganda, The Engineering of Consent.*

He had two basic insights from which everything else followed:

First: modern society, with its millions, is essentially ungovernable. The public must instead be controlled by manipulation. The men who do this manipulating, in government or not, are the true leaders, philosopher-kings. They need not manipulate all the people, only the few thousand who set the agenda. The drivers of history are not the people, in other words, nor the elite who influence the people, but the PR men who influence the elite who influence the people. "Those who manipulate [the] unseen mechanism of society constitute an invisible government which is the true ruling power," wrote Bernays. "We are governed, our minds molded, our tastes formed, our ideas suggested, largely by men we have never heard of."

Second: the people can be made to behave as you want them to behave via the subconscious of the public mind—no one else believed such a thing existed—which can be directed with symbols and signs. "If we understand the mechanism and motives of the group mind," asked Bernays, "is it not possible to control and regiment the masses according to our will without their knowing about it?"

Editor & Publisher called Bernays the "young Machiavelli of our time." *The Atlantic* titled its profile on him "The Science of Ballyhoo." In a letter to FDR, Supreme Court Justice Felix Frankfurter characterized Bernays and others in his trade as "professional poisoners of the public mind." To someone like Frankfurter, a public relations man was a cross between a hypnotist and a snake-oil salesman. In 1933, a Hearst reporter told Bernays that *Crystallizing Public Opinion* was a favorite book of Joseph Goebbels, the minister of propaganda in Nazi Germany, who, the reporter said, was using Bernays's ideas to design his campaign against the Jews. "It shocked me," Bernays wrote, "but I knew any human activity can be used for social purposes or misused for antisocial ones."

Edward Bernays, born in Vienna, Austria, in 1891, spent his first birthday on the ship that carried him to New York. He was Jewish, but neither poor, nor huddled, nor part of the masses he would spend his lifetime manipulating. His family was, in fact, illustrious, counting among its forebears Heinrich Heine and the chief rabbi of Hamburg. His father, a wealthy grain merchant, had a sister, and she married a Viennese man named Sigmund Freud. In other words, Freud was the

PR man's uncle. In his writings, Bernays recalled vacations to a family summer house in the Austrian Tyrol, where he spent time with Uncle Sigmund. "Although Freud was almost a quarter century my senior, we got along like two contemporaries," Bernays wrote in his autobiography. "Freud and I took long walks together through the woods that surrounded Carlsbad, he in pepper-and-salt knickerbockers, green Tyrolean hat with feather and ram's horn stuck in the hat band, brown hand-knit socks, heavy brown brogues and sturdy walking stick—and I in my Brooks Brothers suit. We walked over the sloping hills, talking all the way."

Bernays claimed he crafted his philosophy under the influence of Freud, specifically the notion of a public subconscious, a concept Freud himself would surely have rejected.

Bernays grew up in apartments all over the Upper West Side of Manhattan. He was a short man, five four in fancy shoes, a trim hyphen of a mustache. His first job was in publishing, as editor of the *Medical Review of Reviews*, a magazine filled with research articles on goiter pain. He exceeded his mandate at the magazine, championing an unsolicited play—a play sent to a medical journal!—that dramatized syphilis via a dozen characters who pay for one night of sin. It was called *Damaged Goods*. Bernays said he published the play as an act of conscience, but he clearly saw it as a way out of the boring world of medical jargon and into the bright lights of Broadway. He described it as a warning to the young and a call to acknowledge those syphilitics who suffer quietly among us. The publication of the play was reported in newspapers and journals. Bernays then contacted a theatrical producer who had turned down the play previously and convinced him that, with all the media attention, *Damaged Goods* could be marketed as a public service. Bernays filled the seats at the first performance with doctors and social workers, who then sat on panels and wrote editorials. *Damaged Goods* was a hit. You had to see it even if you didn't want to. It was performed at the White House for President Wilson. Bernays had pioneered a trick he would use throughout his career. If you want to advance a private interest, turn it into a public cause.

He worked on other plays, including Jean Webster's *Daddy-Long-Legs*, a precursor to *Little Orphan Annie*. Audiences were asked to make a contribution to the Daddy-Long-Legs Fund—look for the cans in the lobby. In the end, it was not plays that interested Bernays: it was trends, driving opinion. In 1915, he opened a public relations firm. There had been others—the literary bureau of Mutual Life Insurance, 1888; the Publicity Bureau, 1900; Ivy Ledbetter Lee's Parker and Lee, 1905— but Bernays's firm was the most influential. He coined the term "public relations." Before that, practitioners had been known as "press agents." A press agent is a boozy hack with a big mouth; a public relations expert is a scientist. Early clients included Sergei Diaghilev's Ballets Russes, which Bernays made famous in America, and Enrico Caruso, whom Bernays tagged "the man with the orchid-lined voice."

In 1928, Bernays was hired by George Washington Hill, the owner of the American Tobacco Company, to expand the cigarette market. Especially irksome to Hill was the convention that kept women from smoking in public, behavior considered unladylike. Hill tried to sell smoking to women as a way to shed pounds, strike a pose, stay alert, but nothing worked. Bernays told Hill that he should instead link his private interest—get women to smoke more—to a public cause. With this in mind, he planted newspaper articles that challenged the taboo against female public smoking, arguing that cigarettes were neither a dirty habit nor a weight-loss tool, but a symbol of empowerment. He took out an ad, calling women to "smoke out": the female citizens of New York were asked to leave their offices one afternoon and stroll along Fifth Avenue, puffing all the way. This was followed by "smokeouts" across the country. Bernays claimed he had not invented the issue— women really did want to smoke in public—but had merely exploited an existing sentiment, "crystallizing public opinion" and "manufacturing consent," just as Joseph Goebbels did not invent the hatred of the Jews in Germany but merely exploited an existing sentiment, crystallizing public opinion and manufacturing consent for the Holocaust.

By the 1930s, Bernays was a leading media figure in the United States. His clients included General Motors, General Electric, United States Radium, Eugene O'Neill, Georgia O'Keeffe, Mutual Benefit Life Insurance, Columbia Broadcasting System, National Broadcasting, *Cosmopolitan*, *Fortune*, *Good Housekeeping*, *Ladies' Home Journal*, *Time*, Woolworth, Macy's, and the government of India. He described his grand strategy as indirection. If General Motors hired Joe Schmo to sell cars, Joe Schmo would give an interview to *Road & Track*, telling them the specs of the Thunderbird, engine size in cubic inches, zero-to-sixty, and so on. Given the same job, Bernays would lobby Congress for higher speed limits, making it more fun to own a Thunderbird. Rather than fight for a single season of sales, he would make the world more friendly to his product. In the 1950s, a consortium of publishers—including Harcourt Brace and Simon & Schuster—concerned about a dip in numbers, hired Bernays. Did he go into schools and make the case for books? No, he talked to the architects and contractors who were designing the new suburban homes and convinced them a house is not modern if it does not include built-in bookshelves.

Indirection.

Zemurray hired Bernays in 1944. Their first meeting took place in Zemurray's office on Pier 3 in Manhattan. "Mr. Zemurray sat at a flat-top desk in a large room overlooking the Hudson," Bernays wrote. "A tall, well-built man, six feet two or three, he towered over me as he stood to greet me. His accent was slightly guttural, a hangover from immigrant days, I learned later. He had great surety about himself, and after a few minutes of conversation I recognized I was in the presence of a wise, strong, mature man. Zemurray was an extraordinary man," Bernays continued, "experienced in the rough and tumble action of the banana business, and with a broad, liberal, philosophical bent. In years of meeting tycoons, I had met few who combined as he did the ability to think abstractly and to translate ideas into actions."

Bernays was asked to help grow the banana market, which he did in all the usual ways: by stressing the nutritional value of warm-weather fruit, by bemoaning the bland nature of American breakfast. But his job changed dramatically in the mid-1940s when the Guatemalan president Juan Arévalo pressed for land reform. Bernays had been worried about the atmosphere on the isthmus since his first days with the company. His belief in indirection kept him focused on the big picture. The fisherman worries about the size of the catch; the philosopher worries about the soul of the river. "I kept insisting to Zemurray that revolutionary movements would spread in Middle America, as they had in other parts of the world," Bernays explained. "Despite his wisdom and mature judgment, Zemurray kept pooh-poohing this warning. The Indians, he said, were too ignorant; they had no channels of communication, no press or radio, which drew dissidents together in other parts of the world. How could ideas of communism be spread from one person to another—ignorant persons at that—without primary channels of communication?"

When Zemurray finally accepted the seriousness of the Guatemala situation, he called Bernays into his office and asked him what should be done.

Bernays said he needed to study the problem.

Zemurray told him to go down, take a look, and report back.

Bernays spent several weeks on the isthmus, traveling compound to compound, talking to banana men, laborers, government officials, peasants, people in town. He took notes, sketched ideas. "This whole matter of effective counter-Communism propaganda is not one of improvising," he wrote in a 1952 memo to Ed Whitman, "[but requires] the same type of scientific approach that is applied, let us say, to the problem of fighting a certain plant disease through a scientific method of approach."

In other words, blast them till they're as blue as parakeets.

Bernays devised a strategy built on his trademark tricks. By 1952, Jacobo Arbenz was the issue, yet the solution was not direct confrontation. That would only increase Arbenz's standing, threatening United Fruit. But if the company could turn its corporate challenge (Arbenz is confiscating land) into a problem for the United States (Communists are infiltrating the isthmus), the U.S. government would take care of the rest. Never mind that Arbenz claimed no allegiance to the Communist Party; never mind that Arbenz cited Franklin Roosevelt as among his heroes; never mind that many of the Arbenz policies that United Fruit found so offensive were patterned on the New Deal—the signs were evident for those who knew where to look. (Doesn't the Comintern allow adherents to obfuscate their true nature in the process of infiltration?) There was, for example, the fact that Arbenz included Communists in his government and seemed to support the spirit of communism as a whole; there was the fact of land reform, which replicated the policy of Communist governments everywhere; there was also the rhetoric, the interviews and the speeches—Arbenz sounded like a Communist;

there was the statecraft, too, which, like a star speeding away, shifted red. In 1953, when Joseph Stalin died, Arbenz declared a day of mourning in Guatemala. As it says in the book of Matthew, "You shall know them by their fruits."

Bernays set various goals: convince the American people of the Communist presence in Guatemala; convince members of Congress the issue is a winner; convince the CIA, which can actually do something on the ground, it's time to act. Bernays wouldn't make the world better for bananas, he would make the world better for American politicians, who would make the world better for the CIA, which would make the world better for bananas.

Indirection.

If Zemurray seemed less actively involved in Guatemala than he had once been in Honduras, that's probably because he had moved into a new stage of life, taken on a new role in the company: no longer on the ground with the machete and vaqueros, he had gone into the shadows, where he operated as a puppet master, watching, waiting, giving a tiny nod—plausible deniability—that serves as the green light. He vanished into the background, became the manipulator described in the most paranoid rants. For the first time in his life, he worked entirely through underlings and advisers. He must have known the company was on dangerous ground. Guatemala was something new and terrible even in the history of the banana trade. The company was perverting the politics and social life of the country just as it had already polluted its soil and fields.

The campaign began with a media blitz, a press junket, a pamphlet, a film. "The Public Relations Department had only one task," wrote Thomas McCann, "to get out the word that a Communist beachhead had been established in our hemisphere."

U.F. financed the publication of *Report on Guatemala*, a sliver of a book written by a journalist who later asked to have even his pseudonym removed. It was delivered to every member of Congress. You could see them in their chairs, feet up, reading the opening line: "A Moscow-directed Communist conspiracy in Central America is one of the Soviet Union's most successful operations of infiltration outside the Iron Curtain countries."

(Ed Whitman, the head of U.F.'s in-house public relations department, produced a film called *Why the Kremlin Hates Bananas*. When a new generation came to power at the company, every print was searched out and destroyed.)

Bernays planted stories in big publications in New York, which were picked up across the country. *The Herald Tribune, The Atlantic, Time*—all ran pieces. "The core of Bernays's strategy was the selection of the most influential media communications in America," wrote McCann, "the *Times*, several other newspapers, two or three major newsmagazines, the wire services and the electronic networks—followed by a high-level saturation campaign to expose those media's reporters to the company's version of the facts."

Bernays had great influence at *The New York Times*. According to *The Father of Spin* by Larry Tye, Bernays's wife, Doris, was related to Arthur Hays Sulzberger, the newspaper's publisher. This put Bernays and Sulzberger in the same social circles, at the same openings and parties, where Bernays approached the publisher, took him aside, made the case. *It's the biggest threat in the world, Arthur, and for God's sake, it's not being covered!* "He brought the Guatemalan situation to the attention of *Times* publisher Sulzberger as early as 1951," wrote McCann. "The *Times* agreed to have one of their leading editors look into the matter closely, and Sulzberger himself made an inspection tour at the company's invitation."

Sulzberger sent the reporter Crede Calhoun to the isthmus, resulting in a series of articles about the Red menace, articles that Bernays called "masterpieces of objective reporting," that were clipped and sent to other reporters across the country, resulting in still more "masterpieces of objective reporting." When the *Times* staffer Sydney Gruson, the paper's bureau chief in Mexico, became suspicious of these stories and wrote a piece of his own with a pro-Arbenz spin, Frank Wisner, a CIA operative heavily involved in Guatemala, complained to Allen Dulles, the head of the CIA and previously a member of the U.F. board of directors; Dulles spoke to his friend General Julius Ochs Adler, the business manager of the *Times*, telling Adler that Gruson and his wife,

Flora Lewis, were liberals who could not be trusted on this subject. Adler had a conversation with Sulzberger, who then kept Gruson off the story, ordering him to stay put in Mexico, claiming, dubiously, that there might be a Mexican angle to the Guatemala affair. (You following this?) According to *Bitter Fruit*, Sulzberger described it as a patriotic act.

Shades of Vietnam, shades of Iraq, shades of every war in which the consent is manufactured, in which people are cattle-prodded down the warpath with words like MENACE (*zap!*), CONTAGION (*zap!*), DOMINOS (*zap!*). "In almost every act of our daily lives," wrote Bernays, "whether in the sphere of politics or business, in our social conduct or our ethical thinking, we are dominated by the relatively small number of persons . . . who understand the mental processes and social patterns of the masses, who harness old social forces and contrive new ways to bind and guide the world."

Bernays's plan began to show results by the summer of 1951. The situation on the isthmus, unheard of a few months before, moved onto the national agenda, where it was described not as a threat to a corporate interest, nor as a threat to the region, but as a threat to the American way of life. "As a result of many recent articles and editorials, a point of high visibility has now been temporarily achieved as regards the deplorable pro-Communist conditions prevailing [in Guatemala] and the potential dangers stemming there-from, both to the United States and the United Fruit Company," Bernays wrote in a memo dated July 23, 1951. He added, "[But it's] an axiom in government and politics that for publicity to be effective, it should be translated into an action program." He suggested three steps: "(A) a change to US ambassadorial and consular representation, (B) the imposition of congressional sanctions in this country against government aid to pro-Communist regimes, (C) US government subsidizing of research by disinterested groups like the Brookings Institute into various phases of the problem."

Who was Edward Bernays's real audience?

Whom did he need to sell?

It was, in my opinion, less the American people than the American government, and less the American government than a handful of men working for the CIA.

If the system had been working correctly, the Office of Strategic Services would have been disbanded at the end of the Second World War. That's how it had always happened in the past—when the war ends, the spies are defrocked and sent home. But the system was not working correctly or, more accurately, the war never really ended—it instead faded into another war, the cold war, the way, in a disco, one song bleeds into the next and the people never stop dancing.

In 1947, when Greece was threatened by a Communist takeover, President Harry Truman, who had planned to disband the OSS, turned it into the CIA instead, creating a new feature of national life, the civilian spy agency. (The only comparable institution had been Naval Intelligence, which grew out of the Spanish-American War.) The CIA was created by the National Security Act, which, in addition to making the organization permanent, changed its mission. Expanded it. Blew it up. Whereas the OSS had been authorized "to collect and analyze strategic information and to plan and conduct special operations," the CIA was given a mandate at once vague and ambitious. The new agency, Truman told Congress, will "help free peoples to maintain their free institutions and their national integrity against aggressive movements that seek to impose on them totalitarian regimes." In this way, the spy agency went from being a guy who knows stuff to a being a guy who does stuff about the stuff he knows. In this way, the agency, which had been ears and a brain, became ears and a brain and hands.

Remember what Pinocchio did as soon as Geppetto carved him a pair of hands?

He reached out and pinched the toymaker.

Allen Dulles, who served in the OSS in the Second World War, was the second man to head the CIA (Beetle Smith was the first). Before joining the government, Dulles worked various legal jobs, including as a counselor to United Fruit, in which capacity his brother John Foster Dulles also worked. Despite this, the banana lands remained something of terra incognita for the CIA. The OSS had not operated in South America, which had been under the jurisdiction of the FBI. When planning operations in the region, which became increasingly important during the cold war, the CIA had just one useful model: the banana companies, which had been behaving like spy and paramilitary agencies on the isthmus for generations. Some experts consider Zemurray's overthrow of the Honduran government a model for almost all the CIA missions that followed. In 1911, Sam deployed many tactics that would become standard procedure for clandestine operations: the hired guerrilla band, the phony popular leader, the subterfuge that convinces the elected politician he is surrounded when there are really no more than a few hundred guys out there. Like the CIA, Zemurray did a lot with a little because that's the best way to leave no fingerprints—and because a little is all he had.

It was, in fact, hard to distinguish United Fruit from the CIA in those years. The organizations shared personnel as well as equipment and intelligence. Throughout the Guatemala affair, the CIA used United Fruit ships to smuggle money, men, and guns. When the CIA's funding fell short of its budget, U.F. made up the difference. After all, the organizations had a common goal: to drive anyone who threatened the status quo off the isthmus. It did not take much to convince the CIA that Jacobo Arbenz was a threat. The agency was founded with just such situations in mind. "As long as Khrushchev or his successors use their subversive assets to promote 'wars of liberation'—which means . . . any overt or covert action calculated to bring down a non-Communist regime," Allen Dulles explained later, "the West should be prepared to meet the threat."

The CIA began operating in Guatemala in the early 1950s, cultivating dissidents and smuggling weapons aboard the Great White Fleet. Guns and bombs were shipped to Nicaragua in boxes marked AGRICULTURAL EQUIPMENT. Men working for the dictator Anastasio Somoza (FDR: "He's a son of a bitch, but he's our son of a bitch") loaded the weapons onto banana mules and walked them across the border to Guatemala. There were other efforts, too, including a failed attempt to bribe Arbenz, to pay him from a Swiss bank account to moderate his policies. Truman put a stop to all such covert programs. In his final years as president, he seemed to become alarmed by his creation, by this rogue Pinocchio, which, given feet as well as hands, ears, and eyes, increasingly operated on its own initiative.

The situation escalated in 1953, when Dwight Eisenhower became president. (U.F.'s chief obstacle had not been Arbenz, but Truman.)

Eisenhower's policy was more aggressive. Whereas Truman pledged to contain the Communists, Eisenhower promised to confront them. He called the policy "rollback." He reexamined the Guatemala situation soon after he arrived in the White House. Eisenhower gave the go-ahead for Guatemala in August 1953, at a meeting of something called the 10/2 Committee. Operation Success would replace the Arbenz government, defeating communism on the isthmus. The go-ahead did not make the overthrow inevitable—exit ramps were built in along the way, in case Arbenz buckled or things changed—but the long black train had left the station.

Soon after Operation Success was green-lighted, Tommy Corcoran, who served as Zemurray's go-between with the CIA, met with a member of the 10/2 Committee named Albert Haney. U.F. then began funneling money to agents working on Guatemala. "We always had to be careful," Corcoran said later. "We had to know what was going on but we couldn't [seem to] be in on it because if the plan failed, this could hurt us. . . . The Fruit Company didn't refuse to tell the CIA what it thought, but it couldn't afford to let itself be caught."

By then, there was a perfect model for the overthrow of Arbenz: Operation Ajax, in which CIA agents deposed the prime minister of Iran, Mohammed Mossadegh, after Mossadegh nationalized oil fields belonging to British corporations, specifically British Petroleum. Approved by Eisenhower at the urging of John Foster Dulles, Operation Ajax returned the shah of Iran to power. The success of this operation, carried off as the overthrow of Arbenz was being planned, must have encouraged the 10/2 Committee. It suddenly seemed so easy. It was, in fact, a near-exact parallel. Just cross out the old names and write in the new ones: bananas instead of oil, U.F. instead of B.P. (Like Ajax, Operation Success would be a military coup disguised as a popular revolt.)

Command of Operation Success was offered to Kermit Roosevelt Jr. (Teddy's grandson), who had led Ajax. Roosevelt gave it a pass, later saying he came to fear the hubristic mood of the Eisenhower administration. Describing John Foster Dulles in a debriefing, Roosevelt wrote, "His eyes were gleaming; he seemed to be purring like a giant cat. Clearly he was not only enjoying what he was hearing, but my instincts told me that he was planning [something]."

Backroom control of Operation Success was given to Tracy Barnes (Yale '34), who tapped a number of other agents to participate, including E. Howard Hunt (Brown '40), who chronicled the mission in *Undercover*. The first order of business was finding a replacement for Arbenz, a dissident with roots in the country who could be plugged into the engine after the defective piece was removed, à la Manuel Bonilla. Estranged Guatemalan military men and exiles were interviewed. Among the early favorites was Miguel Ydígoras Fuentes, a general who opposed Arbenz in the presidential election. In his book *My War with Communism*, Ydígoras Fuentes recalled a visit to his house by three men—two agents from the CIA and an executive of the United Fruit Company. The agents promised to make Ydígoras Fuentes president of Guatemala if he agreed to purge the Communists and restore United Fruit's property, among other things. The general turned down the offer, calling the terms "abusive and inequitable." He said it would seem like a naked takeover by the banana company.

The CIA eventually selected Carlos Castillo Armas, a thirty-nine-year-old disaffected officer in the Guatemalan military living in exile in Honduras. Because he agreed to all the conditions and because, according to Hunt, he "had that good Indian look . . . , which was great for the people." What's more, Castillo Armas had an interesting biography, always a helpful distraction for the media. (If you don't want them to find the truth, give them a better story.) Here was a poor Indian who found his calling in the military, a religious man who opposed communism because it was godless. In 1950, Castillo Armas led a group of soldiers against Arévalo. He was defeated and sixteen of his men were killed, himself among them. Or so it seemed. While being dragged across a field to the cemetery, he moaned. He was taken to a hospital, put back together with string and glue, tried for treason, sentenced to death. He escaped six months later, just two days before he was to be executed, slipping out of prison through an abandoned tunnel of the International Railways of Central America, which had been founded by Minor Keith, whose dream was to build a train from New York to Tierra del Fuego. Think about it! Here was Keith, the former vice president of U.F., collaborating through the ages, with Zemurray, providing the tunnel that saves the general who overthrows the president and restores the banana land. Castillo Armas went to Colombia, then Honduras, where he took many jobs, eventually finding steady work as a salesman in a furniture store, which is where the CIA tracked him down in 1953.

He was flown to Florida, then driven to a CIA base in a palmetto grove, where he sat with the clean-cut young men running Operation Success. The outlines of the plan were explained: Castillo Armas would be placed at the head of a liberation movement invented by the CIA, given $3 million in cash, guns, grenades, and, at the right time, technical and air support. If he needed more guns, these would come from the United Fruit Company. Castillo Armas would train his army on island bases in Lake Managua, Nicaragua. A handful of American pilots were meanwhile stationed in Puerto Cabezas, Nicaragua, the same strip later used during the Bay of Pigs invasion. CIA operatives were scattered among a dozen locations, in camps and safe houses, where they prepared the psychological tricks crucial to Operation Success. Exiled Guatemalan newspapermen wrote fake stories that warned of the swelling ranks of the rebel army; printers made up flyers to be dropped from airplanes in the first hours of the war; engineers recorded sound effects—Hunt called them "terror broadcasts"—to be played during the invasion. Panicked newsmen, terrified crowds, exploding bombs—the same sort of tricks Orson Welles used during his *War of the Worlds* radio drama.

Equally important was the part played by John Foster Dulles's State Department. Meetings of the Organization of the American States, discussions at the UN, American calls for investigation and sanction. Weapon sales to Guatemala were banned. At Dulles's insistence, Eisenhower replaced his ambassador to Guatemala (just as Bernays wanted) with John Peurifoy, who arrived in Guatemala City in late 1953 with a single mission: convince Jacobo Arbenz that he has just one more chance to moderate.

Peurifoy, who had become the American ambassador to Greece after that country's civil war, dressed in gaudy neckties, loud sports jackets, and candy-colored slacks. He was a specialist, a symbol as much as a diplomat. His coming heralded the end of a regime. If he behaved like a man trying to prove something, it's because he was. When Joseph McCarthy made his famous speech in Wheeling, West Virginia, claiming the State Department was filled with Communists, it was a smear of Peurifoy, who was State's head of personnel. He cabled Mc-Carthy asking for the names: if he did not trust the State Department with such information, wrote Peurifoy, McCarthy should at least give the names to the FBI. McCarthy never acknowledged the cable and accused the State Department of covering up instead. In the years that followed, Peurifoy was a man in search of vindication. Whether he was in Athens or Guatemala City, he seemed determined to prove he was the fiercest Communist fighter in the world.

A few weeks after Peurifoy arrived in Guatemala, Arbenz invited the ambassador and his wife, Betty Jane, to the official residence for dinner. It was the only time the men would ever meet. The meal, later known as the six-hour dinner, was a decisive encounter. I could go into great detail setting the scene—it was, for all the talk of the peasant ethos of the regime, a palace affair—but I believe it enough to set the names of the principals side by side. John and Betty Jane Peurifoy seated across from Jacobo Arbenz Guzmán and María Cristina Villanova Castro.

The dinner started with cocktails just after eight p.m. By the time Ambassador Peurifoy and his wife stood to leave, it was two in the morning. Arbenz did most of the talking. It was as if he had just this one chance to state his grievance. Did he talk too much? Of course he did. He was like one of those James Bond villains who give away every detail because they know, just know, they've brought it off. It was not only the topic of conversation that bothered Peurifoy—it was the manner. No matter the subject, Arbenz always found his way back to the United Fruit Company, whose railroads are greased with blood and whose ships run on burning souls. The ambassador objected, refuted, argued, scoffed, and bickered with the president and the president's wife as Betty Jane sat quietly.

According to Flora Lewis, who profiled Peurifoy in *The New York Times Magazine*, the ambassador tried "to make the Guatemalan Government see that whether it whipped or embraced the United Fruit Company, the United States cared supremely about only one thing—ousting Communists from positions of control."

Peurifoy was supposed to figure out whether Arbenz was in league with the Communists, was a Communist, or was just a dupe. By the end of the evening, with the black sky glowering over the spires of the capital, he was more certain than ever. "Peurifoy came away convinced that, far from being an unwilling and unwitting tool of the Communists, Arbenz was firmly established as the determined leader, not the follower, of developments in Guatemala," Lewis wrote.

Peurifoy got back to the embassy at two thirty. By three, he was at his desk, writing his report. Addressed to John Foster Dulles, it would be passed from the State Department to the CIA to the White House. A five-page memo sent by secure cable, the report chronicled the dinner with Arbenz. "The President stated that the problem in this country is one between the Fruit Company and the Government," wrote Peurifoy. "He went into a long dissertation giving the history of the Fruit Company from 1904; and since then, he complains, they have paid no taxes to the Government. He said that today when the Government has a budget of $70 million to meet, the Fruit Company contributes approximately $150,000. This is derived solely from the one-cent tax applied to each stem of bananas which is exported. . . .

"If Arbenz is not a Communist," Peurifoy added, "he will certainly do until one comes along."

You can read this last sentence in two ways. Either the way Peurifoy probably intended, which is jaunty, full of attitude—hey, this guy is trouble—or you can deconstruct it, thus seeing what the ambassador was really saying, even if he did not realize it: *Arbenz is NOT a Communist, but let's treat him like one anyway.*

Peurifoy ended the memo with a bit of wee-hour lyricism that was picked up and quoted in diplomatic circles: "The candle is burning slowly and surely, and it is only a matter of time before the large American interests will be forced out [of Guatemala] completely."

If you want to fight a preemptive war, you should probably have a casus belli, a triggering episode or event—best if it can be photographed—that you can point out to your public and say, *This is why!* In Guatemala, it was a shipload of military equipment sent from Czechoslovakia but seized by the U.S. Navy before it could land in Puerto Barrios. The ship, a Swedish vessel called the *Alfhem*, had falsified its papers and switched flags at various ports, but the CIA tracked its every move. Its holds were inspected, its contents seized: bombs, rifles, ammunition, antitank mines, and artillery that seemed to prove Soviet support of the Guatemalan government. Arbenz said the *Alfhem* proved only that no other nation would sell him weapons, because of the American-led embargo. He said he needed weapons to fight the imminent invasion of Castillo Armas and his army. "Arbenz's emissaries had been busy behind the Iron Curtain procuring large quantities of Czech arms and munitions," wrote E. Howard Hunt. "This development was watched with apprehension, for if the armaments reached Arbenz before we were able to mount an invasion, the odds would be even more heavily weighted against Castillo and his men."

Never mind that the above passage shows the invasion was fixed *before* the guns were seized. Never mind, too, that most of the weapons were junk that never would have worked. Spread on the deck of the seized ship, the guns proved the perfect photographic evidence, whipping the American public into a frenzy. As Bernays said, the masses are led by symbols, the most primary of which—you can get as Freudian with this as you want—is the steely shaft of a Commie's pistol.

On April 26, 1954, President Eisenhower, addressing Congress, said, "The Reds are in control in Guatemala, and they are trying to spread their influence to San Salvador as a first step to breaking out of Guatemala to other South American countries."

On June 15, the CIA was given the final go-ahead for Operation Success. "I want you all to be damn good and sure you succeed," Eisenhower told Allen Dulles and a few others. "When you commit the flag, you commit it to win."

Che Guevara had arrived in Guatemala City less than a year before. He walked for hours, talked all night. He described it as the place where a person could breathe the "most democratic air in Latin America." It was here that he met the tough young Cubans, the leaders of Fidel Castro's army, whose cause he would take as his own. Castro was in prison in Isle of Pines, Cuba, but his soldiers had been granted refuge by President Arbenz. In these men, Guevara found the perfect mix of theory and action, ideology and bravado. He moved into their apartments, can be seen in photos sharing sleeping bags and meals with the exiled army. In this way, the seizure of U.F.'s land did more than damage the ledger books of the fruit company. It lit a fuse that burned through the continent. It gave Guevara a cause. It was the Cubans who first called him "Che," which means something like "Hey!" As in, *Hey, Guevara, let's go overthrow the Ubico flies!*

Sam was in New Orleans, monitoring the action from afar. Each morning, he read the papers and met with underlings. Each afternoon, he got the news from Bernays and Corcoran and others, took it all in, then offered ideas and suggestions of his own, saying, *Fine, fine, fine.*

Operation Success was not a war—it was a shadow play, a farce. It was three weeks of smoke and mirrors, flash and noise. It was the United States making a point about communism and Eisenhower drawing a contrast with Truman. It was the United Fruit Company getting back what it had lost.

It began with a couple of Second World War fighter props piloted by retired air force men flying low and loud, dropping smoke bombs and paper flyers (*GET OUT!*) on Guatemala City. This was followed by strafing runs, bombs. If you saw three planes in the sky, you were seeing the entire rebel air force. Then came the psychological tricks meant to confuse the people and terrify Arbenz and his loyalists. Hidden speakers boomed out the sound of guns and shells. Fake newscasts filled the entire bandwidth, some calling for the overthrow of the dictator, some claiming the dictator had already been overthrown. Others heralded the arrival of Castillo Armas and his men in the capital, where they were being greeted by jubilant crowds.

Arbenz went on the radio to explain the nature of the struggle. It's not about ideology, he said, it's about money. It's not about the United States, it's about El Gringo, the Banana Man. "In whose name have they carried out these barbaric acts?" he asked. "What is their banner? We know very well. They have used the pretext of anti-communism. The truth is very different. The truth is to be found in the financial interests of the fruit company."

Castillo Armas, having mustered his army on a U.F. banana plantation in Honduras, marched across the border into Guatemala. His soldiers and weapons were carried on U.F. trains and U.F. boats. He met little resistance. It was less a war than a walk in the country, afternoons of daisy picking, a parade in the mountains. Guatemala 1954 would be the last of the easy overthrows. Because the peasants did not want war, because the government believed it could not win, because Arbenz was willing to go farther than anyone had gone but was still not willing to go all the way.

Arbenz aged ten years in the last five days. Retreating to the presidential palace, he spent these hours in a drunken stupor, wandering the halls, muttering about gringos. He was disheveled and could not sleep. Now and then, he went on the radio. "Our enemies are led by the arch-traitor Armas," who is leading a "heterogeneous Fruit Company expeditionary force" against the country, he said, his words obscured by the static of CIA jamming. "Our crime is having enacted an agrarian reform which affected the interests of the United Fruit Company."

He was buffeted by news, some of it real, some of it fake. He could no longer tell the difference. The cord that ran from his soul to his brain, which had always been taut as a guitar string, snapped with a twang. He was not sure if he should surrender, or retreat to the hills, or take his own life. He was not sure anyone would notice or care. That was the beauty of psychological warfare—it devoured the enemy from within. He ordered the army to open the arsenals and give the guns to the peasants. The leaders of the army, aristocrats who feared the gringo less than they feared the mob, refused. When the officers stopped responding to Arbenz's orders, he knew it was time to go. On June 27, 1954, he addressed his people for the last time. "For fifteen days a cruel war against Guatemala has been under way," he said on the radio. "The United Fruit Company, in collaboration with the governing circles of the United States, is responsible for what is happening to us."

He resigned as soon as he got off the air, turned control of the government over to General Carlos Díaz, crossed the street to the Mexican embassy, and asked for asylum. By that time, Castillo Armas was on the outskirts of Guatemala City.

John Foster Dulles spoke to the American people a few days later. He said he wanted to explain the news from the isthmus, but he seemed less concerned with the progress of the war than with disassociating the Eisenhower administration from the United Fruit Company. Arbenz had clearly hit a nerve. "The Guatemalan government and Communist agents throughout the world have persistently attempted to obscure the real issue . . . by claiming that the United States is only interested in protecting American business," said Dulles. "We regret that there have been disputes between the Guatemalan government and the United Fruit Company. . . . But this issue is relatively unimportant."

John Foster Dulles called John Peurifoy.

Here is what he said: "Magnificent job!"

According to E. Howard Hunt, Operation Success marked "the first time, since the Spanish Civil War, [that] a Communist government had been overthrown."

When Arbenz arrived at the airport the next morning, he was an emotional wreck, a physical ruin. He flinched when trucks backfired, blinked timidly in the blue terminal light. Before being allowed to board a plane for Mexico, he was stripped to his underwear and marched before a crowd of reporters: the flashbulbs went *POP, POP, POP!* It was a final humiliation, the psychological warriors saying goodbye, a pointless bit of cruelty that set the tone for the rest of a desultory life. The wanderings of Jacobo Arbenz, his life in exile, symbolize the fate of the isthmus, squeezed between the ideologues and the banana men.

He landed in Mexico with his wife and children. His daughter Arabella was his favorite. She gave him comfort. Whatever he suffered, he told himself he was suffering it for her. Life was unpleasant for him in the country. Mexico was an ally of the United States—no one wanted him there. After less than a year, he set off again, this time for Switzerland. He lived in one of those mountain towns that have long served as refuges for deposed royalty. The Swiss authorities said he could stay only if he renounced his Guatemalan citizenship. He refused and continued on to Paris, where he lived on the Right Bank, went for walks, and drank heavily in cafés, another exile muttering to himself. He was shadowed by the police. Arabella loved Paris, but her father could not live with the constant surveillance. He continued on to Czechoslovakia, where he believed he would be welcomed as a martyr. The Czechs did not want him, either. It was clear from his first days in Prague. It was said the Czechs were afraid he would demand a refund for their faulty weapons. He went to Russia, where he lived in Moscow while his children attended a school for foreigners four hundred miles away. Here, too, he was followed. In the West, he was the revolution. In the East, he was the man who could not be controlled, the fool who had taken the rhetoric seriously. That's why I call him a symbol: he was like the isthmus itself, a small territory overhung and underhung by huge continents, fought over, then abandoned.

By being in Russia, he seemed to confirm what he would always deny: that he was a Communist and had been playing a game, that all the talk of the fruit company was nothing but a tactic. In fact, he was in Russia only because no other country would have him. He hated the climate there; he was always cold. He longed for the eucalyptus and the tropical shower, the colors of the Caribbean. He appealed to the leader of every nation in Latin America and was finally accepted in Uruguay, on the condition that he neither lecture, publish, teach, nor work. He lived in Montevideo from 1957 to 1960.

When Castro triumphed in Cuba in 1959, it seemed that the wandering of Jacobo Arbenz was finally over. These were, after all, the same Cubans whom Arbenz had sheltered in Guatemala City; the same Cubans who once regarded Arbenz as a hero. Though he was indeed greeted by a throng in Havana, life in Cuba was not as he expected. Arbenz was portrayed less as a hero or a precursor than as a cautionary tale, a failure: because he resigned when he should have stayed and fought, because he was scared and confused at the end, because he turned to the bottle when he should have gone into the hills. In Cuba, Arbenz was considered a perfect example of how not to behave.

When he told his family they were moving to Cuba, Arabella refused. She was tired of wandering from city to city, of living in backwaters without culture. There was a terrible fight. When the family left for Havana, she went by herself to Paris instead. She would become a model, an actress, a movie star. She was twenty, a really beautiful girl. She appeared in just one film, *Un Alma Pura*, as the title character, Claudia. She fell in love with Jaime Bravo, the most famous matador in the world. A master with the cape, a man of close passes. Bravo was known for having affairs with starlets. His romance with Arabella Arbenz was legendary, stormy, filled with threats and scenes. The couple was a tabloid sensation.

In September 1965, Arabella, twenty-five years old, followed Bravo to Colombia, where he was performing in the corridas. The couple got into a fight in a restaurant in Bogotá. Arabella stormed out and came back with a gun. She pointed it at Bravo, who put up his hands, saying, "No, Arabella." She then put the gun in her mouth and pulled the trigger.

She was buried in Mexico City. Jacobo Arbenz was given special permission to attend the funeral. He was devastated, threadbare, wire and bone. He leaned over the coffin as it was lowered into the ground and whispered, *"Hasta pronto, mi hijita."* He moved back to Mexico City in 1971, where he could walk the holy ground where his daughter was buried. He was drunk all the time, wasted on pills, tortured by regret. On January 27, 1971, he was found drowned in the bathtub of his hotel room in Mexico City, fifty-eight years old, a bottle of whiskey at his side.

Castillo Armas fulfilled his part of the bargain soon after he secured power. His soldiers tracked down and arrested or killed the military officers and politicians who championed the Guatemalan Revolution. He rounded up or chased away the ideological vagabonds who streamed into the country in the days of delirium that followed Decree 900. He had soon established a police state, imposing the sort of lockdown that would make the rise of another Arbenz impossible. He abolished political parties and trade unions, closed newspapers and banned books he considered dangerous, including the collected works of Fyodor Dostoyevsky and Victor Hugo. He took care of the fruit company, stripping U.F. workers of their right to bargain collectively and shuttering the Banana Workers Federation. Seven of the labor organizers who had been attempting to unionize the banana field hands—there were scores of them; they gave the plantation managers fits—were found dead in Guatemala City. By 1955, the hundreds of thousands of acres seized from the company had been returned.

Rarely does a skirmish end so decisively, with the disputed issues resolved in such a satisfactory fashion. It was the most lopsided victory in the history of United Fruit. Too lopsided. Did Zemurray realize the danger his company faced, not as a result of its losses but as a result of its wins? Which had been too splashy, too much of a good thing. As Guatemala settled back into its prerevolutionary slumber, U.F. found itself in the position of the fisherman who had gone out to catch a trout for dinner but hooked a shark instead.

Sam should have known, must have known. The coup in Guatemala violated a rule he had practiced all his life: do not draw unnecessary attention. In the days that followed the defeat of Arbenz, American newspapermen and government officials seemed to wake from a dream, filled with questions: Just who was Arbenz? Was he an actual threat? Was the Soviet Union really involved? Where's the proof? Whose interests were served? Those of the taxpayer or those of the United Fruit Company? Some reporters who traveled on junkets with Edward Bernays felt betrayed. According to Thomas McCann, "Our willingness to exaggerate the Communists' importance and to create incidents—coupled with the willingness of the American press to amplify our cries of wolf throughout the United States—led not only to the collapse of the Arbenz regime, but created such a subsequent environment in the United States that, when a real Communist threat actually did appear three or four years later in Cuba, the American public and some members of the press were unwilling to believe the truth."

Guatemala was a hinge moment, an event that first appeared a great success for the company—the door swings open—but later proved a terrible misfortune—the door slams shut. At the time of the coup, U.F. led its industry by every measure: in profits, market share, volume (and it wasn't even close). Within a generation, it would trail Standard Fruit in nearly every category. The overthrow had all the ingredients of irony: meant to prevent the establishment of a Communist beachhead in the hemisphere, it would help create just such a beachhead in Cuba. Meant to make Guatemala friendly for the company, it would engender such hostility that the company was eventually forced to abandon the isthmus altogether.

Che Guevara volunteered to fight soon after the first plane appeared in the sky over Guatemala City. Turned away by the army, he tried to organize a group of friends to travel to the front. Few would go. Lesson number one: the cowardice of the people is figured in the equation of the Banana Man. "In Guatemala it was necessary to fight," he wrote, "but hardly anybody fought. It was necessary to resist, but hardly anybody wanted to do that." According to Jon Lee Anderson, author of *Che Guevara: A Revolutionary Life*, Guevara spent the war patrolling

Guatemala City as part of a civilian guard, checking doors, making sure all lights were out during air raids. Shells fell most nights. It was the first time Guevara, who was twenty-six, had come under fire. Lesson number two: he loved it. In a letter to his girlfriend, he said he was "ashamed for having as much fun as a monkey."

Castillo Armas and his soldiers swept into the capital in June 1954. The streets were chaotic, confused. Guevara, who assumed Arbenz would retreat with his loyalists to the hills—"Without a doubt, Colonel Arbenz is a guy with guts," he wrote, "and he is ready to die in his post"—was shocked when the president fled to Mexico.

Guevara spent several weeks stumbling from here to there, defeated, depressed, unsure what to do or where to go. He came to despise Arbenz and the members of his generation. There is nothing more pathetic than a hero who has failed. The nature of the Cuban Revolution was, to a degree, determined in these hours. The lessons taken from Guatemala would be remembered in Havana: the danger of weakness; the illusion of compromise; the need to kill the enemy when he is down—destroy the remnants, finish the job. The gringo must believe you're crazy enough to go all the way, to pull the pillars of the temple down on your own head, which, translated into the language of the cold war, was Castro telling Khrushchev to *fire the goddamn nukes!* Che Guevara said it was Guatemala that taught him "to go to the roots of the question and decapitate in one stroke those in power and the thugs of those in power."

"'Moderation' is another one of the terms that colonial agents like to use," he told a group of students. "All those who are afraid, or who are considering some form of treason, they are moderates."

Guevara was arrested in the last hours of the war. "Marching overland, the troops of Castillo Armas seized control of the capital and captured Arbenz and his followers—including an asthmatic Argentine medical student and Communist camp follower named Ernesto Che Guevara," wrote E. Howard Hunt. "Among the Guatemalan victors there was much sentiment for dealing summary justice to them all, but a C.I.A. man on the spot dissuaded Castillo from initiating what might well have turned into a nationwide bloodbath. Stripped and searched at the airport, Arbenz, Guevara and their followers were allowed to board planes into exile. Guevara was granted political asylum in

Mexico, where he soon joined the partisans of Cuban rabble-rouser Fidel Castro."

Douglas Hallett, who worked for Charles Colson, Richard Nixon's special counsel, recalled the following, which he heard from Colson: "When [Hunt] was a C.I.A. agent presiding over the 1954 overthrow of President Arbenz of Guatemala, he had held a group of prisoners on the airstrip just as he was about to leave the country. He decided to show mercy and freed them. A few years later, he learned that one of the prisoners he let go was Che Guevara, the Cuban revolutionary; he said that had been enough to convince him never to allow himself to become compassionate again."

Hunt later called freeing Guevara, when he should have put a bullet in his head, the regret of his life.

Both sides took the same lesson from the war: compassion is weakness, mercy a disease. You must be willing to go all the way.

What happened to Che Guevara?

Well, you know.

He joined up with Fidel Castro in Cuba, fought and won, spoke at the United Nations, walked around New York City, stayed at the Hotel Theresa in Harlem, was photographed wearing a beret. This photograph was later silkscreened onto a T-shirt. (Approximately one-third of the people you went to college with purchased this T-shirt.) In 1966, having grown restless, he decided to go to Bolivia to rejoin the universal war. He believed the liberation of South America was at hand. Castro hosted a drunken goodbye dinner. The comrades ate pig and drank beer. At dawn, as the sun was rising over Havana, Guevara got in the back of his car and told his chauffeur, "Drive, dammit!" He traveled in disguise. His passport identified him as Ramón Benítez, a sober man in glasses with heavy frames. In La Paz, he was introduced as Adolfo Mena González, a middle-aged economist from Uruguay. He took a picture of himself, in disguise, in the mirror of his hotel room. He resembles an academic gone to seed, in V-neck sweater and slacks. His cigar glows, wind dances in the hotel curtains.

He hiked into the hills, where he took charge of a small rebel force. He fought battles. He was under fire. Was he as happy as a monkey?

Not when he was captured, that's for sure. He cursed with imagination. He was skinny with a long beard and looked like a mystic or carnival freak. A CIA agent flew in to interrogate the prisoner. Many torturous ideological discussions followed. The Bolivians decided to execute him. "It's better like this," said Guevara. "I never should have been captured alive."

"I no longer hated him," the American intelligence agent said. "His moment of truth had come, and he was conducting himself like a man. He was facing his death with courage and grace."

Che Guevara was killed on October, 9, 1967, his last words recorded by the CIA: "Tell Fidel he will soon see a triumphant revolution in America, and tell my wife to remarry and try to be happy."

Crucial players in the Guatemala affair had died by then: John Peurifoy, driving his Thunderbird in Thailand, where he'd taken a posting; Castillo Armas on a street in Guatemala City on July 27, 1957. He was walking to dinner with his wife. An assassin shot him seven times. The death of Armas launched an era of civil war that persisted for generations in Guatemala, brutalizing the nation and leaving two hundred thousand dead. In October 1995, as life seemed to return to normal, Arbenz's body was exhumed and flown to Guatemala City, where it was buried beneath a shrine as a huge crowd looked on.

19

Backlash

As the details of Operation Success became public, the Eisenhower administration faced withering criticism. Reporters began to make connections. Allen Dulles, John Foster Dulles, Thomas Cabot—all had worked for United Fruit before they worked for the United States. Unless, of course, they never stopped working for United Fruit. Eisenhower promised to investigate. Then, five days after Arbenz abdicated—five days!—the Justice Department filed a massive lawsuit against United Fruit, charging the company with violating the antitrust laws. (Just what Zemurray feared when the State Department pushed him to merge with his biggest competitor.) The White House denied any connection between Operation Success and the legal action, but the point seemed clear: the Eisenhower administration was demonstrating its independence from the banana men. According to Tommy Corcoran, "Dulles began the antitrust suit against UFCo just to prove he wasn't involved with the company."

Was Eisenhower punishing United Fruit for duping him, or was he sacrificing the company with his own reelection in mind? To know this, you must determine the following: Who was in control in Guatemala? Had United Fruit manipulated the CIA, or had the company been used—a tool in a cold war? Most historians long believed the coup was staged at the behest of the company, as it was no longer politically feasible for the banana men to field a mercenary army of their own. But some suggest the trickery went the other way. Marcelo Bucheli, a professor at the University of Illinois and the author of *Bananas and Business*, told me that it was most likely the CIA that used United

Fruit: for its money, its ships, its railroads, its know-how. Used it to fight a battle in the cold war, then dumped it when things got too hot. In this scenario, the antitrust suit was the last act of a covert operation: the spies severing connection to their co-conspirator as the local cops move in. *No, officer, I've never met this man before.*

The Justice Department claimed United Fruit operated by monopoly in Guatemala. The company did not refute the charge but instead cited the Oliver Wendell Holmes Supreme Court opinion from early in the century to argue that American courts had no jurisdiction, as all the practices in question occurred overseas. Edward Bernays was given the assignment of swaying public opinion. He planted stories in newspapers around the country and pressed for editorials that asked why the very company that helped drive the Communists from Central America was being targeted by prosecutors with no understanding of how the world actually works. We should be thanking God for the fruit company, not breaking it up.

But times had changed. The old magic was gone. Whereas the company had once been considered the tip of the spear, the cutting edge of American capitalism, staffed with clean-cut men bringing civilization to the waste places, it had since come to be seen as a relic, a leftover from the colonial world destroyed in the Second World War. It was an image problem that became acute. U.F. was increasingly considered an embarrassment, a throwback to the ugliest days of old lamplit America. Thomas McCann recalled a plantation manager, responding to a suggestion that banana workers be given more freedom, saying, "Shit, man, suppose Leroy don't want to carry the ball? He don't want to—what're you going to do?"

The antitrust suit was settled in 1958, when U.F. agreed to sign a consent decree. While admitting no wrongdoing, the company promised to establish, within ten years, a competitor at least one-third its own size in Guatemala. To accomplish this, U.F. promised to sell 33 percent of its fields and facilities to an "independent fruit company." This would mean the end of United Fruit as it had been envisioned first by Preston, then by Keith, then by Zemurray. It took a generation to work out the details. Not wanting to advantage its main competitor, Standard Fruit—later purchased by Dole—United Fruit eventually sold the remainder of its properties in Guatemala to Del Monte, then a distant third in the trade. Within a few years of the sale, United Fruit had fallen out of first place in market share, a position it had held since the start of the century. The lead went back and forth after that, but United Fruit never regained its dominance. In 1950, the company cleared $66 million in profit. By 1955, that number had fallen to $33.5 million. In 1960, United Fruit earned just over $2 million. The story that began in the right-of-way along the Costa Rican railroad had come to an end.

Brown

20

What Remains

While no one was looking, Samuel Zemurray had grown painfully, shockingly, bitterly old. It's like this: you leave the house in the morning and are young and fit and strong, and you whistle as you walk down Magazine Street, then turn a corner, and *bang*, run right into your own decrepit seventy-eight-year-old self going the other way.

He retired from the banana trade. For the last time. He left Boston forever. He left New York forever. He left Honduras, Costa Rica, Guatemala, Cuba, Ecuador, Colombia forever. He was like a man wandering though a mansion, closing doors. At a certain age, no matter which direction you walk, you are walking away.

Sam had one of those seemingly endless careers that span eras: in the beginning, it was the Wild West of banana cowboys and mercenaries raising hell on the isthmus, the America of Owen Wister and Bret Harte; in the end, it was the CIA and the triumph of the corporation and the air-conditioned nightmare, the America of Clive Cussler and Tom Clancy. He did not just live through this change, which is the rise of America told another way—he helped make it happen. Perhaps he's best understood as a last player in the drama of Manifest Destiny, a man who lived as if the wild places of the hemisphere were his for the taking. It was in this spirit that he built his company into a colossus, so big its size became the most important fact of life on the isthmus. The United Fruit Company's dominance in Central America made a mockery of regional governments, and was humiliating and infantilizing in ways that were hardly understood at the time. It was worse than the old European colonialism, which at least came with a sense of obligation. Those who lived in the banana lands were ruled not by foreign nationals bringing "civilization" and the word of God but by businessmen who looked on their fields with a cold moneymaking precision.

Sam did not see himself this way, of course. He considered himself a bearer of modern industry, creating jobs and wealth in a place deprived of both. But there is the world as you see it and the world as it is. It was not all Zemurray's fault: he had inherited a machine built by his predecessors. If he had questioned the workings of this machine, he would have been a great man, but he was not a great man; he was a complicated man blessed with great energy and ideas. He did not question the machine because he did not understand what it was doing to the people who lived in its gears. When things got so hot the truth could not be missed, he saw himself, for one terrible moment, as he was seen: a pirate, a puppet master, a banana king. In an instant, the work of your life reveals itself to be the opposite of what you had always considered it. He reacted with a burst of activity. He tried to change his legacy at the end of the game—built roads and hospitals, train depots, water systems—but it was too late. The story of United Fruit had been written. "I feel guilty about some of the things we did," he said. "All we cared about was dividends. Well, we can't do business that way today. We have learned that what's best for the countries we operate in is best for the company. Maybe we can't make the people love us, but we will make ourselves so useful to them that they will want us to stay." These are the words of a card shark who has realized, at dawn, that the power has shifted, that the pictures on the face cards have lost their meaning. The boss who dominated for decades became a person at the mercy of historical forces, the will of the people, who had hardly figured in his calculations.

Sam Zemurray has two legacies: as a leader in the business world of America, he was a stunning success, a pioneer, everything he considered himself; as a leader in Latin America, a man so powerful he became a political factor, his legacy is darker. Far darker. Regardless of his intentions, he aligned himself with the forces of reaction. As a man, he was admired, even respected—this had to do with his love for Honduras and its people. As the boss of United Fruit, he was abhorred.

Even now, years after the company as he knew it has ceased to exist, Hugo Chávez is denouncing El Pulpo. Many books about United Fruit give short shrift to Zemurray, though he was its body and its brain for twenty-five years, a lifetime in the corporate world. He is mentioned in passing, as a colorful character who once ruled banana land as Jeroboam once ruled the Kingdom of Israel. (We still find his seal on ancient coins in the ruins.) That's because, in the popular imagination, Zemurray was able to separate his legacy from that of United Fruit. An amazing feat. It's as if the company founded by Preston, Baker, and Keith were a monster that, once set loose, gobbled up everything in its way, even Sam the Banana Man.

In his final years, Zemurray liked to walk in Audubon Park, or linger in coffeehouses in the French Quarter, an old man with his buttermilk and *Times-Picayune*. He stood on the wharf watching the Mississippi River. The evening came slowly, a shade of blue at a time. The lights went on in Algiers, where African slaves were once kept in chains. The world is young but the history of man is long. His Parkinson's got worse. He was nothing but tremor. The planet was trying to shake him off. His thoughts were cloudy. He had lived so long and done so much and now he was tired. He had huge hands that became huge fists which he brought down on the table when he was frustrated, because the thought was there, but he couldn't dig it out. *Goddamn it, Sarah, is this how it's going to be?* He went to bed early. He stayed in bed late. He was a burned-out engine. Now and then, when you close your eyes in New Orleans as the rain drums on the roof, you feel as if you are back in the jungle, on the first day of your career, and this time you will do everything right.

Did Sam Zemurray have regrets?

He lived one of the great lives of his time. He devoured his years, consumed as much as he could reach. He was not as famous as many, but I would put his story beside the most heralded. He never recovered from the death of his son, but that was not a regret. It was a blow, suffered in the service of his country in a war.

If he had a regret, it might have been that he did not raise his children as Jews. Here was a man who lived every aspect of the Jewish experience in America. He came with the great influx from Eastern Europe, prospered with his times, was devastated by the war. He married a Jewish woman, belonged to a synagogue, said Kaddish for his dead. He was a Zionist. Israel was important to him, and he was important to Israel. And yet he did not teach his children or grandchildren to be Jewish—to marry Jews, raise Jews, worship as Jews, fret as Jews. And none of them did. I do not think Sam did this intentionally, or wanted it to happen. It was just one of the things that unfolded when he was away on the isthmus. He was too busy to pay attention, did not care enough to notice, until he was old and it was too late. His particular line diverged from the story of his people, has been swallowed by the freedom of America. I believe that was Zemurray's regret, the sadness of his final years. He accomplished everything, and let everything go.

Of course, this is just me imagining myself into the mind of a man I never met and can never really know. Perhaps I have it wrong. Perhaps it's merely a lack of imagination and courage that causes me to see the sheep gone astray as a tragedy. Perhaps neither confusion, regret, nor sadness waits beyond the Judean hills—perhaps it's Disneyland for the soul, utter fulfillment, total escape. In the end, Zemurray traded his ancient heritage for a place in the upper reaches of the establishment. As my grandfather would say, "The son of a bitch got away!" Perhaps this had been his goal from the beginning, a crucial aspect of his American dream. Perhaps Judaism, with its ancient past and dusty books and moral codes and stooped men in dim rooms, was a prison he longed to escape. Perhaps his work for Israel was merely a tax, the price of getting away. But I doubt it.

Let me explain in a Jewish way—with a story. I heard it from Marjorie Cowen at Tulane. When Zemurray was old, Sam Jr.'s children moved into the house at 2 Audubon Place, where they were raised by a nanny. One day, Zemurray, who did not know his grandchildren well, banged on the door of Sam III's room with his cane. The boy, twelve or thirteen, stood in the threshold. Zemurray studied him, then asked, "What religion are you, anyway?"

"Christian," said the boy.

Zemurray turned and went down the stairs, muttering.

By this time, Doris Zemurray Stone, Sam's daughter, with degrees from Radcliffe, had become a scholar of Mesoamerican art and culture. She moved to Costa Rica, where she lived on a plantation with her husband, Roger Thayer Stone. Doris was an ethnographer and anthropologist, an expert in the lost cultures of the isthmus, some centered in the very valleys Zemurray bought for a song, cleared, and planted. Is it ironic? Her tremendous work of memory and recovery was made possible by his tremendous work of amnesia and destruction. For Sam, the past was at best irrelevant, at worst a fantasy. He was a materialist. All we have and know is what you see today. For Doris Stone, the past mattered. It's like this: first conquer, then kill, then gather the artifacts and open a museum.

Doris and her husband had a child, Samuel Zemurray Stone, and he, too, became a scholar of Central American history. A member of the Princeton Class of 1954, Sam Stone published several books, including *The Heritage of the Conquistadors: Ruling Classes in Central America from Conquest to the Sandinistas* and *Telltale Stories from Central America: Cultural Heritage, Political Systems, and Resistance in Developing Countries*. It's strange to read Sam Stone's books about the isthmus. He wrote as if he had no connection to the story, as if every person gets a clean start. Some passages feel like condemnations of his own grandfather, the source of the wealth that made such musing possible. "Many outsiders continue to repeat that these countries need and want foreign investment," wrote Stone, who died in Costa Rica in 1996, "and the constant discord between the United Fruit Company . . . and most of the Central American governments passes almost unnoticed in the United States. . . . In spite of a variety of expressions of such sentiments, United States (and Japanese) corporations in Central America, due to the small size of the Isthmian countries, still aspire to become the biggest employers. Although they provide foreign exchange and create jobs, it hurts the Central American to make him feel he has not been capable of utilizing his own resources, and foreign interference in national politics adds insult to injury."

Sam Stone's most interesting theory regards the political dynamics of the region. Having traced the genealogies of powerful local leaders, he showed that the countries of Central America have always been ruled by a handful of families, each of which can trace its roots back to a conquistador who traveled with Cortés. Starting around 1910, these families, who long ruled in partnership with the military, began to be replaced by banana men, who used their wealth and influence to strike their own deals with the generals, overthrowing the aristocrats, becoming aristocrats themselves. Unlike the old families, the banana royalty had no roots in the region. In this way, the ancient regime was superseded by a band of capitalists, who got rich and got out, and whose only obligation was to the shareholders back in Boston or New Orleans. ("All we cared about was dividends.")

Sam Stone had two children, the great-granddaughters of Sam the Banana Man, whom they never knew: Alison Stone of El Salvador, who is on the board of Tulane, and Stephanie Stone Feoli, a historian of Latin American art, who lives in New Orleans, where I met her while working on this book. We talked in a coffee shop on the campus of Tulane. In her forties, slender and pretty, she did not have much to say about her great-grandfather—a few legends, a few myths, a general sense of him as a hero to some, a more complicated figure to others. Talking to her, you realize that Samuel Zemurray occupies a strange middle ground. He died a long time ago. There are very few people alive who knew him face-to-face. But he's not yet the true historical figure he will become when the last living witness is gone. There are four rungs: newly dead; dead but remembered; dead and all those who knew you dead; dead and all those who knew those who knew you dead. When I asked Stephanie Feoli about her great-grandfather's legacy, she told me it was too soon to tell. Everything that happens makes the past a different story. For Stephanie's daughter, her great-great-grandfather will be a relic, less known to her than the dead presidents of the United States. That's the way a living, breathing, jungle-clearing, government-toppling banana man turns into just another picture on the wall.

At the time of his death, Sam Jr. was married with two young children, Anne and Sam III. In the years that followed, the family evaporated. Anne went first, in a car crash. She was a young woman, newly married. It was another disaster piled on the shoulders of Sam Jr.'s widow, Margaret Thurston Pickering, who was fragile to begin with. She traveled in elite circles, flirting with madness. She served on the staff of Norbert Wiener, a storied scientist at MIT, and worked at *The Atlantic* as a manuscript reader. Her last address was the Robert B. Brigham Hospital in Boston, where she died in June 1968, at age fifty-four. Her obituary, which ran in the *Times* ("Mrs. Zemurray Jr., Widow of Major"), made no mention of her daughter, which struck me as sad. It was as if Anne Zemurray had never been born.

This left only Sam III, a little boy alone, the sole survivor. I have seen him in a picture that ran in *Life* in 1951, where he is posed with his sister and grandparents—Sarah and Sam—on a field in the Zemurray plantation. You look at this picture as if looking back at the past, the past not only of this family but also of the country and of the South: the boy at the feet of the tycoon, his grandmother and sister, the dogs, the stiff smiles, the mackinaw coats, the tall grass and oak trees. It's a vision from another world. I saw him again in a documentary about the house at 2 Audubon Place. Dignified and old, he looked distant and thoughtful. But the years in between are something of a mystery. Sam III's family was among the most notable in the South, but he drifted away.

When I tracked him down in Savannah, Georgia, where he has lived with his wife for many years, he was stewing over an NPR interview he had recently heard in which a historian described Samuel Zemurray in the worst terms. "Robber baron," that was the word that particularly galled Sam III. He repeated it as if stunned by the collision between his family narrative—Sam, the fish that ate the whale—and the public narrative that has taken shape over the years. At first, this made Sam III eager to talk to me. He would clarify, explain, set the record straight. We made plans, considered dates. I would fly down, sit on the porch, stay in a country motel, drive a rented Taurus to his house each morning, drink lemonade with mint leaf. Perhaps I would buy a seersucker suit. But as time went by, Sam III took longer and longer to return my calls, and I never could pin him down to a date. Then he stopped returning calls altogether. I left message after message, sent e-mail after e-mail.

I finally got a call from a relative of the Zemurrays. He had been in touch with the family and wanted to explain why Sam III had gone silent. This is from memory—I was in a hotel in Miami—so I won't use quotation marks, but here's the gist: Sam III and the people around him had decided it was not in his best interest to talk. Sam had suffered a lot of tragedy in his life—so many people around him had died—and in such a situation, the healthiest course is probably to avoid the past altogether.

Among other things, I had wanted to ask Sam III about the patriarch's heritage, and his work for Israel. Did any of this survive in the family, or was it like the skim on top of the pond that cooks off by eight a.m.?

When you ask why the Jews, of all the people of the ancient world, have persisted into modern times, you can come up with various reasons: maybe it's the power of the tradition, maybe it's the will of God, or maybe it's just that Jews had no choice, were locked in ghettos, confined to towns and professions where they had to marry other Jews. Even when the walls came down in Europe, Jews were hemmed in by prejudice and fear. But in America, where we're all mutts, Jews were offered real freedom: not only to worship and travel and work, but from history. Jews could be Jews in America, or they could stop being Jews, which, for many, turned out to be the ultimate emancipation.

To me, Sam Zemurray's life is the true story of the American dream—not only of the success but of the price paid for the ambition that led to that success. By the people of the isthmus, by the men who battled him in the Banana War, and by Zemurray himself. Did Sam really think he could get away without paying? He scaled the heights, but lost so much in the process—first his son; then his family, which came apart a sheet at a time. As Arthur Miller wrote in *The Price*, "If you don't understand the viewpoint, you don't understand the price." For Zemurray, that viewpoint, to some degree, would always remain the world as seen from the window of the farmhouse in Russia, where every Jew knew that without a family, without a legacy, without a son to say Kaddish over you in the end, even the greatest man was nothing.

Of course, Sam Zemurray's public legacy was not his children or grandchildren. It was his work, all gathered under the banner of United Fruit. Which must have made it painful to see the company fail in the final years. From his porch in New Orleans, he could watch a lifetime of toil swept away by the incoming tide: Guevara, Castro. This was a man who left and returned several times—because work is life and retirement is accepting the shortcomings and failures as part of the permanent record. When Zemurray took over United Fruit in 1932, the company was fading. It would have gone under if he had not breathed it full of energy. He gave it twenty-five years of prosperity. But it was his spirit that kept the beast moving. When he went away for good, the company began to die.

Zemurray sold all his stock in United Fruit soon after he retired. He wanted a clean break, to end his life in the business, and so on, but it was more than that. Zemurray did not feel his money was in good hands at the company. He knew what was coming after him and did not like it. He had the melancholy of a person who has no choice but to leave the world in the wrong hands. The men who would follow him were smaller, weaker, products of a different culture. "When the disparities between styles became too great," wrote Thomas McCann, "Zemurray finally sold out all his Fruit Company stock. He was too old to fight battles. [His] career was bracketed by men who failed to grasp what United Fruit was about and who failed at leadership."

21

≡

Bay of Pigs

A corporation is a product of a particular place and a particular time. U.S. Steel was Pennsylvania in the 1890s. Microsoft was Seattle in the 1980s. It's where and when their sense of the world was fixed. The company brain is hardwired. Which is why a corporation, though conceivably immortal, tends to have a life span, tends to age and die. Unless remade by a new generation of pioneers—in which case it's a different company—most corporations do not outlive the era of their first success. When the ideas and assumptions prevalent at the time of their founding go out of fashion, the company fades.

United Fruit/Cuyamel was a product of Central America circa 1911. No matter the problem, the top executives behaved as if they were still operating in the Honduras of Manuel Bonilla. A concession, a bribe, a mercenary army, a revolution—always the broad sword, the blunt instrument. It was a methodology that became impossible in the wake of Guatemala, though few seemed to realize it until they tried the same trick in Cuba.

Fidel Castro's father, Ángel, worked for United Fruit as a tenant farmer, growing sugarcane for the company and sending his son to U.F. schools. Fidel was a product of El Pulpo, in other words, ripening beside the stalks, the son of the caretaker who will return to depose the master and walk in muddy boots across the carpets of the big house. In 1959, Castro nationalized every U.F. plantation, building, and piece of equipment in Cuba. The company estimated its losses at $60 million. The CIA, still commanded by Allen Dulles, put together a plan. Approved by Eisenhower, green-lighted by Kennedy, it amounted to a group of Cuban exiles, Brigade 2506, landing in Cuba at the Bay of Pigs, sparking a popular uprising that would hopefully overthrow Castro. Called Operation Zapata, it was led by Howard Hunt, who secured money, guns, and ships from United Fruit. According to McCann, a New Orleans–based seaman named J. Arthur Marquette, who served as U.F.'s go-between with the CIA, met with Robert Kennedy. Marquette later complained about Kennedy's arrogance and "dirty long hair."

Zemurray was not involved in this. He was old and ailing, had sold his stock. If he played a role, it was by his absence. In the fiasco that followed, Zemurray was in the same position as Eisenhower: both men created a system no one else could control; both had been irreplaceable.

Brigade 2506 reached the Bay of Pigs on the morning of April 17, 1961. Fourteen hundred men were carried on four ships, two of them supplied by United Fruit. It was a bad place to attack, isolated, with reefs close to shore. Several skiffs were damaged before the exiles even made it to the beach. They had to wade in heavy equipment. Many reached land exhausted. They dug foxholes and tried to survive as bombs fell. Dulles asked the president for emergency air support. Kennedy refused—this is where he drew the line with the agency. Brigade 2506 surrendered the following morning: 114 dead, 1,200 taken prisoner. U.F. lost both its ships. It was the company's last attempt at regime change, a pathetic bookend to Honduras in 1911.

United Fruit started selling its property in the Torrid Zone soon after. What Arbenz had taken by force, the company began relinquishing on its own, returning to the model that preceded Preston and Keith: instead of owning land, hospitals, and towns, instead of dealing with the challenge of life on the isthmus, the company would contract local farmers—"associate producers"—to supply bananas. U.F. sold 37,440 acres in 1962, a year after the Bay of Pigs. By 1967, the company, which once owned three million acres on the isthmus, owned less than eighty-two thousand. By 1970, the company was out of the region as a landowner altogether.

I visited Honduras, stood in the ruins of the compounds, wandered through the banana towns, which were as forlorn as ghost towns in Colorado. It was a kingdom that ended in the way of the British Empire, slowly, then all at once. Everyone came, then everyone left. The country is just as poor as the first banana man found it, rutted roads lined with shanties, overgrown fields, empty swimming pools. The golf courses of the fruit company have been abandoned. Switch grass grows tall on the fairways.

22

The Earth Eats the Fish That Ate the Whale

Thomas Lemann, who worked for Zemurray in the final years of his life, is one of the few people still living who spoke to the Banana Man as Moses spoke to the Lord. He last saw Sam at a funeral in 1961. "He couldn't walk anymore, not even with a cane," Mr. Lemann told me. "And he could barely talk. He was in a wheelchair. He had been powerful, but it was gone. When I bent down to shake his hand, he couldn't even hold my grip. His mouth was open and his eyes were glazed."

Samuel Zemurray died on November 30, 1961. He was eighty-four years old. His fortune was estimated at $30 million, half of which was donated, per his instruction, to the Touro Infirmary in New Orleans. The rest went to his heirs, to his causes, and to the endowment of the Zemurray Foundation, which is still giving grants. His obituary was carried on the AP wire: "Samuel Zemurray, former president of the United Fruit Company, who came to the United States as a penniless Russian immigrant and accumulated a $30,000,000 fortune selling bananas, died here last night of Parkinson's disease," it read. "In the banana belt of the Caribbean, Sam Zemurray was known as 'the fish that swallowed the whale.'"

He was buried in Metairie Cemetery—you drive past it as you head into the city from the airport—beside his wife, son, and granddaughter Anne. It's a storied cemetery, where Zemurray lies among the most colorful figures in the history of the city. William Claiborne, the first governor of Louisiana; Richard Taylor, the son of President Zachary Taylor and a hero of the Mexican and Civil wars; Jefferson Davis, the president of the Confederacy; Mel Ott, one of the great sluggers in baseball history. Being in this ground, among these famous dead, feels like a final acceptance of a man who was never accepted in any of the clubs, nor welcomed in society, a man who was taunted by cries of "Sam the Banana Man" as he pushed his ripes through the slums of Mobile.

23

Fastest Way to the Street

After Zemurray's death, United Fruit seemed like a man without a mission, wandering from here to there, having suffered a blow to the brain. The big problem, the problem that caused so many others (Panama disease), was finally solved by Standard Fruit, which took the initiative in U.F.'s lost years of overthrow and consent decree. The disease was not cured but was made irrelevant by the introduction of a banana called the Cavendish, which grows wild in Southeast Asia. Though inferior to the Big Mike in many ways—it's neither as tasty, nor as big, nor as hardy—the Cavendish is unaffected by Panama disease. It has a much higher yield, too. A Cavendish rhizome produces twice as many fingers as a Big Mike, meaning the banana companies could operate on half as much land, with obvious political implications.

A. J. Chute, a scientist who worked for U.F. before going to Standard Fruit, began to experiment with the Cavendish in the 1950s. Standard shipped the first Cavendish stems in 1953, but these reached the market bruised. Whereas the Big Mike was tough and could be stored on the deck of a ship, the Cavendish was fragile. Which is why, in the 1950s, Standard Fruit introduced the banana box. I don't want to talk too much about this—a box is a box—but it was a revolutionary development in the trade. It changed the way bananas were sorted, stacked, and shipped. Not inventing the banana box was an embarrassment for U.F. The company had lost its edge. "In place of the innovations that marked its early years, the character of the company became imitative," explained Thomas McCann. "It merely repeated earlier moves and tactics. The company had lost every semblance of invention. In the areas of production, sales and transportation, as in politics, United Fruit was doing business at the same old stand, but in fifty years the neighborhood had changed beyond recognition." By the early 1960s, Standard Fruit was shipping only the Cavendish. In 1962, United Fruit followed suit. The last Big Mike was sold in America in April 1965, and presumably eaten soon thereafter.

United Fruit struggled under the weight of its own history, its own image. Once considered among the most enlightened corporations in America, it came to be seen as one of the worst. Backward. Racist. Retrograde. In November 1969, the U.F. offices at Pier 3 were bombed by radicals of the Weatherman variety. Their complaint was the Vietnam War, which had nothing to do with United Fruit, but that did not matter to the bombers. U.F. had transcended its business and become a symbol of the System. That same year, Tulane Students for a Democratic Society issued a manifesto demanding the school divest of any money given it by Zemurray. "There is every reason to believe," reads the crazed document, "that the William Gause who appeared on campus Nov. 7, 1967, recruiting for the CIA is the same William Gause who was UFCo's Southern Passenger Traveling Agent in the 1930s."

In the 1970s, Pier 3 itself was destroyed. Torn up by giant machines and dumped into the Hudson River, it became part of the landfill that made ground for the World Trade Center. Thomas McCann remembers walking though the building before it was demolished. Zemurray's office was just as the old man left it, a shrine filled with ghosts. "He was monumental, one of the greatest people I ever met," McCann told me, "and his furniture was huge, too. Enormous. I asked what would happen to it. They said it would be dumped into the river. I asked if I could have the desk. They were sore as hell. The thing weighed a ton. But they did it. They put it on a truck and brought it to Boston, and I've worked on it ever since."

On September 24, 1969, someone began buying stock in United Fruit. By the end of the day, 733,000 shares had been purchased, the third-largest transaction in the history of the New York Stock Exchange to that point. At first, no one knew the identity of the buyer, though his purchase made him the owner of the company. The next morning, he called Boston to introduce himself. His name was Eli Black.

Black was a Polish immigrant descended from ten generations of rabbis and was a rabbi himself. He led a congregation on Long Island for three years, before quitting the pulpit, changing his name from Blachowitz, and enrolling in Columbia Business School. He took a job on Wall Street after he graduated and made millions in investment banking. He was forty-eight when he purchased United Fruit. He merged the company with others he already owned and called the conglomerate United Brands, which he ran from an office in the Pan Am Building above Grand Central Station in New York. He was touchy about his previous life as a religious leader. When McCann mentioned Black's background to a reporter, Black took him aside and said, "Forget the rabbi business."

Black paid around $540 million for United Fruit, which many suggested was far too much. (He overpaid, according to experts, by perhaps $200 million.) He must have had plans to overhaul the company, add value, resell it, but he was like a man who has caught an anvil. Down they went together. According to McCann, the company lost $24 million in 1971. Black slashed budgets, sold land, cut divisions. In 1973, OPEC embargoed oil to the United States, driving up United Fruit's shipping costs, further cutting into the company's profits. Several of the nations of the isthmus—emulating OPEC—then formed a cartel of banana-producing nations called UPEB (Union of Banana Exporting Countries). Members pledged to tax the banana companies a dollar per box. It would destroy United Fruit. Black made his case to leaders of the member states, paying special attention to the president of Honduras, Oswaldo López Arellano. It was a bleak time for the storied company.

On Monday morning, February 3, 1975, Eli Black filled his briefcase with heavy books, told his driver to take him to the Pan Am Building, rode the elevator to the forty-fourth floor, locked his office door, removed his overcoat, hat, and scarf, smashed a window with his briefcase, cleaned up the shards of broken glass, tossed his briefcase through the broken window, then followed it out. The police said he was in the air for six seconds. The towers of Park Avenue sped past, the concrete rose to meet him. He was traveling a hundred miles per hour when he hit the street. According to a report written by Detective John Duffy, "the

head had been split, it went from front to back, right down the middle."
He landed in rush-hour traffic. A beat cop bitched to a reporter on the
scene—his words can stand as a critique of the banana men in general—"It's a hell of a thing to do. Jumpers don't care. They don't think of
anyone down below."

No one could make sense of the suicide. Why would he do it? Eli
Black seemed wealthy, popular, loved. More than five hundred people
attended his funeral. The eulogy was given by Rabbi Leonard Rosen-
feld, who had flown in from Jerusalem. "How many persons pushed Eli
to a desperate option?" the rabbi asked. "How many contributed to his
untimely tragedy—and who called on Eli to choose the wrong door?"

The mystery was resolved that April when the Securities and Exchange Commission filed charges against United Brands, which, according to the complaint, paid the president of Honduras $1.25 million
to reduce the banana tax and destroy the cartel, with another $1.25
million to be paid later. "Black knew he had fallen far short of success
in every area that mattered to him," wrote Thomas McCann. "The former rabbi was embroiled in bribery and corruption. The great achievement of his business lifetime, United Brands, was struggling to stay
afloat in a sea of debt. His directors were in revolt, his management
had lost respect for him, his friends had deserted him, his personal fi-
nances were at least as bad as those of the company, his ability to win
people's confidence disappeared, and he had nowhere left to turn." The
scandal, which came to be known as Bananagate, drove the president
of Honduras from office. Trading of United Brands was suspended for
a week on the New York Stock Exchange. The share price plummeted
when it resumed, hitting a low not seen since Zemurray made his trip
to Boston in 1932. The company admitted wrongdoing to the SEC and
agreed to pay a $14,000 fine. $14,000! Eli Black killed himself for what,
in the world of bananas, seemed like a minor bit of skulduggery, business as usual on the isthmus.

That's the end of United Fruit. I mean, yes, more happened, and
happens still. The company bounced from owner to owner. After posting a $200 million loss in 1983, it was taken over by Carl Lindner, a
billionaire investor who began his career in his father's ice-cream shop.
Lindner moved the company to Cincinnati and changed its name to
Chiquita Brands International, Inc. In 2001, the company declared

bankruptcy. It came out of it a year later. Lindner had retired by then. Ice-cream men get old, too. More recently, Chiquita was accused of paying protection money to FARC, the Colombian terrorist organization, buying immunity for its executives, endangering the nonprotected executives of other companies. But for me, the story of U.F. ended when the rabbi hit Park Avenue.

Epilogue

The story of Sam Zemurray is the story of New Orleans. It was booming when he found it and it's foundered since he died. It's a body without a soul. It's a skinny man in fat-man pants. The buildings are grand, the streets are endless, but the people are gone. According to the last census, the city has fewer than three hundred thousand inhabitants—a 40 percent drop since its peak in the 1950s. No longer the world strider and shipbuilder, no longer the capital of commerce and Queen of the Gulf Ports, no longer the preferred destination of pirates, no longer the oasis of Kentucky woodsmen, it's been mummified, pickled, turned into a diorama that tells the story of its own existence. It lives on its memories, tearing off and selling pieces of its skin. Run-down, dilapidated, depleted, and yet still wonderful. Because no other city in America looks like it. Because its houses are haunted and its people are strange and its sunsets are bloody and its waters are black and its music is madness and its food is incredible. Because it was once inhabited by mercenaries and parrot kings and machine gunners and the greatest banana man the world has ever known. If New Orleans was New York, Samuel Zemurray would be John D. Rockefeller. What happens when you attach your legacy to a city and that city dies?

Saddest of all is the United Fruit Building on St. Charles Avenue north of Canal Street. You can see the entrance from a passing car. The doorway is arched, the stone etched with filigree, a frieze of tropical plenty. It's the sort of entrance that was built when this city was sure of its future and U.F. was king, the first of the truly global concerns, with a hundred ships and a million acres and a hundred thousand employees. But when you step through the arch, you find nothing but a shabby foyer, a building dumb to its own glory, its rooms rented to foreign consulates, nondescript law firms, a bank. When I went into the bank and looked at the ceiling—there was once a Diego Rivera–like mural there that showed a banana steamer coasting a palm-fringed bay—the teller seemed irritated.

"What are you looking at?"

"I wanted to see if the United Fruit mural was still up there."

"What's United Fruit?"

Sam Z, Sam the Banana Man, El Amigo, the Big Russian, the Gringo—he was not an easy person, nor is his biography without controversy. To some, it's the story of a great man, a pioneer in business, a hero. To others, it's the story of a pirate, a conquistador who took without asking.

What does it say about America?

It's a question I have asked myself repeatedly as I researched, interviewed, traveled, and wrote. In the end, I decided that his career is the history of the nation, the promise and the betrayal of that promise, experienced in the span of a single life. It starts a hundred years ago, when America was a rising power, and ends the day before yesterday, with the confidence of the people sapped. It might look bad but, as Zemurray understood, as long as you're breathing, the end remains to be written. Sam's defining characteristic was his belief in his own agency, his refusal to despair. No story is without the possibility of redemption; with cleverness and hustle, the worst can be overcome. I can't help but feel, after all the talk of America's decline, that we would do well by emulating Sam Zemurray—not the brutality or the conquest, but the righteous anger that sent the striver into the boardroom of laughing elites, waving his proxies, shouting, "You gentlemen have been fucking up this business long enough. I'm going to straighten it out."

A Note on Sources and Acknowledgments

In writing these pages, I have drawn on hundreds of books, newspaper articles, magazine stories, interviews, government documents, and corporate reports, as well as less conventional sources. Especially helpful was the work of the beat writers and war reporters who covered these events as they unfolded, including writers from *The New York Times*, *The New Orleans Statesman* and *The Daily Picayune*, *The Times-Picayune*, *The Wall Street Journal*, *Time*, *Forbes*, *Fortune*, and *Life*. Also helpful were unpublished dissertations archived at various libraries, as well as diaries, collections of letters, and personal correspondence at Tulane University and the University of Tennessee, Knoxville. The letters of Lee Christmas were especially illuminating on the early years in Honduras. Also thanks to people at great research institutions, public and private, where material relating to these years is collected: the Library of Congress; Harvard Library, which has a collection of United Fruit photos; the Howard-Tilton Memorial Library at Tulane University, which keeps the entire run of *Unifruco*, United Fruit's magazine, regularly published for more than forty years; the Securities and Exchange Commission's digital archive, where I found documents concerning antitrust investigations of United Fruit and the banana trade, as well as legal filings concerning Bananagate; the archive of the U.S. Congress, where I found transcripts from subcommittee hearings on the proposed "banana tax"; the U.S. Army websites; and the Ellis Island archive. Through the U.S. Customs Department and Ancestry .com, I was able to trace the comings and goings of Sam and Sarah and look at nearly every passport and manifest filled out by the Banana Man.

Equally valuable were people who sat for interviews and served as guides, directing me through a storied epoch of American history: Thomas Lemann, who did legal work for Zemurray in his later days; Nick Lemann, dean of the Columbia Journalism School, who directed me to his father, Thomas (when talking about his son, Mr. Lemann, who is in his eighties, would say, "So what does the dean think about it?"); Frank Brogan, among the last of the banana cowboys—he probably knew Zemurray and his son better than anyone else still living; Hortensia Calvo at the Roger Thayer Stone Center for Latin American Studies at Tulane; Kathe Lawton, at Tulane's Middle

American Research Institute; the staff at the New Orleans Museum of Art, where Zemurray's collection of Mayan artifacts was on display while I was researching; Marcelo Bucheli, historian, author, and expert on all things United Fruit—Bucheli maintains the United Fruit Historical Society, an outstanding website dedicated to the company's history; Mike Valladares, who served as a translator and guide in Honduras; Mark Varouxakis, traveling companion and translator; Mark Kilroy, who hosted me in New Orleans and was a friend throughout; David Spielman, for his enthusiasm, counsel, and terrific help with research; Stephanie Stone Feoli and her husband, Ludovico Feoli, chair of the Center for Inter-American Policy and Research at Tulane; E. Wyllys Andrews, a retired Tulane professor in Latin American studies; Eamon Kelly, the former president of Tulane; Richard Greenleaf at Tulane; Marjorie Cowen at Tulane; Samuel Zemurray III; Peter Jacobson; William Hess, the president of the American Zionist Movement; Morris Leibman, who, working for the Justice Department, investigated the Huey Long assassination; Gadi Marle, who explained Zemurray's contributions to Zionism from an Israeli perspective; Manuel Bonilla III, the grandson of the former president of Honduras, who lives in Tegucigalpa; and Thomas McCann, a firsthand witness to many of the events I've described.

Special thanks to my friends at FSG: Miranda Popkey, Jesse Coleman, Debra Helfand, Lisa Silverman, Charlotte Strick, Jeff Seroy, Sarita Varma, and especially Jonathan Galassi, who did what only he can do with a manuscript. I'm truly indebted to Cynthia Cotts. She fact-checked this book in a way that would make Albrecht proud. Cynthia challenged me editorially as well, making me do, metaphorically, those last fifty push-ups that Coach Ditka tells us can be the difference between kicking ass and getting your ass kicked. Effusive thanks to Jennifer Rudolph Walsh, who is wonderful. Thanks also to those who helped in ways more general and perhaps more demanding: Jessica Medoff, who read this book about a billion times; David Lipsky, who was up all night in the pilothouse; Jonathan Newhouse; Graydon Carter; Dana Brown; Julie Just; Kevin Baker; Jerry Weintraub; Herb and Ellen Cohen; Sharon and Bill Levin; Steven Cohen and Lisa Melmed; Renee Blumenthal; Robert Blumenthal; David Blumenthal; Cary Goldstein; Alec Wilkinson; and Ian Frazier. And also to my sons Micah, Nate, and Aaron, who helped me plant a banana tree behind our house in Connecticut, the progress and swift demise of which taught me a crucial lesson about the banana business and art in general: if you don't get the thing in the right soil, it's going to die. And, of course, to Francis Albert Sinatra.

Notes

Prologue

5   *Custom House Street*: Custom House Street is now called Iberville.

5   *it was known as Storyville*: Storyville was closed at the order of the U.S. Navy during the First World War. It had become a danger to sailors, many returning from leave with syphilis. The area was cleared in the 1930s to make way for public housing. The Iberville Projects are perhaps the most dangerous blocks in the United States. Tourists in New Orleans who mistakenly wander into these streets, which have been made to look something like the streets of the French Quarter—but it would have to be late, and you would have to be drunk—occasionally meet with foul play. When I toured some Zemurray "sites" with a friend who happens to be a New Orleans cop, he refused to accompany me into the Iberville Projects "'cause the sun is going down, and I love my kids."

5   *a company printed a blue book*: See Rose, *Storyville*; Carter, *The Past as Prelude*.

5   *a man in a dinner jacket played piano*: Many consider Storyville the birthplace of jazz. It was in bordellos, where the clientele needed mood music, that American jazz really got going.

6   *"Well, compadre, this is the first time"*: Langley and Schoonover, *The Banana Men*; Kinzer, *Overthrow*.

7   *The engines started and the boat glided*: Sources include Langley and Schoonover, *The Banana Men*; McCann, *An American Company*; Deutsch, *The Incredible Yanqui*; Federal Writers' Project, *New Orleans City Guide (1938)*; Kinzer, *Overthrow*; Asbury, *The French Quarter*; Sublette, *The World That Made New Orleans*; "Bonilla to Lead Revolt"; "Bonilla Gone with Hornet." I also hired a boat and followed the route the mercenaries took out of the city.

1: Selma

14   *According to those who knew him*: For example, Frank Brogan, who worked for Zemurray in New Orleans and Honduras.

14   *According to newspaper and magazine accounts*: Kobler, "Sam the Banana Man."

2: Ripes

21 *During the next delay*: Sources for these stories include ibid.; Chapman, *Bananas*; as well as interviews.

3: The Fruit Jobber

24 *Almost all were foreign born*: Early last century, a jobber, pushing a cart on Hester Street in New York, hawking his wares in pidgin English, woke the jazz drummer Frank Silver, who shared it with his friend Irving Cohn, who turned it into the song "Yes, We Have No Bananas."

24 *It was the only work*: In 1905, when yellow fever swept New Orleans, the banana men became scapegoats. There was even talk of banning the trade from the city. In response, industry leaders organized a tour of the isthmus. Politicians from Louisiana, Mississippi, and Alabama were ferried to the banana ports in Nicaragua and Costa Rica, where they were entertained by brass bands and shown towns that were clean and fever free. A photo diary of the trip is in the Tulane University Latin American Library.

24 *"one of the few statesmen"*: Freedman, *Roosevelt and Frankfurter*.

25 *"He's a risk taker"*: These words were spoken before the U.S. Congress, at hearings to determine whether United Fruit constituted a monopoly.

4: Brown to Green

27 *In him, Zemurray would have recognized*: On Ashbell Hubbard, see Moore, *History of Alabama and Her People*, Vol. 2.

29 *With Thatcher*: Sources for this section include Karnes, *Tropical Enterprise*; Dodd, *Tiburcio Carías*; Wilson, *Empire in Green and Gold*; Langley and Schoonover, *The Banana Men*; May and Plaza Lasso, *The United Fruit Company in Latin America*; as well as magazine and newspaper articles.

5: Bananas Don't Grow on Trees

31 *The scientific name for the plant*: Sources on the history and biology of the banana include Adams, *Conquest of the Tropics*; Wilson, *Empire in Green and Gold*; *Unifruco*, the United Fruit magazine; and discussions with agronomists at the botanical garden in La Ceiba, Honduras.

32 *"Northeast India, Burma"*: Wilson, *Empire in Green and Gold*.

32 *It's an herb*: My son Aaron tells me bamboo is the tallest grass in the world, but I am fairly certain I'm right. He is eight, but that's not why I think he's wrong.

33 *That's what happened to the Big Mike*: For recent developments in the saga of the Cavendish, see Peed, "We Have No Bananas."

33 *In 1516, Friar Tomás Berlanga*: Chapman, *Bananas*; Wilson, *Empire in Green and Gold*; Koeppel, *Banana*.

34 *When Berlanga was made bishop of Panama*: Davies, *Fyffes and the Banana*.

6: The Octopus

40   *He landed in Port Antonio, Jamaica*: On the founders of United Fruit, see Crowther, *The Romance and Rise of the American Tropics*; Wilson, *Empire in Green and Gold*; Adams, *Conquest of the Tropics*. For a contemporaneous look at Captain Baker, see *The World Today*, a monthly magazine that ran a profile of the captain in Vol. 6, January–June 1904.

44   *For now, let the Keiths be heroes*: On Minor Keith, see Stewart, *Keith and Costa Rica*; Crowther, *The Romance and Rise of the American Tropics*; Wilson, *Empire in Green and Gold*; Langley and Schoonover, *The Banana Men*; Adams, *Conquest of the Tropics*.

44   *This made him a hero in Costa Rica*: See Stewart, *Keith and Costa Rica*; also, "Minor C. Keith Dies." Much of Keith's fortune was wiped out in the stock market crash of 1929—lucky that he died the summer before, believing his family would be rich forever. His widow, by the end of her life, had to take in washing.

44   *Minor argued with the man*: The fact that he carried an American flag seems significant. For years, a painting of this scene, done by a famous Costa Rican artist, hung in the National Museum in San José, Costa Rica. It was later moved to the Customs House, then to the home of a private citizen. It disappeared fifty years ago.

45   *"Gentlemen, please pardon me"*: Keith's railroad has become a tourist attraction in Costa Rica. It remains the most romantic way to cross the isthmus. See Elliott, "Costa Rica's Jungle Train."

50   *"A conspiracy in this country"*: *American Banana Co. v. United Fruit Co.*

7: New Orleans

53   *Erudite and refined*: See Korn, *The Early Jews of New Orleans*.

54   *U.F. had private facilities*: Federal Writers' Project, *New Orleans City Guide* (1938).

54   *The most colorful of them*: On Jake "the Parrot King" Weinberger, various newspaper stories and books were helpful, including Crowther, *Romance and Rise of the American Tropics*; Wilson, *Empire in Green and Gold*; Langley and Schoonover, *The Banana Men*; Adams, *Conquest of the Tropics*. Several articles from *The Daily Picayune* were helpful as well. Also important was my own interview with Frank Brogan.

55   *Mother's Birth Place: Mexico*: Galveston, named Galvez Town for Bernardo de Gálvez y Madrid by José de Evia, the explorer who planted the Spanish flag there in 1785, was part of Mexico when Zemurray's mother-in-law was born.

8: The Isthmus

59   *Zemurray traveled to Honduras*: On Zemurray's timeline: It can be difficult to establish exact dates for the early years. Sources occasionally disagree—a by-product, no doubt, of Sam's passion for secrecy. For example, *The Banana Men* (Langley and Schoonover) has him first visiting Honduras in 1910, while *Bitter*

Fruit (Schlesinger and Kinzer) puts him there in 1905. According to *An American Company* (McCann), Zemurray traveled to Honduras in 1905, then returned to buy land in 1910. After comparing various accounts with newspaper articles and documents, I have arrived at a timeline I consider the most authoritative possible.

59   *Puerto Cortés had become a criminal refuge*: For information on Puerto Cortés in the wild years, see Langley and Schoonover, *The Banana Men*; Crowther, *The Romance and Rise of the American Tropics*; O. Henry, *Cabbages and Kings*; Smith, *O. Henry*.

60   *"That segment of the continent"*: O. Henry negotiated a deal with American law enforcement and returned to the United States after making restitution.

61   *It remained a point of pride*: This story comes via Frank Brogan, as do several others in this section.

61   *Following the coast, he sailed past*: The three companies that would dominate the modern trade—they have now become Chiquita Brands International, Dole Food Company, Inc., and Del Monte Foods.

62   *In a letter to Queen Isabella of Spain*: Morison, *Admiral of the Ocean Sea*.

62   *"Rain, thunder, and lightning"*: Columbus had his fourteen-year-old son with him on the trip. See Thomas, *Rivers of Gold*, and Morison, *Admiral of the Ocean Sea*.

62   *Neither Cortés nor his father*: For information on Cortés, see Las Casas, *A Short Account of the Destruction of the Indies*; Thomas, *Conquest*.

63   *If I have used the word "Cordillera" a lot*: "Cordillera" comes from the Spanish word *cordón*, "cord," as in the cord of muscle that runs up the spine of the isthmus.

9: To the Collins

67   *"Sam adapted himself to the ways of life"*: "Zemurray vs. Boston."

71   *Without it, the plantation dies*: See United Fruit Company, *The Story of the Banana*; Crowther, *The Romance and Rise of the American Tropics*.

71   *They're there, we're here!*: McCann, *An American Company*. This was a favorite phrase of Zemurray's. It seemed to encapsulate his greater complaint about how most men do business.

72   *There was a club for top executives*: This story comes from *Telltale Stories from Central America* by Samuel Z. Stone, Zemurray's grandson.

72   *"I noticed that the railroad depots"*: García Márquez, *Living to Tell the Tale*.

73   *Which of course means gangsters*: The Mafia made its American debut in New Orleans. By the late 1800s, stevedores were paying protection, which they called "gangster tax."

10: Revolutin'!

76   *In 1894, British marines*: See Meeker, *And Points South*.

77   *The resulting exchange*: See Crowther, *The Romance and Rise of the American Tropics*; McCann, *An American Company*; Chernow, *The House of Morgan*; Kinzer, *Overthrow*; Whitfield, "Strange Fruit." Also, Pringle, "A Jonah Who Swal-

lowed the Whale," a profile of Zemurray that ran in the defunct *American Magazine* in September 1933. Zemurray gave an interview for this piece, and many of the details come from him.

78   *"Mr. Secretary, I'm no favorite"*: In quotes because these are the exact words as later reported by Zemurray.

80   *Zemurray would have found the men*: "Filibuster" derives from the Dutch word for freebooter. By 1880, it came to mean that select group of North Americans who were fighting in Central and South America.

80   *"half Indian and half Negro"*: Langley and Schoonover, *The Banana Men*.

80   *"the hotbed of revolution"*: "New Orleans Junta Plots."

81   *Between 1890 and 1925*: Deutsch, *The Incredible Yanqui*.

82   *When he turned up*: For details on Lee Christmas, see ibid.; Crowther, *The Romance and Rise of the American Tropics*; Wilson, *Empire in Green and Gold*; Langley and Schoonover, *The Banana Men*; Koeppel, *Banana*; Karnes, *Tropical Enterprise*; Kinzer, *Overthrow*. Also, "Lee Christmas Dies, Soldier of Fortune"; and "Gen. Lee Christmas, a Dumas Hero in Real Life."

82   *In the end, he was the greatest*: His stories appeared in the *Blue Book Magazine of Fiction and Adventure*, or *Blue Book*, which was published from 1905 to 1975, where his work ran beside that of the likes of Robert Heinlein and Agatha Christie. He died in Lamar, Missouri, where he retired after the Second World War. His obituary was headlined "Col. Richardson Served 6 Nations, Soldier of Fortune, 59, Dies—Captor of Managua Jammed Gun into Villa's Stomach" (*New York Times*, April 23, 1949).

83   *When Christmas found Richardson*: Interesting on Richardson is a long profile that ran in *The New York Times* on October 31, 1915, under the headline "The 'Machine-Gun Man of the Princess Pats.'" Such young men were in no way distinguishable from Billy the Kid, Wyatt Earp, and other adventurers who made their name on the frontier.

83   *According to an appreciation*: McNutt, "Profiles: Sam Drebin."

84   *"Manuel Bonilla is now in New Orleans"*: "Bonilla to Lead Revolt."

84   *Called the* Hornet: The ship, a private yacht before being conscripted into the U.S. Navy, saw successful action in Daiquiri and Siboney, Cuba. There is a website dedicated to all navy ships that went by the name *Hornet* ("The name HORNET is one of the most distinguished in American naval history"), starting with a sloop that saw action in the War of Independence. After detailing the career of Zemurray's ship in the Spanish-American War, the website concludes, "In 1910 she was sold out of service" (http://www.usshornetassn.com). See also Feuer, *The Spanish-American War at Sea*; Manners, *Poor Cousins*.

86   *"coincident with the departure"*: "Bonilla Gone with Hornet."

86   *"I shot the roll on you"*: This dialogue has been reported in several books, including, Deutsch, *The Incredible Yanqui*. The original source is probably the interview Zemurray gave *Forbes* in 1936.

88   *He thought he'd scored perfectly*: The story appears in Deutsch, *The Incredible Yanqui,* as well as in interviews given by Christmas. As for the particular colors he failed to identify, these vary from telling to telling, if named at all. I have included those that seem most relevant to his railroading job.

93   *"Guerrero . . . defended the town"*: F. G. Masquelette as quoted in the *New York Times,* February 1, 1911.

95   *The treaty was defeated*: For details on Dávila during the war, see Langley and Schoonover, *The Banana Men;* Karnes, *Tropical Enterprise;* Deutsch, *The Incredible Yanqui;* Schlesinger and Kinzer, *Bitter Fruit;* Kinzer, *Overthrow;* "Honduran Factions Agree to Armistice"; "New Orleans Junta Plots"; "Bonilla Gone with Hornet"; "Davila Suspected of Plan to Decamp"; as well as my own interviews.

95   *"Dávila, who is willing"*: "Americans Abroad."

96   *As of 1926, Honduras*: U.S. Department of State, *Papers Relating to the Foreign Relations of the United States.*

11: To the Isthmus and Back

101   *If Zemurray could be shown*: This tax concerned more than bananas; it was a huge affair proposed on many goods. See *The American Economist,* Vol. 51, January–June 1913, published by the Anti-Tariff League of New York, which makes a strong case against the tax.

101   *"I think Mr. Zemurray desired it"*: For investigation into the tariff, I relied on many sources, including the transcript of *Proceedings of the Committee on the Merchant Marine and Fisheries,* 1913.

103   *When he failed to appear*: These details come from various articles and books, but the real color, the sense of the man, comes from Frank Brogan.

104   *"Mr. Zemurray was pleased"*: U.S. Department of State, *Papers Relating to the Foreign Relations of the United States.*

106   *Cuyamel was harvesting eight million*: "Cuyamel Accepts United Fruit Offer."

108   *"Hell, I'm having so much fun"*: Zemurray as quoted in Pringle, "A Jonah Who Swallowed the Whale."

12: The Banana War

110   *Zemurray's work was done*: On Victor Cutter, see "United Fruit Obeys"; Barton, "A Big, Human Fellow Named Cutter"; Adams, *Conquest of the Tropics;* Wilson, *Empire in Green and Gold.*

110   *"on which the owner"*: "United Fruit Obeys."

112   *When the Banana War came*: The most vivid material on the war comes from Frank Brogan, who heard the stories from Guy Molony. Most of the material was covered in the daily press.

114   *He bought it twice*: See Dosal, *Doing Business with the Dictators;* "Zemurray vs. Boston"; Pringle, "A Jonah Who Swallowed the Whale." Also, Whitfield, "Strange Fruit"; Langley and Schoonover, *The Banana Men;* Wilson, *Empire in Green and Gold;* Karnes, *Tropical Enterprise.*

115 *This was a preferred Zemurray tactic*: On Montgomery and Cuyamel, see *United States v. Illinois Central*. Also, Dosal, *Doing Business with the Dictators*.

119 *A figure worth considering*: Langley and Schoonover, *The Banana Men*; Koeppel, *Banana*; as well as many articles that ran at the time of the merger.

13: King Fish

124 *It was his favorite room*: The house was a place of fantasy for playwright Lillian Hellman, who grew up in New Orleans and was related to Zemurray by marriage. Jake Weinberger was her uncle Charlie's brother. Through her uncle, Hellman knew Sam Zemurray, who, according to Deborah Martinson, author of *Lillian Hellman: A Life with Foxes and Scoundrels*, was a romantic figure in Hellman's childhood. Martinson says Hellman loved the "tales and rumors . . . [of] killings and gunships . . . Guy Machine-Gun Molony, Lee Christmas." Martinson quotes a letter Hellman wrote Zemurray, in which she asked a favor. "Many times," wrote Hellman, "when I was in Boston, I wanted to telephone you, but it always seemed intrusive . . . but through the years I have so often heard people speak of you, and always felt an irrational, distant in-law pleasure in what they said." According to Martinson, Uncle Willy, an unforgettable presence in Hellman's memoir *Pentimento*, was a composite character partly based on Zemurray.

125 *It's where he took associates*: On the house and the plantation, see Johnson, "If Walls Could Talk"; Barry, *Rising Tide*; Mohr and Gordon, *Tulane*. Information also comes from Marjorie Cowen, the wife of the current Tulane president, Scott Cowen. She gave me a tour of the house. Mrs. Cowen produced a documentary film about the house, which was also helpful. The plantation is now a national park best visited in the spring, when the azaleas bloom. See also the National Park Service, *National Register of Historic Places: 1966–1991*.

127 *His friends called him Pig Iron*: I was given a quick, illuminating description of Sam Jr. by his great-grandniece, Stephanie Stone Feoli, and her husband, Ludovico Feoli. See also Davis, *The Story of Louisiana*, Vol. 2.

127 *They were married on June 25, 1936*: A wedding announcement ran in *The New York Times* on June 26. The marriage marked the ascent of the Zemurrays into the upper stratum of American society.

128 *He seemed to be aware of the concept of* tzedakah: Here's how *tzedakah* is described in the *Jewish Virtual Library*: "The word *tzedaka* derives from the Hebrew word *tzedek*, 'justice.' Performing deeds of justice is perhaps the most important obligation Judaism imposes on the Jew. '*Tzedek, tzedek* you shall pursue,' the Torah instructs (Deuteronomy 16:20). Hundreds of years later, the Talmud taught: '*Tzedaka* is equal to all the other commandments combined.'"

129 *It's called the Samuel Zemurray Jr.*: "Radcliffe Gets $250,000."

130 *Still considered among the best schools of its kind*: See Malo, *El Zamorano*.

131 *On occasion, he met with the president himself*: Eggenberger, *Encyclopedia of World Biography*; Marcus, *United States Jewry, 1776–1985*.

131 *He was one of the unofficial advisers*: Zemurray was brought to the White House by Felix Frankfurter, who had previously praised the Banana Man to President Roosevelt.

132 *"How many men ever"*: The speech can be seen and heard at http://www.youtube.com/watch?v=VIMi7fBA6e4 (last accessed February 3, 2012).

133 *To Long, "the people"*: Sources on Huey Long include Williams, *Huey Long*; White, *Kingfish*; as well as the very funny opening pages of Liebling, *The Earl of Louisiana*; and Long, *Every Man a King*.

133 *"In the evenings they literally sat around"*: Barry, *Rising Tide*.

133 *Why the Zemurray millions*: Long, *Every Man a King*.

136 *I once knew one of the investigators*: Morris Leibman was a friend and mentor of mine in Chicago. He was a founding partner, with Newton Minow, of one of the law firms that merged to become the present-day Sidley Austin.

136 *Others suggest a darker conspiracy*: For an edgier take on Long, see Deutsch, *The Huey Long Murder Case*.

14: The Fish That Ate the Whale

138 *It grew by accretion*: Federal Writers' Project, *New Orleans City Guide* (1938).

130 *The company was caught in a death spiral*: For corporate numbers, see the *Wall Street Journal* and *New York Times* stories; "United Fruit Annual Reports" (1929–1933); Wilson, *Empire in Green and Gold*; Whitfield, "Strange Fruit"; Langley and Schoonover, *The Banana Men*. Also, "Zemurray vs. Boston."

141 *"If you trust him, trust him"*: This dialogue was recounted by Zemurray to a reporter for *The American Magazine* (Pringle, "A Jonah Who Swallowed the Whale").

142 *Wing welcomed Zemurray*: McCann describes the scene in *An American Company*. More information on this scene, which, in the way of the Gunfight at the O.K. Corral, has been chronicled again and again, can be found in Langley and Schoonover, *The Banana Men*; Koeppel, *Banana*; "United Fruit Obeys"; "United Fruit's Control Shifts."

143 *"[I didn't want to watch]"*: On the showdown in Boston, see Langley and Schoonover, *The Banana Men*; Koeppel, *Banana*; McCann, *An American Company*; "United Fruit Obeys."

15: *Los Pericos*

148 *Given the opportunity*: On banana diseases and how the various companies reacted, see Voss, "Report on Aerial Application Procedures and Equipment"; Calpouzos, "Studies on the Sigatoka Disease of Bananas and Its Fungus Pathogen"; Pillay and Tenkouano, *Banana Breeding*; Taylor and Scharlin, *Smart Alliance*; Jenkins, *Bananas*; Mohr and Gordon, *Tulane*; Stewart, *Keith and Costa Rica*; Koeppel, *Banana*; Kobler, "Sam the Banana Man"; *Unifruco*, Winter 1927.

149 *"Please, Sport, don't confuse me"*: McCann, *An American Company*. Zemurray

frequently referred to people as "Sport," which is only one of the things he had in common with Jay Gatsby.

150 *United Fruit hired the biologist*: Karnes, *Tropical Enterprise*.

154 *You see it in the climactic scene*: According to McCann, the company, in exchange for the use of its facilities, asked only that Bogart sit for a short interview, conducted by McCann, for *Unifruco*. Bogart drank all day, was too loaded to do his scene—a stunt double was used—then swore at McCann when he approached with his notebook, saying, in essence, Get the fuck out of here, kid.

154 *Elia Kazan wanted to use the dock*: Watch the movie carefully and you will realize one of the ships unloaded by the dockworkers is carrying bananas, which would give the union boss leverage with the owner, as a delay of even a few hours could mean the ruin of the cargo.

16: Bananas Go to War

157 *War Crops*: Zemurray with Smith, "War Crops from Our Neighbor's Garden." For further information on United Fruit in the war, see Chapman, *Bananas*; May and Plaza Lasso, *The United Fruit Company in Latin America*.

157 *As part of FDR's National War Board*: See "Jamaica Acts to Send Men Here." This episode shows Zemurray behaving like a banana man in the classical sense. In the first years of the industry, when the Indians refused to work the fields, or were sickened by the work, Minor Keith imported workers from Jamaica and other islands, which is why the Caribbean coast of the isthmus seems less Central American than Caribbean today.

157 *Sam gave everything he had*: Meanwhile, as U.F. diversified away from bananas, executives sought to fix the brand in the public mind. Enter sultry "Chiquita Banana," the company mascot, which debuted in print ads and radio jingles in 1944. This character, created by Dik Browne, the cartoonist who created Hägar the Horrible, was nakedly based on the Brazilian nightclub singer Carmen Miranda, whose fame (she danced and sang in thickly accented English) had swept the nation. Like Miranda, Chiquita wore a fruit basket on her head; like Miranda, Chiquita high-kicked in heels; like Miranda, Chiquita tossed her fluted skirt, showing the doughboys a little too much thigh as she sang her silly song. (See Pieterse, *White on Black*; Jenkins, *Bananas*; Wilson, *Empire in Green and Gold*.)

17: Israel Is Real

161 *"I paid my first visit to New Orleans"*: Am I the only one who finds the phrasing funny?

162 *In 1926, he gave*: "To Aid Power Plant on Jordan River."

163 *In the early 1940s, Sam used*: On Zemurray's contributions to Zionism, see Feldstein, *The Land That I Show You*; Hammer, *Good Faith and Credit*; Whitfield, "Strange Fruit"; as well as various newspaper articles.

163 *several hundred Jewish refugees*: Most of these émigrés had moved to the United States by 1960. About seventy Jews live in Sosúa today, the remnant of the wartime

community. According to the Jewish Virtual Library, "Those who did remain in Sosúa and held on to their land have made a fortune. Erik Hauser, an original settler from Vienna, now owns an entire block of the lucrative downtown area, where hotels and restaurants were built on his original eighty acres. He is Sosúa's wealthiest resident." (See Lauren Levy, "The Dominican Republic's Haven for Jewish Refugees," Jewish Virtual Library.)

164 *"the victorious Allies"*: Hochstein and Greenfield, *The Jews' Secret Fleet*.

166 *"Zemurray helped raise the purchase price"*: McCann does not have this right. The *Exodus* was turned back, which is what made it such a powerful symbol—these Holocaust survivors were returned to the land of their tormentors. The *Exodus* was the model for the ship portrayed in Leon Uris's book *Exodus*, the basis for the Otto Preminger movie of the same name. I was able to interview the captain of the *Exodus* before he died.

166 *The most famous vessel*: On Zemurray and the Bricha, see Hochstein and Greenfield, *The Jews' Secret Fleet*; Hammer, *Good Faith and Credit*; Skolnik, *Encyclopaedia Judaica*, Vol. 21; Weizmann, *Trial and Error*; Weisgal, . . . *So Far*. Additional information comes from newspaper stories and discussions with Gadi Marle,

169 *Behind them, behind the creation*: For this section, see Klich, "Latin America, the United States, and the Birth of Israel"; Didion, *Salvador*; Morris, *1948*; Chapman, *Bananas*; Hochstein and Greenfield, *The Jews' Secret Fleet*; Weizmann, *Trial and Error*.

18: Operation Success

174 *If you wanted to open*: Sources for this section include Gleijeses, *Shattered Hope*; Schlesinger and Kinzer, *Bitter Fruit*; Cullather, *Secret History*; Grandin, *Empire's Workshop*; Chapman, *Bananas*; May and Plaza Lasso, *The United Fruit Company in Latin America*; McCann, *An American Company*.

174 *There were no workers*: See Koeppel, *Banana*; Perez-Brignoli, *A Brief History of Central America*; Gleijeses, *Shattered Hope*; Schlesinger and Kinzer, *Bitter Fruit*.

176 *He said he would govern*: Perez-Brignoli, *A Brief History of Central America*.

179 *"All the achievements of the Company"*: Schlesinger and Kinzer, *Bitter Fruit*.

180 *In return, the company was reportedly paid*: To make a point, Arbenz ordered that his own family estate be confiscated under the decree.

182 *"There's a battle waging"*: Anderson, *Che Guevara*. In addition to books mentioned above, sources include Castañeda, *Compañero*; and Guevara, *The Complete Bolivian Diaries*.

184 *"I had the opportunity"*: Anderson, *Che Guevara*.

185 *"Right after he became Undersecretary of State"*: On Tommy the Cork and political hires, see McKean, *Tommy the Cork*; Hunt, *Undercover*; Schlesinger and Kinzer, *Bitter Fruit*; Whitfield, "Strange Fruit"; McCann, *An American Company*; "The Cork Bobs Back."

186 *When Clements died*: See Schlesinger and Kinzer, *Bitter Fruit*.

188 *If you want to advance*: Sources on Edward Bernays include Tye, *The Father of Spin*; as well as Bernays's own books, especially *Propaganda* and *Biography of an Idea*.

189 *He took out an ad*: Bernays paid models to participate in his "smokeouts," assuring that the less attractive would fall in like sheep. I came across the following exchange in John O'Hara's *BUtterfield 8*, published in 1935:

"Didn't you notice that girl that went by with the foreign looking man? She was smoking a cigarette."

"She gets paid for that."

"Paid for it?"

"Yes, paid for it. I read that in Winchell's column—"

190 *"Mr. Zemurray sat at a flat-top desk"*: Bernays, *Biography of an Idea*.

193 *When the* Times *staffer*: Gruson, "How Communists Won Control of Guatemala." He actually suggested that Guatemala had gone Red.

196 *"As long as Khrushchev"*: This quote, an expression of a long-held sentiment, appears in Dulles, *The Craft of Intelligence*.

200 *Whether he was in Athens*: On Ambassador Peurifoy, see Higgins, *Perfect Failure*; Quigley, *The Ruses for War*; Schlesinger and Kinzer, *Bitter Fruit*; Chapman, *Bananas*; Lewis, "Ambassador Extraordinary."

201 *"The President stated"*: Kinzer, *Overthrow*.

201 *The ship, a Swedish vessel*: Original documents regarding the affair and the surrounding drama in Guatemala can be found on the website of the State Department's Office of the Historian, http://history.state.gov. These events were covered in several of the above-mentioned books, including *Bitter Fruit* and *Shattered Hope*. See also "Swedish Freighter Anchors off Key West"; "Reaction in Other Capitals"; Gruson, "Guatemala Says U.S. Tried to Make Her Defenseless"; Waggoner, "U.S. White Paper Alerts Americas to Aims of Reds."

202 *He described it as the place*: Anderson, *Che Guevara*.

204 *"Our crime is having"*: For Arbenz, see Pellecer, *Arbenz y yo*; Simon, *Guatemala*; Hunt, *Undercover*; Schlesinger and Kinzer, *Bitter Fruit*; Chapman, *Bananas*; Anderson, *Che Guevara*; Lewis, "Ambassador Extraordinary"; Kennedy, "Arbenz Blames U.S. for His Fall."

204 *"For fifteen days a cruel war"*: See Hunt, *Undercover*; Schlesinger and Kinzer, *Bitter Fruit*; Gleijeses, *Shattered Hope*.

206 *He lived in Montevideo*: Arbenz's wanderings were chronicled by the newspapers of the day. See, for example, "Arbenz Would Be Swiss"; Gruson, "Arbenz to Make Home in Prague." Pictures of Arabella Arbenz can be found on a website dedicated to Jaime Bravo, http://matadorjaimebravo.com.

207 *On January 27, 1971*: For recent developments, see Malkin, "Guatemala to Restore Legacy of President U.S. Helped Depose."

208 *Within a generation*: Standard Fruit, a privately owned company based in New Orleans, was purchased by Castle & Cooke between 1964 and 1968, then renamed Dole. See Karnes, *Tropical Enterprise*.

19: Backlash

214 *U.F. was increasingly considered an embarrassment*: For this section, see Ambrose, *Eisenhower*; Tye, *The Father of Spin*; Hunt, *Undercover*; Schlesinger and Kinzer, *Bitter Fruit*; Taylor and Scharlin, *Smart Alliance*; McCann, *An American Company*. McCann is especially good on the twilight years, as he was then working with top management at the company. See also "United Fruit Yields in Suit."

20: What Remains

227 *He had the melancholy*: Frank Brogan and Thomas Lemann were helpful on Zemurray's last days.

21: Bay of Pigs

230 *Kennedy refused*: Many conspiracy theories regarding the assassination of JFK center around this episode—Kennedy's decision to withhold air power, which meant the death of exiles on the beach at the Bay of Pigs. In several scenarios, the CIA retaliates by recruiting Lee Harvey Oswald, a former employee of United Fruit and a figure in a New Orleans netherworld where Zemurray had been a power. Often mentioned is the fact that in the guest book at the Russian embassy Oswald visited in Mexico City, the assassin's name appears beside the name William Gaudet, suggesting the men came together. William Gaudet, probably a CIA agent, had been publisher of the *Latin American Report*, a propaganda sheet bankrolled, in part, by United Fruit. "When Oswald visited the American Embassy in Mexico City shortly before he assassinated John F. Kennedy, the signature appearing immediately next to Oswald's own on the Embassy visitors' register is that of William Gaudet," wrote Thomas McCann in *An American Company*. "As of this writing [1976], the coincidence has not been explained." If I am not delving into this too deeply, it's because I do not want to chase my tail around the ceiba tree.

230 *It was the company's last attempt*: On the Bay of Pigs, see Kornbluh, *Bay of Pigs Declassified*; Rasenberger, *The Brilliant Disaster*; McCann, *An American Company*; Schlesinger and Kinzer, *Bitter Fruit*; Anderson, *Che Guevara*; Kinzer, *Overthrow*; Dulles, *The Craft of Intelligence*; Hunt, *Undercover*.

230 *U.F. sold 37,440 acres*: "Gringo Company."

22: The Earth Eats the Fish That Ate the Whale

233 *William Claiborne, the first governor of Louisiana*: Information comes from my trip to the burial ground, as well as Gandolfo, *Metairie Cemetery*. Also, Findagrave.com.

23: Fastest Way to the Street

236 *In November 1969*: "They Bombed in New York."

236 *"He was monumental"*: After leaving United Fruit, McCann worked as a movie producer. In 1975, he made *The Watergate Cover-up Trial*, a film about Richard

Nixon, using the Watergate tapes as a script. (McCann told me this story.) When he needed a desk for Nixon, he used the furniture from Pier 3. In the film, you can see Zemurray's desk appearing as Nixon's desk, which seems both right and wrong.

237   *Members pledged to tax*: UPEB fell apart when Ecuador, then the largest banana producer in the world, refused to join.

237   *"the head had been split"*: Black's suicide was said to be the model for the first scene of *The Hudsucker Proxy*, the Coen Brothers movie.

238   *"It's a hell of a thing to do"*: This quote, as well as details regarding the suicide of Eli Black, come from Thomas McCann, our conversation and his book. Sources on Eli Black include Langley and Schoonover, *The Banana Men*; Chapman, *Bananas*; Koeppel, *Banana*; Jenkins, *Bananas*; Kinzer, *Overthrow*; Kilborn, "Suicide of Big Executive."

238   *More than five hundred people*: "Eli Black's Rites Attended by 500."

238   *The mystery was resolved*: See "Complaint Names United Brands Company," which summarizes the charges against the company. Also Cole, "S.E.C. Suit Links a Honduras Bribe to United Brands."

239   *Ice-cream men*: I tried to interview someone from Chiquita for this book. My request led to e-mail exchanges with Andrew Ciafardini, manager of investment relations and corporate communications at Chiquita Brands International in Cincinnati, Ohio. In the end, my request was not granted.

239   *More recently, Chiquita was accused*: See Gentile, "Families Sue Chiquita in Deaths of Five Men."

Bibliography

Adams, Frederick Upham. *Conquest of the Tropics: The Story of the Creative Enterprises Conducted by the United Fruit Company.* Garden City, NY: Doubleday, 1914.

Ambrose, Stephen. *Eisenhower: Soldier and President.* New York: Simon & Schuster, 1990.

American Banana Co. v. United Fruit Co., 213 U.S. 347, 357–58 (1909).

The American Economist, Vol. 51. American Protective Tariff League, 1913.

"Americans Abroad." *New York Times*, February 19, 1911.

Ancestry.com.

Anderson, Jon Lee. *Che Guevara: A Revolutionary Life.* New York: Grove Press, 1997.

———. "The Power of García Márquez." *New Yorker*, September 27, 1999.

"Arbenz Would Be Swiss." *New York Times*, January 6, 1955.

Asbury, Herbert. *The French Quarter: An Informal History of the New Orleans Underworld.* New York: Knopf, 1936.

Asturias, Miguel Angel. *The Green Pope.* New York: Delacorte, 1971.

Baker, John Newton. "Your Public Relations Are Showing." *Rotarian Magazine*, June 1949.

"Banana Split." *Time*, February 17, 1958.

"Bananas Are Back!" *Time*, March 18, 1946.

Barry, John M. *Rising Tide: The Great Mississippi Flood of 1927 and How It Changed America.* New York: Simon & Schuster, 1997.

Barton, Bruce. "A Big, Human Fellow Named Cutter." *American Magazine*, August 1925.

Basso, Hamilton. "Encounter in Puerto Cortés." *New Yorker*, October 12, 1957.

"Battle on Near Ceiba." *New York Times*, August 5, 1910.

Bernays, Edward L. *Crystallizing Public Opinion.* New York: Boni and Liveright, 1923.

———. *Propaganda.* New York: Horace Liveright, 1928.

———. *Public Relations.* Norman: University of Oklahoma Press, 1952.

———. *Biography of an Idea: Memoirs of Public Relations Counsel Edward L. Bernays.* New York: Simon & Schuster, 1965.

———. *The Engineering of Consent*. Norman: University of Oklahoma Press, 1969 [1947].

Biuso, Emily. "Banana Kings." *Nation*, February 28, 2008.

"Bonilla Gone with Hornet." *New York Times*, December 24, 1910.

"Bonilla Indicted for Hornet Affair." *New York Times*, February 19, 1911.

"Bonilla Sails for Belize." *New York Times*, May 24, 1907.

"Bonilla to Agree to an Armistice." *New York Times*, February 5, 1911.

"Bonilla to Lead Revolt." *New York Times*, November 15, 1910.

Brown, Francis. "Looking at Industrial Leaders from the Right and Left." *New York Times*, June 21, 1936.

Brunhouse, Robert Levere. *Pursuit of the Ancient Maya*. Albuquerque: University of New Mexico Press, 1975.

Bruno, Stephanie. "The President's Residence." *Times-Picayune*, November 2, 2007.

Bucheli, Marcelo. "Good Dictator, Bad Dictator: United Fruit Company and Economic Nationalism in Central America in the Twentieth Century." Working Paper 06-0115. University of Illinois at Urbana-Champaign, College of Business, 2006.

Cable, George Washington. *Old Creole Days*. New York: Pelican Books, 1991 [1897].

Calpouzos, L. "Studies on the Sigatoka Disease of Bananas and Its Fungus Pathogen. Soledad Cienfuegos, Cuba: Atkins Garden and Research Laboratory, 1955.

Cannon, Carl L. "Lee Christmas, Soldier of Fortune." *New York Times*, March 15, 1931.

Carter, Hodding, ed. *The Past as Prelude: New Orleans 1718–1968*. New Orleans: Pelican Publishing, 1968.

Castañeda, Jorge G. *Compañero: The Life and Death of Che Guevara*. New York: Knopf, 1997.

Castilla, Alfredo Trejo. *El Señor Don Samuel Zemurray y la soberanía de Honduras*. Tegucigalpa, 1926.

"Castro-Zelaya Scare." *New York Times*, February 25, 1913.

Chambers, Glenn Anthony. *Race, Nation, and West Indian Immigration to Honduras, 1890–1940*. Baton Rouge: Louisiana University Press, 2010.

Chapman, Peter. *Bananas: How the United Fruit Company Shaped the World*. New York: Canongate, 2007.

Chernow, Ron. *The House of Morgan: An American Banking Dynasty and the Rise of Modern Finance*. New York: Grove Press, 1990.

Cole, Robert J. "S.E.C. Suit Links a Honduras Bribe to United Brands." *New York Times*, April 10, 1975.

"College Boxers Ready for Tourney." *New York Times*, April 8, 1932. Sam Zemurray Jr. appears in this story.

"A Colony of Defaulters." *New York Times*, September 16, 2003.

"Complaint Names United Brands Company." *SEC News Digest*, April 10, 1975.

"The Cork Bobs Back." *Life*, April 11, 1960.

Cortés, Hernando. *Five Letters of Cortés to the Emperor*. Translated by J. Bayard Morris. New York: W. W. Norton, 1969.

Crowther, Samuel. *The Romance and Rise of the American Tropics.* Garden City, NY: Doubleday, 1929.

"Cuba: Confiscation!" *Time,* June 1, 1959.

Cullather, Nick. *Secret History: The CIA's Classified Account of Its Operations in Guatemala 1952–1954.* Palo Alto: Stanford University Press, 1999.

"Cuyamel Accepts United Fruit Offer." *New York Times,* November 26, 1929.

"Cuyamel Fruit Co." *Wall Street Journal,* August 11, 1924.

Dando-Collins, Stephen. *Tycoon's War: How Cornelius Vanderbilt Invaded a Country to Overthrow America's Most Famous Military Adventurer.* Philadelphia: Da Capo, 2008.

Davies, Peter N. *Fyffes and the Banana: Musa Sapientum: A Centenary of History, 1888–1988.* Atlantic Highlands, NJ: Athlone Press, 1990.

"Davila Suspected of Plan to Decamp." *New York Times,* January 29, 1911.

"Davila's Sincerity Doubted." *New York Times,* February, 14, 1911.

Davis, Edwin Adams. *The Story of Louisiana.* Vols. 1 and 2. New Orleans: J. F. Hyer, 1960.

Davis, William C. *The Pirates Laffite: The Treacherous World of the Corsairs of the Gulf.* Orlando, FL: Harcourt, 2005.

Deras, Ismael Mejía, Ricardo D. Alduvín, and Rafael Heliodoro Valle. *Policarpo Bonilla: Algunos apuntes biográficos.* Mexico City: Imprenta Mundial, 1936.

Deutsch, Hermann B. *The Incredible Yanqui: The Career of Lee Christmas.* New York: Longmans, Green, 1931.

———. *The Huey Long Murder Case.* New York: Doubleday, 1963.

Díaz, Bernal. *The Conquest of New Spain.* Translated by J. M. Cohen. New York: Penguin Books, 1963.

Didion, Joan. *Salvador.* New York: Simon & Schuster, 1983.

Dodd, Thomas J. *Tiburcio Carías: Portrait of a Honduran Political Leader.* Baton Rouge: Louisiana State University Press, 2005.

"Doris Zemurray Stone Dies." *Union College Magazine,* January 1, 1995.

Dos Passos, John. *USA: The Trilogy.* New York: Library of America, 1996 [1930–1933].

Dosal, Paul J. *Doing Business with the Dictators: A Political History of United Fruit in Guatemala, 1899–1944.* Wilmington, DE: SR Books, 1993. See Chapters 5, "United Fruit, Cuyamel and the Battle for Motagua, Part One," and Chapter 8, "Battle for Motagua, Part 2."

Dulles, Allen W. *The Craft of Intelligence: America's Legendary Spymaster on the Fundamentals of Intelligence Gathering for a Free World.* New York: Harper and Row, 1963.

Eggenberger, David, ed. *Encyclopedia of World Biography: 20th Century Supplement.* Vol. 1. Palatine, IL: J. Heraty, 1987.

"Eli Black's Rites Attended by 500." *New York Times,* February 6, 1975.

Elliott, Vicky. "Costa Rica's Jungle Train." *New York Times,* July 28, 1985.

Epstein, Edward Jay. "Garrison." *New Yorker,* July 13, 1968.

Euraque, Darío A. *Reinterpreting the Banana Republic: Region and State in Honduras, 1870–1972.* Durham: University of North Carolina Press, 1996.

"Executive Changes at United Fruit Company." *New York Times*, April 24, 1951.

"Farming: The Fruit King." *Time*, March 11, 1946.

Federal Reporter. Circuit Courts of Appeals and District Courts of the United States. Vol. 230, April–May 1916. St. Paul: West Publishing, 1916.

Federal Writers' Project, Works Progress Administration. *New Orleans City Guide (1938).* Boston: Houghton Mifflin, 1938.

Feibelman, Julian B. *The Making of a Rabbi.* New York: Vantage Press, 1980.

Feldstein, Stanley. *The Land That I Show You: Three Centuries of Jewish Life in America.* Garden City, NY: Doubleday, 1978.

Feuer, A. B. *The Spanish-American War at Sea: Naval Action in the Atlantic.* Westport, CT: Praeger, 1995.

"Fighting in Honduras." *New York Times*, August 8, 1910.

Findagrave.com.

Fonseca, Mary. *Louisiana Gardens.* Gretna, LA: Pelican, 1999.

"Food Trade Heads Aid Farm Revival." *New York Times*, July 10, 1933.

Freedman, Max, ed. *Roosevelt and Frankfurter: Their Correspondence, 1928–1945.* Boston: Little, Brown, 1967.

Gandolfo, Henri A. *Metairie Cemetery, An Historical Memoir. Tales of Its Statesmen Soldiers, and Great Families.* New Orleans: Stewart Enterprises, 1981.

García Márquez, Gabriel. *One Hundred Years of Solitude.* Translated by Gregory Rabassa. New York: Harper, 1970.

———. *Living to Tell the Tale.* Translated by Edith Grossman. New York: Knopf, 2003.

"Gen. Christmas Captured." *New York Times*, August 12, 1910.

"Gen. Lee Christmas, a Dumas Hero in Real Life." *New York Times*, January 15, 1911.

Gentile, Carmen. "Families Sue Chiquita in Deaths of Five Men." *New York Times*, March 17, 2008.

Gleijeses, Piero. *Shattered Hope: The Guatemalan Revolution and the United States, 1944–1954.* Princeton: Princeton University Press, 1991.

———. *The Cuban Drumbeat.* London: Seagull Books, 2009.

Grandin, Greg. *Empire's Workshop: Latin America, the United States, and the Rise of the New Imperialism.* New York: Henry Holt, 2006.

Greene, Laurence. *The Filibuster: The Career of William Walker.* New York: Bobbs-Merrill, 1937.

"Gringo Company." *Time*, April 20, 1962.

Grow, Michael. *U.S. Presidents and Latin American Interventions: Pursuing Regime Change in the Cold War.* Lawrence: University Press of Kansas, 2008.

Gruson, Sydney. "How Communists Won Control of Guatemala." *New York Times*, March 1, 1953.

———. "School Turns out Tropical Farmers." *New York Times*, November 24, 1953. About the Zamorano.

———. "Guatemala Says U.S. Tried to Make Her Defenseless." *New York Times*, May 22, 1954.

———. "Arbenz to Make Home in Prague." *New York Times*, November 27, 1955.

"Guatemala: Battle of the Backyard." *Time*, June 28, 1954.

"Guatemala: Machete Blow." *Time*, August 31, 1953.

"Guatemala: Unifruit Under Fire." *Time*, November 12, 1951.

Guevara, Che. *The Complete Bolivian Diaries, and Other Captured Documents*. Edited by Daniel James. New York: Stein and Day, 1969.

———. *Che: The Diaries of Ernesto Che Guevara*. North Melbourne, Australia: Ocean Press, 2009.

Hadari, Ze'ev Venia, and Ze'ev Tsahor. *Voyage to Freedom: An Episode in the Illegal Immigration to Palestine*. Totowa, NJ: Vallentine Mitchell, 1985.

Hallett, Douglas. "A Low-Level Memoir of the Nixon White House." *New York Times*, October 20, 1974.

Hammer, Gottlieb. *Good Faith and Credit*. New York: Cornwall Books, 1985.

"Hands Across the Gulf." *Time*, January 20, 1941.

"Harvard Gets a Woman." *Time*, April 26, 1948.

Hearn, Lafcadio. *Inventing New Orleans: Writings of Lafcadio Hearn*. Edited by Frederick Starr. Jackson: University Press of Mississippi, 2001.

Hellman, Lillian. *Pentimento*. Boston: Little, Brown, 1973.

Higgins, Trumbull. *Perfect Failure: Kennedy, Eisenhower, and the CIA at the Bay of Pigs*. New York: W. W. Norton, 1987.

Hill, Gladwin. "Rise of the Banana King." *Hartford Courant*, February 13, 1938.

Hochstein, Joseph M., and Murray S. Greenfield. *The Jews' Secret Fleet: The Untold Story of North American Volunteers Who Smashed the British Blockade*. New York: Gefen Books, 1988.

"Honduran Factions Agree to Armistice." *New York Times*, February 9, 1911.

"Honduran Revolt Starts." *New York Times*, December 30, 1910.

"Hondurans Consider Peace." *New York Times*, February 6, 1911.

"Honduras: Peace Offering." *Time*, December 11, 1944.

Humphrey, Chris. *Moon Handbooks: Honduras*. Berkeley: Avalon Travel, 2003.

Hunt, E. Howard. *Undercover: Memoirs of an American Secret Agent*. New York: Berkley, 1974.

———. *American Spy: My Secret History in the CIA, Watergate, and Beyond*. New York: Wiley, 2007.

Immerman, Richard H. *The CIA in Guatemala: The Foreign Policy of Intervention*. Austin: University of Texas Press, 1982.

"In Private Equity, the Limit of Apollo's Power." *New York Times*, December 8, 2008.

"Internationalists of New Orleans." *Fortune*, June 1952.

"Jamaica Acts to Send Men Here." *New York Times*, March 26, 1943.

James, C. L. R. *The Black Jacobins: Toussaint L'Ouverture and the San Domingo Revolution*. New York: Random House, 1963.

Jenkins, Virginia Scott. *Bananas: An American History*. Washington, DC: Smithsonian Books, 2000.

Johnson, Suzanne. "If Walls Could Talk." *Tulanian*, September 12, 2007.

"Join National Committee." *New York Times*, December 22, 1941.

Kaplan, Dana Evan. "The Determination of Jewish Identity Below the Mason-Dixon Line: Crossing the Boundary from Gentile to Jew in the Nineteenth-Century American South." *Journal of Jewish Studies* 52, no. 1 (Spring 2001): 98–121.

Karnes, Thomas L. *Tropical Enterprise: Standard Fruit and Steamship Company in Latin America*. Baton Rouge: Louisiana State University Press, 1978.

Kennedy, Paul P. "Arbenz Blames U.S. for His Fall." *New York Times*, November 8, 1954.

Kilborn, Peter T. "Suicide of Big Executive." *New York Times*, February 14, 1975.

Kinzer, Stephen. *Overthrow: America's Century of Regime Change from Hawaii to Iraq*. New York: Times Books, 2006.

Klich, Ignacio. *Latin America and the Palestinian Question*. London: Institute of Jewish Affairs, 1986.

———. "Latin America, the United States, and the Birth of Israel: The Case of Somoza's Nicaragua." *Journal of Latin American Studies* 20, no. 2 (1988): 389–432.

Klich, Ignacio, and Jeffrey Lesser. *Arab and Jewish Immigrants in Latin America: Images and Realities*. New York: Routledge, 1998.

Kobler, John. "Sam the Banana Man." *Life*, February 19, 1951.

Koeppel, Dan. *Banana: The Fate of the Fruit That Changed the World*. New York: Hudson Street Press, 2007.

Korn, Bertram Wallace. *The Early Jews of New Orleans*. New York: American Jewish Historical Society, 1969.

Kornbluh, Peter, ed. *Bay of Pigs Declassified: The Secret CIA Report on the Invasion of Cuba*. New York: New Press, 1998.

Krehm, William. *Democracies and Tyrannies of the Caribbean in the 1940's*. Toronto: Lugus Libros, 1999.

Lachoff, Irwin, and Catherine C. Kahn. *The Jewish Community of New Orleans*. Charleston, SC: Arcadia Publishing, 2005.

LaFeber, Walter. *The Cambridge History of American Foreign Relations. Volume 2: The American Search for Opportunity, 1865–1913*. New York: Cambridge University Press, 1993.

Langley, Lester D., and Thomas Schoonover. *The Banana Men: American Mercenaries and Entrepreneurs in Central America, 1880–1930*. Lexington: University Press of Kentucky, 1995.

Las Casas, Bartolomé de. *A Short Account of the Destruction of the Indies*. Edited and translated by Nigel Griffin. New York: Penguin, 1992 [1552].

"Lee Christmas Dies, Soldier of Fortune." *New York Times*, January 22, 1924.

"Lee Christmas No Better." *New York Times*, August 19, 1923.

Lemann, Nicholas. "Southern Discomfort." *New Yorker*, March 13, 2000.

Leonard, Thomas M. *The History of Honduras*. Santa Barbara, CA: ABC-CLIO, 2011.

Levy, Lauren. "The Dominican Republic's Haven for Jewish Refugees." The Jewish Virtual Library.

Lewis, Flora. "Ambassador Extraordinary: John Peurifoy." *New York Times Magazine*, July 18, 1954.

Lewis, Paul. "John M. Fox, Innovator in Developing Frozen Juice." *New York Times,* January 19, 2003.

Liebling, A. J. *The Earl of Louisiana.* Baton Rouge: Louisiana State University Press, 1970.

Litvin, Daniel. *Empires of Profit: Commerce, Conquest and Corporate Responsibility.* New York: Texere, 2003.

Long, Huey P. *Every Man a King: The Autobiography of Huey P. Long.* New York: Da Capo, 1996 [1933].

Louisiana Supreme Court. *Records,* 1906, Vol. 42, p. 1162. Information on early business operations of Sam Zemurray.

Malkin, Elisabeth. "Guatemala to Restore Legacy of President U.S. Helped Depose." *New York Times,* May 23, 2011.

Malo, Simón. *El Zamorano: Meeting the Challenge of Tropical America.* Melbourne, Australia: Sinbad Books: 1999.

Manifesto: Three Classic Essays on How to Change the World—Che Guevara, Rosa Luxemburg, Karl Marx and Friedrich Engels. North Melbourne, Australia: Ocean Press, 2005.

Manners, Ande. *Poor Cousins.* New York: Coward, McCann, 1972.

Marcus, Jacob Rader. *United States Jewry, 1776–1985.* Detroit: Wayne State University Press, 1990.

Marion Samson Collection of General Lee Christmas and President William Walker, MS-0014. University of Tennessee Libraries, Knoxville, Special Collections.

Martinson, Deborah. *Lillian Hellman: A Life with Foxes and Scoundrels.* New York: Counterpoint, 2005.

May, Stacy, and Galo Plaza Lasso. *The United Fruit Company in Latin America.* Charleston, SC: Nabu Press, 2010.

"May Attack Honduras." *New York Times,* December 20, 1910.

Mayo, Anthony J., Nitin Nohria, and Laura G. Singleton. *Paths to Power: How Insiders and Outsiders Shaped American Business Leadership.* Boston: Harvard Business School Press, 2006.

McCaffety, Kerri, and Cynthia Reece McCaffety. *The Majesty of St. Charles Avenue.* Gretna, LA: Pelican, 2001.

McCann, Thomas P. *An American Company: The Tragedy of United Fruit.* New York: Crown, 1976.

McCullough, David. *The Path Between the Seas: The Creation of the Panama Canal, 1870–1914.* New York: Simon & Schuster, 1977.

———. *Truman.* New York: Simon & Schuster, 1992.

McKean, David. *Tommy the Cork: Washington's Ultimate Insider from Roosevelt to Reagan.* South Royalton, VT: Steerforth Press, 2004.

McNutt, William Slavans. "Profiles: Sam Drebin." *New Yorker,* May 2, 1925.

Meeker, Oden and Olivia. *And Points South.* New York: Random House, 1947.

"Milestones." *Time,* December 8, 1961. Obit of Sam Zemurray.

"Minor C. Keith Dies." *New York Times,* June 15, 1929.

Mohr, Clarence L., and Joseph E. Gordon. *Tulane: The Emergence of a Modern University, 1945–1980.* Baton Rouge: Louisiana State University Press, 2001.

Moore, Albert Burton. *History of Alabama and Her People.* Vol. 2. American Historical Society, 1927.

Morison, Samuel Eliot. *Admiral of the Ocean Sea: A Life of Christopher Columbus.* Boston: Little, Brown, 1942.

Morris, Benny. *1948: The First Arab-Israeli War.* New Haven: Yale University Press, 2008.

"Mrs. Zemurray Jr., Widow of Major, 54." *New York Times,* June 29, 1968.

Naipaul, V. S. *The Middle Passage.* New York: Macmillan, 1963.

———. *The Loss of El Dorado: A Colonial History.* New York: Knopf, 1970.

National Park Service. *National Register of Historic Places: 1966–1991.* Nashville: American Association for State and Local History, 1992.

Nelson, Donald F. *To the Stars: Over Rough Roads: The Life of Andrew Atchison, Teacher and Missionary.* Cambridge, MA: TidePool Press, 2008.

Neruda, Pablo. *The Poetry of Pablo Neruda.* Edited by Ilan Stavans. New York: Farrar, Straus and Giroux, 2003.

"New Orleans Junta Plots." *New York Times,* June 12, 1911.

"New York Major Killed." *New York Times,* February 4, 1943.

"No More Revolutions for Gen. Christmas." *New York Times,* July 25, 1923.

O'Brien, Thomas F. *The Revolutionary Mission: American Enterprise in Latin America, 1900–1945.* New York: Cambridge University Press, 1996.

O. Henry. *Cabbages and Kings.* Garden City, NY: Doubleday, 1914.

"1,000 More to Join Refugees' Colony." *New York Times,* January 31, 1941.

O'Toole, G. J. A. *The Spanish War: An American Epic 1898.* New York: W. W. Norton, 1984.

Peckenham, Nancy, and Annie Street. *Honduras: Portrait of a Captive Nation.* New York: Praeger, 1985.

Peed, Mike. "We Have No Bananas." *New Yorker,* January 10, 2011.

Pellecer, Carlos Manuel. *Arbenz y yo.* Guatemala City: Artemis-Edinter, 1997.

Pérez-Brignoli, Héctor. *A Brief History of Central America.* Translated by Ricardo B. Sawrey A. and Susana Stettri de Sawrey. Berkeley: University of California Press, 1989.

Pieterse, Jan Nederveen. *White on Black: Images of Africa and Blacks in Western Popular Culture.* New Haven: Yale University Press, 1995.

Pillay, Michael, and Abdou Tenkouano, eds. *Banana Breeding: Progress and Challenges.* Boca Raton: CRC Press, 2011.

"President Tells of Plan to Relieve Farm Labor Shortages." *Wall Street Journal,* March 31, 1943.

"Pride of Boston." *Time,* February 4, 1924.

Pringle, Henry F. "A Jonah Who Swallowed the Whale." *American Magazine,* September 1933.

"Profit Increased by United Fruit." *New York Times,* February 3, 1940.

Quigley, John. *The Ruses for War: American Interventionism Since World War II*. Amherst, NY: Prometheus Books, 1992.

Rabe, Stephen G. *Eisenhower and Latin America: The Foreign Policy of Anticommunism*. Chapel Hill: University of North Carolina Press, 1988.

"Radcliffe Gets $250,000." *New York Times*, March 5, 1947.

Rasenberger, Jim. *The Brilliant Disaster: JFK, Castro, and America's Doomed Invasion of Cuba's Bay of Pigs*. New York: Scribner, 2011.

"Reaction in Other Capitals." *New York Times*, June 19, 1954.

Rorty, James. "Tortillas, Beans, and Bananas." *Harper's Magazine* 203 (September 1951): 76–80. Discusses Zemurray's innovations on the isthmus.

Rose, Al. *Storyville, New Orleans: Being an Authentic Illustrated Account of the Red-Light District*. Tuscaloosa: University of Alabama Press, 1978.

Roueché, Berton. "The Humblest Fruit." *New Yorker*, October 1, 1973.

Sachar, Howard M. *A History of the Jews in America*. New York: Knopf, 1992.

"Saw the Battle of Ceiba." *New York Times*, February 7, 1911.

Saxon, Lyle. *Lafitte the Pirate*. Gretna, LA: Pelican, 1989 [1930].

Schlesinger, Stephen. "Ghosts of Guatemala's Past." *New York Times*, op-ed, June 4, 2011.

Schlesinger, Stephen, and Stephen Kinzer. *Bitter Fruit: The Story of the American Coup in Guatemala*. Revised and expanded ed. Cambridge, MA: Harvard University Press, 2005.

Scott, Peter Dale. *Deep Politics and the Death of JFK*. Berkeley: University of California Press, 1993.

Simon, Jean-Marie. *Guatemala: Eternal Spring—Eternal Tyranny*. New York: W. W. Norton, 1988.

Skolnik, Fred. *Encyclopaedia Judaica*. Vol. 21. Detroit: Macmillan Reference, 2007.

Smith, Arthur D. Howden. *Men Who Run America: A Study of the Capitalistic System and Its Trends Based on Thirty Case Histories*. Indianapolis: Bobbs-Merrill, 1936.

Smith, C. Alphonso. *O. Henry*. Seattle: University Press of the Pacific, 2003 [1916].

Smith, Peter H. *Talons of the Eagle: Latin America, the United States, and the World*. New York: Oxford University Press, 2007.

Smyser, A. A. "Herbert Cornuelle Reflects on Hawaii." *Honolulu Star-Bulletin*, June 6, 1996.

Soluri, John. *Banana Cultures: Agriculture, Consumption, and Environmental Change in Honduras and the United States*. Austin: University of Texas Press, 2006.

Stewart, Watt. *Keith and Costa Rica: The Biography of Minor Cooper Keith, American Entrepreneur*. Albuquerque: University of New Mexico Press, 1964.

Stiles, T. J. *The First Tycoon: The Epic Life of Cornelius Vanderbilt*. New York: Knopf, 2009.

Stone, Samuel Z. *The Heritage of the Conquistadors: Ruling Classes of Central America from the Conquest to the Sandinistas*. Lincoln: University of Nebraska Press, 1990.

———. *Telltale Stories from Central America: Cultural Heritage, Political Systems, and Resistance in Developing Countries*. Albuquerque: University of New Mexico Press, 2001.

Sublette, Ned. *The World That Made New Orleans: From Spanish Silver to Congo Square.* Chicago: Lawrence Hill, 2008.

"Succeeds to Presidency of United Fruit." *New York Times,* May 11, 1948.

"Swedish Freigher Anchors off Key West." *New York Times,* May 28, 1954.

Taylor, Gary J., and Patricia J. Scharlin. *Smart Alliance: How a Global Corporation and Environmental Activists Transformed a Tarnished Brand.* New Haven: Yale University Press, 2004.

"They Bombed in New York." *Time,* November 21, 1969.

Thomas, Hugh. *Conquest: Montezuma, Cortés, and the Fall of Old Mexico.* New York: Simon & Schuster, 1995.

———. *Rivers of Gold: The Rise of the Spanish Empire, from Columbus to Magellan.* New York: Random House, 2003.

"391 Persons Have $1,000,000 Policies." *Wall Street Journal,* September 16, 1931.

"To Aid Power Plant on Jordan River." *New York Times,* June 1, 1926.

"Top Banana." *Time,* May 19, 1967.

Travis, Mary Ann. "Doris, Zemurray, Stone Pavilions Dedicated." *Tulanian,* March 19, 2007.

"Trouble in Green Gold." *Time,* May 16, 1960.

Tucker, Richard P. *Insatiable Appetite: The United States and the Ecological Degradation of the Tropical World.* Berkeley: University of California Press, 2000.

Tulane University Latin American Library, Roger Thayer Stone Center for Latin American Studies, Image Archive, Special Photos from the Yellow Fever Tour of the Isthmus, 1905; Louisiana Research Collection, Letter regarding United Fruit from Tulane Students for a Democratic Society.

Tye, Larry. *The Father of Spin: Edward Bernays and the Birth of Public Relations.* New York: Henry Holt, 1998.

"United Fruit Clears $10,729,000." *New York Times,* July 15, 1941.

"United Fruit Closes 1938 with Business in Advancing Trend." *Wall Street Journal,* February 4, 1939.

"United Fruit Co." *Wall Street Journal,* March 9, 1935.

"United Fruit Co." *Wall Street Journal,* March 14, 1943.

United Fruit Company. *The Story of the Banana.* 2nd ed. Boston: United Fruit Company, 1922.

———. *Chiquita Banana Cookbook.* Boston: United Fruit Company, 1974.

United Fruit Historical Society (Unitedfruit.org).

"United Fruit Net Up in 1940." *Wall Street Journal,* February 8, 1941.

"United Fruit Obeys." *Time,* January 23, 1933.

"United Fruit Official Calls Retail Prices for Bananas Excessive." *Wall Street Journal,* May 12, 1947.

"United Fruit Outlook Improved." *Wall Street Journal,* March 7, 1935.

"United Fruit Paid $58,450 to Hart." *New York Times,* May 30, 1935.

"United Fruit Yields in Suit." *New York Times,* February 5, 1958.

"United Fruit's Control Shifts." *Wall Street Journal,* March 8, 1933.

United States v. Illinois Central, 244 U.S. 82 (1917).

U.S. Congress. House Select Committee on Small Business, 1955. Washington, DC: GPO, 1955. Discussions of Zemurray and early work with Ashbell Hubbard.

U.S. Department of Commerce and Labor, Bureau of Manufacturers. *Consular and Trade Reports,* issues 355–57. Washington, DC: GPO, 1910. Details early business life of Hubbard-Zemurray Co.

U.S. Department of State. *Papers Relating to the Foreign Relations of the United States with the Annual Message of the President Transmitted to Congress December 6, 1910.* Washington, DC: GPO, 1910.

———. *Foreign Relations of the United States, Reports and Correspondence, 1912.* Washington, DC: GPO, 1912.

U.S. House of Representatives, 62nd Cong. *Proceedings of the Committee on the Merchant Marine and Fisheries in the Investigation of Shipping Combinations Under House Resolution 587.* Washington, DC: GPO, 1913.

U.S. Interstate Commerce Commission. *31st Annual Report.* Washington, DC: GPO, 1917. Details early arrangement regarding Zemurray, United Fruit, and ripes.

"U.S. May Get Jamaica Labor." *New York Times,* March 25, 1943.

Veeser, Cyrus. *A World Safe for Capitalism: Dollar Diplomacy and America's Rise to Global Power.* New York: Columbia University Press, 2002.

"Victor M. Cutter." *American Magazine,* August 1925.

Voss, Carrol M. "Report on Aerial Application Procedures and Equipment Used for Control of Sigatoka Disease on Bananas in the Windward Islands and Recommendations for an Improved Program." Berkeley: University of California, Consortium for International Crop Protection, 1981.

Waggoner, Walter H. "U.S. White Paper Alerts Americas to Aims of Reds." *New York Times,* August 8, 1954.

Weisgal, Meyer Wolfe. *. . . So Far: An Autobiography.* New York: Random House, 1971.

Weizmann, Chaim. *Trial and Error: The Autobiography of Chaim Weizmann, First President of Israel.* New York: Harper, 1949.

———. *The Letters and Papers of Chaim Weizmann,* Vols. 1–7. Jerusalem: Israel Universities Press, 1974.

White, Richard D., Jr. *Kingfish: The Reign of Huey P. Long.* New York: Random House, 2006.

Whitfield, Stephen J. "Strange Fruit: The Career of Samuel Zemurray." *American Jewish History* 73, no. 3 (March 1984): 307–23.

Williams, T. Harry. *Huey Long.* New York: Knopf, 1969.

Wilson, Charles Morrow. *Empire in Green and Gold: The Story of the American Banana Trade.* New York: Henry Holt, 1947.

"Would-Be Filibuster Held." *New York Times,* December 7, 1913.

Zagoren, Ruby. *Chaim Weizmann: First President of Israel.* Champaign, IL: Garrard, 1972.

"Zemurray—Pickering." *New York Times,* June 26, 1937.

"Zemurray Succeeds Hart as Head of United Fruit." *New York Times,* February 1, 1938.

"Zemurray vs. Boston." *Fortune*, March 1933.

Zemurray, Samuel. "La Frutera's Record." *Nation*, letter to the editor, March 25, 1950.

Zemurray, Samuel, with Beverly Smith. "War Crops from Our Neighbor's Garden." *American Magazine*, October 1943.

Zemurray, Sarah. *One Hundred Unusual Dinners and How to Prepare Them*. Boston: Thomas Todd, 1938.

———. *Useful Information for Every Household*. Boston: Thomas Todd, 1944.

———. *A Menu for Every Day of the Year*. Boston: Thomas Todd, 1951.